OUTRAGE AND MURDER!

A

Kalendar *of the* PRISONERS

(*Whether for* Felony *or* Misdemeanors)

Now in Custody of HIS MAJESTY's Goaler for the County of *NORTHAMPTON*,

To be Try'd on *Tuesday* the 15th Day of *JULY*, 1735.

William Hunt,

Condemn'd, but Repriev'd 'till further Orders.

William Blinman,

Continued for Want of Security.

Frances Goodman,

(*Committed by* Thomas Hawley, *Esq*; March 15.)

Charged upon Oath to have feloniously stolen one Sheet, one Table-Cloth, one Pillow Drawer, Value Five Shillings, the Property of *William Hart* of *Earl's-Barton*.

Elizabeth Wilkinson, Hanged

(*Committed by* Thomas Hawley, *Esq*; April 9.)

Charged upon Oath of *William Hicks*, for feloniously picking his Pocket, and taking thereout One Pound Seventeen Shillings and Ten-pence, the Property of the said *William Hicks*.

Robert Pittam,

(*Committed by* Smith Fleetwood, *Esq*; April 11.)

Charged upon Oath to have in an unlawful Manner defrauded *Richard Slatter* of Two Blacks Filleys, the Property of *John Slatter*.

Elizabeth Ward,

(*Committed by* John Freeman, *M. D.* April 18.)

Charged upon Oath to have in an unlawful Manner defrauded *Susannah Collins* of Two Guineas in Gold and Thirteen Shillings and Sixpence in Silver, the Property of the said *Collins*.

Thomas Winpress,

(*Committed by* Robert Dextor, *Coroner*, April 25.)

Charged upon an Inquest, found Guilty of Manslaughter.

Elizabeth Fawson, Burnt

(*Committed by* Nathaniel Humphreys, *L. L. D.* and Thomas Richards, *Coroner*, June 26)

Charged with a violent Suspicion of feloniously poisoning her Husband, *Thomas Fawson*; and also upon an Inquest charged with a violent Suspicion of poisoning the said *Thomas Fawson*, the Younger, by giving him a Quantity of White Mercury on the 18th Day of *June*, of which he languished 'till the 21st of the same Month, and then died.

William Clarke,

(*Committed by* Thomas Richards, *Coroner*, July 9.)

Charged, on an Inquest, with murdering, on the 9th of *May* last, *Henry Wright* of *Grendon*, in this County, Plaisterer, by violently and cruelly beating and bruising him.

Preserved at the Northamptonshire Record Office is the Calendar for the 1735 Northamptonshire Assizes, before Mr Justice Reeve. The handwritten verdicts are the work of the Clerk of the Court.

OUTRAGE AND MURDER!

800 years of
CRIMINAL HOMICIDE
and
JUDICIAL EXECUTION
in
NORTHAMPTONSHIRE

Volume One 1202 to 1850

RICHARD COWLEY

PEG AND WHISTLE BOOKS
BARTON SEAGRAVE
KETTERING
NORTHAMPTONSHIRE NN15 6TG

2010

First Published 2010

ISBN 0 9534095 2 X

Published by :
Peg and Whistle Books
20 Grosvenor Way
Barton Seagrave
Kettering
Northamptonshire NN15 6TG

Peg and Whistle Books is an Imprint of Monkshood Publishing

www.monkshood.co.uk

Printed and Bound in Great Britain by

Direct Print On Demand Limited
Saxon Fields
Old Harborough Road
Brixworth
Northamptonshire NN6 9BX

Set in Melior, *Palatino Italic, Perpetua Italic* and **JUBILEE LINES**

CONTENTS

Richard Cowley is a retired Northamptonshire Police officer. Born in Finedon in Northamptonshire, he became an apprentice compositor in the printing trade. Subsequently, he worked in estimating and production planning before becoming a typographer and graphic designer. He still retains a keen interest in printing history and typography.

In 1968 he joined the then Northampton and County Constabulary as a Special Constable before joining the regular constabulary two years later. Always stationed in the north of the county, he served in large towns, small villages, desk jobs and specialist squads, and along the way, picked up his interest in police, criminal and legal history.

He graduated from the Open University with a BA in Modern History, before going on to gain an MA in Victorian Studies from Leicester University. He has written five previous books : *Policing Northamptonshire 1836-1986* (1986); *Guilty M'Lud! The criminal history of Northamptonshire* (1998); *Who's Buried Where in Northamptonshire* (2000); *A History of Northamptonshire Police* (2008); and *Policing EOKA: The United Kingdom Police Unit to Cyprus 1955-1960* (2008). In 2005 he was commissioned by the Home Office to write the official history of the Inspectorate of Constabulary for the 150th anniversary of its establishment; and has just been commissioned to write the history of the British police by a national publisher, which will be published next year.

Now retired, he is the Curator and Archivist of Northamptonshire Police; and also the Curator and Archivist of Northamptonshire Saint John Ambulance, of which he has been a member for 27 years, and which in 2006 awarded him the dignity of a Serving Brother of the Venerable Order of Saint John of Jerusalem.

Married to Valerie, they both enjoy their six grand-children and two great-grand-children; and holiday in Cyprus whenever they can.

INTRODUCTION

Murder, for obvious reasons, has always been considered one of the most serious, if not *the* most serious, of all the crimes mankind is capable of committing. So much so, that it's even in the Bible - 'thou shalt not kill'. And so ingrained was this concept in the mind of ancient man, that there was never seen to be a need to have it written down. Thus, a written law against murder came relatively late upon the scene.

Indeed, the first written laws in the English language only came when the missionaries started arriving in England, or Britain, in the late sixth century. And coming from Rome, these missionaries obviously brought with them their own Roman legal ideas. This caused the English kings to start codifying their own existing legal customs, and writing them down, producing what came to be regarded as written law, but which as the Venerable Bede says was 'in the Roman style - but in English'.

The most important king to do this was Ethelbert, the king of Kent (560-616). Ethelbert's code recorded the customs of his time, which gave each offence what was called a 'wergild'. The wergild was the price in money considered reasonable for the crime, to be paid in compensation to the victim, or in the case of a homicide, obviously to the next of kin. Ethelbert's wergild for killing a man was 100 shillings, but in the case of a homicide, as well as paying the wergild, it was also the custom to give the murdered person's family the right to avenge the killing, and this right extended way out to the sixth cousin.

And it didn't stop there. For a homicide, apart from the wergild, an additional 50 shillings was to be paid to the king. So there we have the legal system also being used as a cash generator for the king/government. Unfortunately, with the public's perception of some speed cameras, things appear not to have changed much in 1400 years.

Also surviving, are the laws of the Kingdom of Wessex under King Ine, about the year 680, which virtually duplicated Ethelbert's

Code. And Alfred the Great's Code for Mercia can be dated as being written between 871 and 899.

But it gradually came to be realised, of course, that homicide was so serious that it must be punished in some other way, not just by a fine. So by the early eleventh century, following the spread of Christianity, homicide (along with other serious crimes, such as house breaking, theft, treason, serious assaults and so on) came to be punishable by death, but only because they were considered sins against God's law rather than as crimes against the king's law. And by this time as well, the right of vengeance for the family was dropping out of use.

Also, as regards homicide, there was not any distinction made between accident and malice aforethought, or as we call it now, murder and manslaughter. The medieval mind reasoned that a man was responsible for any consequence of his actions, whether slight or serious, and irrespective of whether or not it was intended. Case 1294/95B is a good example of this, and it was not until the year 1390, that murder and manslaughter were separated.

And well over 400 years passed before the homicide laws needed adjustment again. Up until 1828, to prove the crime of murder when the body of a newly born baby was found dead in suspicious circumstances, the prosecution had to prove that the baby had been capable of a separate existence away from its mother, no matter how brief, indicating therefore the cutting of the umbilical cord. As most, if not all, illegitimate births were in private anyway, then the 'separate existence' rule was nigh on impossible to prove.

Where the defence of 'being stillborn' was pleaded, such was the lack of medical sophistication of the time, that forensic medical opinion could not always agree as to whether the baby had been stillborn or not. Some women were therefore literally seen to be 'getting away with murder'

The 'separate existence' rule was finally abolished by the 1828 Offences Against The Person Act, which introduced the new offence of 'Concealment of Birth'. The mother of a baby found dead in suspicious circumstances could then be charged with this offence, with its lesser burden of proof, rather than murder or manslaughter, where the need to prove 'separate existence' had been paramount and essential.

And in the early years of the twentieth century, the law was again faced with something entirely new, which it had never met before. How the law coped with fatalities caused by the motor car, can be seen in the decade starting in 1911.

Following a series of highly publicised national cases, the law of homicide was again looked at in the early 1950s. The murder of PC Nathaniel Edgar in 1948; the Timothy Evans/John Christie Case in 1950; and the murder of PC Sydney Miles in the notorious 'Craig and Bentley Case' in 1952, had focused attention on the death penalty for the offence of murder. As a result, the Homicide Act was passed in 1957. This split the crime of murder into two groups; Capital and Non-Capital Murder.

Capital Murder was defined as any of the following : murder in the course of, or furtherance of, theft; murder by shooting or causing an explosion; murder done in resisting lawful arrest; murder done in escaping from legal custody; murder of a police officer or of a person assisting; and murder by a prisoner of a prison warder. Under the Act, Capital Murder attracted the death penalty, whilst Non-Capital Murder attracted 'life' imprisonment.

Agitation for the total abolition of the death penalty continued however, and in 1964, Sydney Silverman introduced a Bill into Parliament for the abolition of the death penalty. And in 1965, this Bill became law as the Murder (Abolition of Death Penalty) Act, which introduced a trial period without capital punishment. In 1969, the death penalty for murder was totally abolished, and in today's 'thinking society', is unlikely ever to return. Murder, however, escalates.

IT IS OF NO USE RELYING ON PEOPLE'S MEMORIES. MEMORIES are notoriously unreliable. For this very reason, therefore, written records were used from the earliest times; and where these documents have been preserved, we are grateful for the opportunity they give us of reading the thoughts and preoccupations of our ancestors. From them, we can extract those things that interest us.

The written records which concern us when dealing with criminal homicides are the official records of the Assize Court, the Coroner's Court, the Supervisors' Rolls and Gaol Deliveries, and much later on, the Assize Calendars and the newspaper reports of the time. The Coroner's Court and the newspapers are obviously still with us, but the Assize Court has been gone these 30 years past.

The Assize Rolls

By the Crown Court Act 1971, the Assizes were abolished (together with the Quarter Sessions, but that court did not have the power to try homicide cases, and so does not concern us), to be replaced by one higher criminal court, the Crown Court. The Crown Court sits with judge and jury and is permanently sitting, unlike the Assizes which only sat twice (or occasionally, three times) a year. The Assizes have a long history.

When the Normans forced themselves upon England in the unforgettable year of 1066, they came as conquerors. And as such, immediately put the indigenous Saxons under the heel by imposing a strong government. William 'the Conqueror' collected together administrators and judges into one committee for the purpose of administering his new country. This committee was called the King's Court (in Latin, Curia Regis) and was the medieval equivalent of today's 'think-tank'. It was the King's Court, for example, which commissioned the Domesday Book, and appointed the auditors who did the actual 'bean counting' in every village.

Within a few years, the King's Court, obviously housed in London, became the senior court of the land, mainly because of the superior competence of the judges who sat in it. And so people who were able to, travelled to London purely to have their cases heard before the King's Court. But surely those people who could not afford to travel, also had the right to expect legal competence? Of course they did. So, if the cases could not come to the judges, then the judges would go to the cases.

Thus, judges from the King's Court were sent out from London on regular trips into the shires and held sessions of the King's Court at the major towns of the country. These trips by the judges eventually became spaced at two sittings per locality per year, and became known as the Assizes, as the word Assize is Norman French for just such a thing - a gathering together of important people for the purpose of law making.

Homicide was considered far too serious a matter to be tried by small local courts, and so all cases of homicide were left to the judges of the King's Court when they came visiting twice a year at the Assizes (except for a small period of time when a system of 'Supervisors' was tried during the reign of Edward II, see below). And to provide the 'official memory', the proceedings of the Assizes were written down onto skins of parchment which were then sewn together end-to-end and rolled up, thus being known as 'rolls'.

Northampton, because it was an important provincial town, was one of the centres chosen to have the Assizes, and the Northamptonshire Assizes were held from the twelfth century right up until the Crown Court came along in 1971. The local police were expected to provide the court ushers at the Assizes, and as a young police officer, I attended the Northamptonshire Assizes in 1971. I did not realise it then, but I do now, that I was attending the last sitting of a court that had been held for over 800 years, nearly 300 of which had been in the very same building as I was then in. And that building was the Sessions House, in George Row, Northampton.

And what a building it is! Completed in 1678, it provided a new home for the Assizes, which had previously been held in Northampton Castle, which, because it was so dilapidated, had just been pulled down. The new building provided two court rooms, one for the criminal cases, and one for the civil cases (called the 'Nisi Prius' court, from the Latin inscription on all civil summonses) as well as offices and robing rooms and so on. But the talking point of the two courts is undoubtedly the plaster ceilings. Started in 1684 by the London plasterer Edward Gouge, it took four years to complete. And one of the features of the ceiling in the main court, is the 'Devil's Mask', having a moveable tongue, which is supposed to wag every time a lie is told in court.

The Sessions House in George Row, Northampton, from a postcard of 1912. Note the very high doorways. It has often been said that they are so high to allow stagecoaches to drive in to the entrance hall. This is not true, no such thing happened, the high doors are part of the design and nothing more. (NLIS)

bottom of previous page

The interior of the Number 1 Court (the criminal court) in the Sessions House.
This view is from the Judge's Chair. In front of him sat the Clerk of the Court (facing into the court). Beyond him sat the barristers; and behind them was the square dock, where the prisoner sat, all of them facing towards the judge. Right at the back of the court, in the gallery, which has no access into it from the floor of the court, was the Gentry Gallery, where only those persons who had a ticket from the Lord Lieutenant of the County, were allowed to sit. The hoi polloi was only allowed in the Public Gallery on the ground floor, underneath the Gentry Gallery. The Public Gallery was divided into two parts, because there was strict segregation - men on one side, and women on the other.
On the extreme left are the two jury boxes. The Grand Jury Box is the upper gallery, having no access to it from the floor of the court; and the Petty Jury Box is beneath it. For an explanation of the two juries, see the book *Guilty M'Lud! The criminal history of Northamptonshire* by an author whose names escapes me.
The Witness Box is on the extreme right. (NP)

The view from the other end of the court, from the Public Gallery towards the Judge's Chair. In January 2009, a programme of restoration was started, hence the scaffolding, and workmen. (NP)

The back of the Dock, showing the stairs down to the dungeons below. How many murderers, thieves and villains have come up these stairs in 300 years? And perhaps even a few innocent people as well! (NP)

A part of the lovely plasterwork ceiling can be glimpsed in the photographs on pages 6 and 7. Directly above the scaffolding in the photograph on page 7, is the 'Devil's Face' mask. This is a close-up, clearly showing the moveable tongue, which is supposed to waggle every time a lie is told in court. Surprisingly, the tongue is still there, and hasn't dropped off through overuse. (NP)

What surviving Assize Rolls there are, are kept in the National Archives at Kew. But these are in medieval court Latin, which is nigh on impossible to decipher unless you are an expert. Northamptonshire is lucky in having one of the oldest of the Assize Rolls still preserved (for the years 1202 and 1203), and is equally lucky in having these rolls transcribed and published in one of the Northamptonshire Record Society publications, so giving ready access to the information contained there.

In the later times, just before the start of the Assizes, a list, or 'Calendar', of prisoners due to appear before the Assizes was published. Assize Calendars are preserved in the Northamptonshire County Record Office, and although the series is far from complete, the existing ones provide a fairly comprehensive list of the homicides appearing before the Northamptonshire Assizes, from the start of the nineteenth century.

The Coroners' Rolls

Coroners' Rolls are also kept in the National Archives kept at Kew, and Northamptonshire is again lucky in having one of the most complete sets of Coroners' Rolls preserved: records of seventy complete years during the period of 1290 and 1420. As with the Assize Rolls, the Coroners' Rolls are in medieval Latin, and we must therefore rely on published interpretations and transcripts.

The office of Coroner is an ancient one, probably starting sometime during the twelfth century. Each county, generally, had four Coroners at any one time, with each borough electing one of its own. Generally speaking, the Borough Coroner's only qualification was to be a Burgess; whilst the County Coroner had to own a certain amount of land within the county. Coroners held office for life, and only 'escaped' either by becoming unqualified or by being removed by the king.

As they still do, the function of the medieval Coroner was to enquire into all sudden or unexplained deaths, that is, homicide, suicide or accident. When a body was discovered, and the first on the scene suspected that the culprit was still nearby, the 'Hue and Cry' was raised, which is a headlong pursuit of any suspected persons, shouting for others to join in, until the offender was caught. The Coroner would then be summoned to the scene, and he would cause a jury to be gathered quickly together from twelve free-men of the locality, who would then examine the body in-situ. The Coroner and jury would examine the body for marks of violence and the possible cause of death, and would record the date, place and time of death as far as they could. The jurors, being locals, were then asked if they could identify the body, determine the cause of death, and if possible, the circumstances surrounding it, and in the case of a suspected homicide, to try to name the suspects.

If it was decided the sudden death was a homicide, the Coroner would order the arrest of any suspect, confiscate all their possessions, and if they had been captured, commit them to gaol to await trial at the next Assizes. If the accused had fled the scene, the Coroner would direct the local law enforcement officer (the county sheriff, bailiff or parish constable) to arrest the person as soon as possible. All this Inquest information would then be copied onto rolls of parchment and await further examination by the professional judges when next they came visiting the county during what was known as the 'Eyres' - as opposed to the Assizes.

Not to put too fine a point on it, the Eyres were more about filling the king's coffers than the administration of justice, and there are reports of villagers fleeing to the woods whenever they heard the Eyre was on their way to see them, as they knew they were in for a financial fleecing. As with the Assizes, each offence could (and was) punished by a fine. Hence the reason why so many Coroners' Rolls have been preserved, as it was not unusual for the Eyre to demand the Coroners' Rolls for the previous few years.

Coming to the throne in 1327, Edward III ordered an Eyre, because he wanted to wage his wars (in France and Scotland), but was short of money. The Eyre visited Northamptonshire in 1329 and 1330, and the record of it has survived, with a modern transcript being published by the Selden Society. From this, we can extract information about any homicides that the Eyre also examined, 680 years ago.

Supervisors' Rolls

During the time of Edward II (1307-1327), experiments in government were tried. Included in this, was a system of 'Supervisors' who were given the power of 'oyer' and 'terminer' to try legal cases in between the twice yearly visits of the Assize judges. 'Oyer' was the power to call or to summon people before them to try their cases; and 'terminer' was the power to determine the outcome, and to pass sentence where necessary.

The majority of the Supervisors were chosen from the land owners of the county, and thus were not trained judges, although they sat on a panel which *was* chaired by a qualified judge. It is interesting to note, however, that as soon as Edward II died in 1327, his son, Edward III, although only fifteen, in realising that local people should try local crimes, started tinkering with the concept of the Supervisors' system, and passed laws which eventually developed the Supervisors' system into that of the Justices of the Peace for each county, who sat in their newly established court held every three months, and thus called the Quarter Sessions. The Justices of the Peace, or Magistrates, were still given powers of 'oyer' and 'terminer' to try the lesser offences before their court of Quarter Sessions, but were still not thought competent enough to try the homicide cases, which were then left fairly and squarely in the hands of the professional judges of the Assize Courts.

In 1940, the Northamptonshire Record Society published the few surviving Northamptonshire Supervisors' Rolls, of 1314, 1316 and 1320. Only a few homicides appeared in these Rolls, however, and these contain absolutely minimal detail. But they will be included, because of the historical interest of the documentary source.

Newspaper reports

Obviously, the further towards our own times we come, official records of the Court and Coroner are kept from public view for a closed period of years. When this happens, we must consult the local newspapers.

Northamptonshire, in the *Northampton Mercury*, has one of the oldest continuously published newspapers in the world, printed since 1720. The *Mercury* was joined by the *Northampton Herald* in

1834, and these two served town and county until amalgamation as the *Mercury and Herald* in the 1920s. So where there are gaps in official records, newspaper accounts will be available.

Apart from these, other printed sources have been consulted of course, and these will be acknowledged in the text. But it is the Assize and Coroners records, together with the newspaper reports, which form the bulk of the sources consulted.

THE LAYOUT OF THE ENTRIES IS SELF-EXPLANATORY, BUT an explanation of the judges' titles must be given. Up until 1873, the English court system included the Court of Common Pleas, the Court of the King's/Queen's Bench and the Court of the Exchequer, each in effect a division of the High Court. The Exchequer Court obviously heard the cases concerning financial matters, whilst the King's/Queen's Bench and the Common Pleas heard the rest, their case loads being the same, only an historical anomaly giving the two divisions instead of one as it logically should have been. But each division was given its own judges, who sat mainly in their own courts, but were competent to sit in either of the other two as the occasion arose.

The judges of the Common Pleas and the King's/Queen's Bench were called Justices and were addressed as Mr Justice so-and-so, with the chief justice being called Mr Chief Justice so-and-so. Because in the Law Reports it was time consuming to write 'Mr Justice so-and-so' all the time, so a shorthand emerged which called the judges by their surname followed by the initial 'J' for Judge/Justice; 'CJ' for Chief Justice and eventually 'LCJ' for Lord Chief Justice. Thus Mr Justice Hawkins was referred to as 'Hawkins J'; Mr Justice Lawrence as Lawrence J; Lord Chief Justice Russell as 'Russell LCJ', and so on.

By some historical accident, judges of the Exchequer division were known as Barons rather than Justices. But the same applies, thus Mr Baron Pollock becomes 'Pollock B', and Lord Chief Baron Abinger becomes 'Abinger LCB'. Although their expertise was in the Exchequer Courts, the Barons could, and often did, sit in the other two divisions, hearing criminal cases. However, in 1875 the Exchequer Court was abolished, so no more Barons were created, but the existing ones kept their title until retirement. The last Baron to be created was Sir John Huddlestone in 1875. He died in 1890, making Sir Charles Pollock the last surviving Baron, who died in 1897.

OBVIOUSLY THERE WERE MANY MORE MURDER CASES IN Northamptonshire, especially during the earliest years, of which no record has survived. But all that changes when the *Northampton Mercury* appears on the scene in 1720.

However, in the early days, the *Mercury* considered the national news (culled from the London newspapers), as more important than local news. So although the Northamptonshire Assizes *were* reported on, some of these reports were very brief and perfunctory, resulting in actual detail being disappointingly and tantalisingly absent.

Thus although a fairly complete list of all the criminal homicides from 1720 onwards can be compiled, the detail about them varies greatly. Nevertheless, every homicide *is* given, because a complete picture of the frequency and nature of the homicides committed, can give a better insight into the very essence of our society more than could any other social barometer.

But having said that, what is *not* included are those sad cases of homicide, followed by the suicide of the offender. These cases obviously went to the coroners' courts, and not to the criminal courts, and are often surrounded with painful family circumstances. It would serve no purpose to examine them in detail.

Because the number of homicides is so great, there will be two volumes in this series. This is the first volume which will cover all the years up to, and including, 1850. The second volume which will be along shortly, will cover the years from 1851 onwards.

In the meantime, read and wonder at the murkier doings of our county ancestors. And do please, please, please remember, that by definition, a murder means that someone's life has been violently taken, with all the pain and grief which that means to those surviving family members.

JUDICIAL EXECUTIONS

Before 1834, the death sentence could be given for offences other than for criminal homicide. So as well as containing all those executions for criminal homicide, this book contains, as far as can be made out, a complete list of all those executions for non-homicide offences which have occurred within the county, and for which documentary evidence has survived.

Obviously there were many, many more executions throughout the centuries, both for homicides and non homicides, because Lords of the Manor had the power of dispensing the death penalty at their manorial courts. But all records of these have now been lost.

There are lots of ways to execute people, but in Northamptonshire, only four have been used : beheading, pressing, burning and hanging. Beheading, of course, has been quite common in British history, but because it was the method of execution reserved exclusively for those of noble blood, it has only been used in Northamptonshire on three occasions.

Thankfully, only been one recorded instance of 'pressing to death' has occurred within the county. This was not done indiscriminately, but for a very specific offence. Death by burning was also done for very specific offences, and seven burnings are recorded in Northamptonshire.

But by far the commonest form of execution was, of course, by hanging. This has always been the favourite English means of judicial execution, and we shall see how the means of administering it changed over time, and indeed how the frequency also changed as social enlightenment twisted and turned in its development over the years.

Although a list of the recorded judicial executions in Northamptonshire appeared in my book *Guilty M'Lud! The criminal history of Northamptonshire*, I never gave any detail of them, which I regretted. This is now rectified, and a full list of all executions within the county will be found in the Index.

Also a confession. Because of a faulty perpetual calendar, a large number of the days of the week given in *Guilty M'Lud!* for the executions, are wrong. This is now corrected, with many apologies.

THE MIDDLE AGES

1201-1500

In this twenty first century of ours, we think we live in violent times. But when compared to the medieval period, our homicide rate shrinks into insignificance. The earliest known surviving documentary record of criminal homicides for the county, is contained in the Rolls for the 1202 and 1203 Northamptonshire Assizes. During those two years, there were sixteen homicides reported to the Assizes. With an estimated population for the county of 20,000 at that time, then an average of eight homicides per year gives a rate of ·4 homicides per 1,000 population.

In the year ending May 2010, there were four criminal homicides from a population of about 650,000, giving a rate per 1,000 of ·006. If the medieval rate of ·4 were applied to today's population, then we would be having 260 criminal homicides per year - 5 murders per week, every week of the year!

The Northamptonshire Assizes for the year 1202 started on the Feast of the Blessed Virgin Mary (Sunday 15 September) and lasted until Saturday 19 October, with only a brief intermission of a few days when cases were heard at Bedford.

In 1930, the Assize Rolls of 1202 and 1203 were translated (they are written in the 'Court Latin' of the day) and published as Volume V of the publications of the Northamptonshire Record Society. As well as the reports of the murders, these Rolls also give a clear insight into the system of law enforcement during King John's time, and before there was any organised system of police as we know it today. The Rolls also show the stage that the English criminal law had reached by then, with its mixing of the emerging Common Law with the ancient trial customs of the previous centuries.

The workings of Frankpledge, Sanctuary and Outlawry are plainly seen, as well as the lesser known system of Englishry, all of which are also clearly seen for their secondary purpose - that of providing the Crown with the excuse for the extortion of money from whatever source it could think of.

There were five judges at these Assizes : Simon of Pattishall; Richard Malebysse; Eustace of Fauconberg; Alexander of Poynton and Henry of Northampton. Which judge heard which case is unfortunately not known.

✣✣ *However, these five judges are an interesting bunch, all being important figures in one way or another. Simon of Pattishall (that is, the Pattishall near to Northampton) was Chief Justice of the Bench of Common Pleas by 1193, and was a Baron of the Exchequer in 1198. He was High Sheriff of Northamptonshire between 1199 and 1204, with King John also making him one of the 'Justices of the Jews'. This meant that he administered the property confiscated from Jewish owners during the many anti-Semitic purges of the Middle Ages. So much so, that in 1199, King John gave two houses in Northampton to Simon after they had been confiscated from Benedict the Jew of Northampton. Simon also received the manor of Rothersthorpe in 1209. But when suspecting Simon of siding with his enemies (the disgruntled Barons, who would eventually force John into signing the Magna Carta), the fickle King John confiscated all Simon's property - but quickly restored it when John realised that because of his disastrous reign, he needed all the friends he could get. It is believed that Simon of Pattishall was one of the very few that accompanied King John to Runnymede in 1215, when he was forced to sign the Magna Carta. King John died in 1216, and it is believed that Simon died just one year later.*

✣✣ *Richard Malebysse was from a Norman family which had come over with the Conqueror, and which had received vast lands in Yorkshire. A rather wild character, Richard had been implicated in a violent massacre of Jewish families in York (no doubt similar to the Northampton Massacre - 1277A); together with other 'naughties', one of which involved a plot to have the Pope excommunicated! Only the payment of vast sums of money to Prince John, who was acting as Regent in the absence of Richard I, restored him to favour, and John made him a Judge. John, when he became King in 1199, sent Richard Malebysse as Ambassador to Scotland, but then fined him for neglecting his Yorkshire estates! Richard Malebysse died in 1209.*

✣✣ *Eustace of Fauconberg was a Yorkshire man who by 1199 had become a Judge at Westminster. In 1218, Henry III would make him Treasurer of England, and Ambassador to France. In 1221 he was made a Canon of Saint Paul's Cathedral, and at the same time was consecrated Bishop of London. He was believed to have carried out the duties of both Judge and Bishop at the same time. He died in October 1228, and was buried in (the old) Saint Paul's Cathedral.*

✣✣ *Alexander of Poynton was already a Judge at Westminster by 1202. He had large estates in Lincolnshire, and in 1213 would be High Sheriff of that county. He must have been one of the very few on the King's side, because in December 1215, he was captured by the Barons and imprisoned in Rochester Castle, and all his property seized. It was only after the entreaties of his son, that he was released and his property restored. It is not known when he died.*

✣✣ *Henry of Northampton was in Holy Orders, and was at the time of the 1202 Northamptonshire Assizes, the Vicar of Saint Peter's Church in Northampton, and a Canon of Saint Paul's Cathedral, where he had already founded a hospital within the Cathedral's precincts. He was certainly a Judge of many years standing by 1202, because his judgements are recorded in Lincolnshire, Cambridgeshire and Huntingdonshire. He was High Sheriff of Northamptonshire between 1205 and 1208, but obviously picked the wrong side, when he threw in his lot with the Barons rather than King John. As a result, all his property was confiscated by the King. This must have ruined him, because there is no more mention made of him in any surviving documents, and he fades from history's view.*

At the Assizes, each Hundred of the county had to send a jury (of twelve men) to describe to the judge all the crime that had occurred in their Hundred since the last Assizes. The descriptions of the criminal homicides, therefore, tend to be sparse, and do not provide much information, or interest. But, for what it's worth, here they are :

1202

1202A Sometime during 1202. Duddington parish
Victim An unknown man
Undetected

The body of an unknown man was found murdered in Duddington Wood. There are no other details known.

What an ignominious start. This is all we know of the very first surviving legally recorded criminal homicide in Northamptonshire - we do not even know his name.

1202B Sometime during 1202. Glendon parish
Victim Richard of Glendon
Undetected

When Richard of Glendon was murdered at Glendon, Sybil, his widow, had accused three men of his murder. The case was dealt with at the Northamptonshire Assizes as follows:

The Jurors of the Rothwell Hundred say that Sybil, widow of the murdered Richard of Glendon, had accused three men of the murder: Richard, son of Henry of Glendon; Roger of Oxhill; and William, son of Henry of Glendon. However, although Sybil had since withdrawn her accusation against Richard, son of Henry, both Roger of Oxhill and William, son of Henry were both outlawed by the Assizes because of her accusations. But both men continued to live in Glendon without Frankpledge, and the villagers of Glendon had failed to deliver up the two men for trial. The village of Glendon is therefore fined for this, as also is Sybil for failing to come to the Assizes to follow up her accusations. However, Stephen, the murdered Richard's brother, is also fined because he continued to accuse Richard, son of Henry of the murder, despite Sybil's withdrawal of her accusation against this Richard, son of Henry. As the Assize Court now accepts the innocence of Richard, son of Henry, Stephen is fined for false accusation.

It is immediately apparent in the 1202 Assizes Roll, that in the early thirteenth century, the use of surnames was still not a common practice, and each individual had to be identified either from their place of birth, their occupation, or their father's name. Surnames as we know them, were not to be commonplace for another one hundred years or so.

Each Hundred of the county (a Hundred was an administrative district within the county) had to send a jury of twelve knights to the Assizes to answer questions about the crimes committed within their Hundred. Failure to answer these questions resulted in a fine. In this instance, the jurors of the Rothwell Hundred (of which Glendon is a parish, and where Richard of Glendon was murdered) were more than equal to their task and not only repeated Sybil's accusations, but also reported to the Assizes judge that the two accused, although outlawed, had openly been living in Glendon without belonging to the Glendon Frankpledge. Only the Assize Court could outlaw anybody, and then only after they had been summoned three times and had failed to appear on each occasion.

The Saxon system of Frankpledge had fallen into disuse after the Norman Conquest of 1066, but by the Assize of Clarendon in 1166, it had been revived. Every man over 16 in a village was supposed to be in the village Frankpledge, where each man was mutually responsible for the good behaviour of the other members, and duty bound to produce any of their number in court when summoned.

If any member of a Frankpledge failed to appear when summoned, then the whole Frankpledge was fined. Such a system was not entirely satisfactory, as disreputable characters were not welcome in any Frankpledge, for obvious reasons, but it was hard, if well nigh impossible, to prevent any such characters from staying in the village. This is what had obviously happened to the Glendon Frankpledge over Roger of Oxhill and William, son of Henry of Glendon, with the result that the whole village of Glendon was fined for allowing two outlaws to stay in the village without them being in the Frankpledge, and for not delivering them to the Assizes.

The next of kin of murdered people were expected to make a formal declaration of the crime to the local Manorial Court, and then 'follow it up' at the Assizes before the judge. In the Assize Court, the accuser then had to offer to prove his/her case either by Trial by Combat, or in some other way that the court saw fit.

At that time, Trial by Combat was still looked upon as one of the main practices to establish guilt or innocence, as was the Trial by Ordeal of the person when/if caught. In the 1203 Assize Roll, there are several reports of Trial by Ordeal, though none for the crime of murder. In this case, Sybil had not followed up her accusations in the Assizes, and was, therefore, fined for that.

Unfortunately, there are no further details of this murder, so we do not know whether the two alleged murderers stood trial or not. On this, history, and the Rolls, are silent.

1202C Sometime during 1202. The Rothwell Hundred
Victim Gilbert of Desborough
Accused Thomas of Nuttall

Gilbert of Desborough was murdered by Thomas of Nuttall (which is in Nottinghamshire) somewhere in the Hundred of Rothwell (presumably, but not necessarily in Desborough). Thomas fled from the district, so the Assizes ordered that he be hunted and caught.

1202D Sometime during 1202. Marston Trussell
Victim An unknown man
Undetected

The Stodfold Hundred Jury say that the body of an unknown man was found murdered at Marston Trussell, and they have no clue as to the identity of the murderer.

1202E Sometime during 1202. Northampton
Victim John the Goldsmith
Accused Walter of Northampton

Walter, accused of the murder of John the Goldsmith, had not yet been captured.

1202F Sometime during 1202. Northampton
Victim An unknown man
Undetected

The body of an unknown murdered man was found dumped in the 'ditch of the nuns of Northampton'.

1202G Sometime during 1202. Warkton
Victim Roger the Reaper
Accused Godfrey of Warkton

Roger the Reaper was murdered by Godfrey of Warkton, who had already been hanged after admitting the murder. His worldly goods, value twelve shillings, were forfeited to the Crown.

This is the first recorded instance in Northamptonshire of a criminal actually being caught. Remember, in those days there was no police force as we know it. England had to wait for well over 500 years before it got any sort of detective/investigative police force ('The Bow Street Runners'), and even then, this was started by a private individual, and not by central government. So murderers actually being caught (let alone convicted) was a rare occurrence, but see cases 1202H and 1202P.

1202H Sometime during 1202. Grafton Underwood
Victim Robert, son of Hugh of Grafton
Accused Richard, son of Gilbert

Robert, son of Hugh of Grafton was murdered by Richard, son of Gilbert, who then sought sanctuary in a church. Richard admitted his guilt and was exiled from the country, and his goods, worth 5s 6d, were forfeited to the crown.

Perhaps one of the best known, but least understood, of ancient legal rights, the system of Sanctuary needs explanation.

A fugitive who gained the sanctuary of a church or other religious institution such as a monastery, could remain there for up to 40 days. During this time the parish had to supply sufficient food to keep him alive, and the four neighbouring parishes had to supply men to keep a constant watch upon the church to see that the fugitive did not escape.

At any time during the 40 days, the fugitive could send for the local coroner, confess his crime, and either give himself up for trial, or swear to 'abjure [leave] the realm'. If he chose exile, then the criminal had to go through the little ceremony of abjuration. This usually took place at the churchyard gate, and before the coroner, the criminal had to say 'I,.......for the crime of.......which I have committed, will quit this realm of England, never more to return, except by leave of the Kings of England or their heirs, so help me God and all His Saints'.

The coroner then assigned a specific port to him, and the criminal had to walk there 'ungert, unshod, bare-headed in his bare shirt, as if he were to be hanged on the gallows'. He was given a fixed time for his journey, normally one day for every 25 miles distance.

Along the route, he was to carry a Cross and was forbidden to stray off the main highway, on which he was safe. If the fugitive wandered off the main road for any reason, then any person was within their legal rights to apprehend him using any force as was necessary. Sometimes, this resulted in serious injury, and worse, to the fugitive. In Northamptonshire, in 1322, the Coroners' Rolls report the case of John of Ditchford, who did exactly that - stray off the main highway. The villagers of Wootton who were watching his sanctuary, chased him over the fields and caught him near to Collingtree. They promptly beheaded him, and in triumph carried his head to the Northampton Coroner. No one was blamed for this - how could they - they had all acted within the law.

The fugitive was passed from parish constable to parish constable along his journey, and each parish where he stopped for the night was legally bound to supply him with food. When he arrived at his port, he had to board the earliest available ship. If there were no ships ready to sail, he had to walk into the sea as though to demonstrate his readiness to leave the country, and had to do this every day until there was a ship sailing.

In 1540, this right of Sanctuary was severely curtailed by abolishing the need to leave the country. Instead all sanctuary seekers were to be kept in a kind of house arrest in any one of eight designated towns throughout the country, one of which was Northampton. For fairly obvious reasons, the townspeople of the eight designated centres objected to having other peoples' 'riff-raff' dumped on them, and so this system was never popular, and was never a success, despite several attempts at 'tinkering' with it.

By an Act of Parliament in 1623, Sanctuary was abolished entirely. Hereafter, 'no sanctuary or privilege of sanctuary, shall be...permitted or allowed in any case'.

1202J Sometime during 1202. Denford
Victim Hugh the Shepherd
Accused Robert of Keystone

Hugh the Shepherd of Denford was murdered by Robert of Keystone (which is in Huntingdonshire) who lived in Denford without being in Frankpledge. He had since run away, so his goods, worth four shillings, had been confiscated, and the village of Denford had been fined for allowing him to live there when not in Frankpledge.

1202K Sometime during 1202. Somewhere in the Navisford Hundred (the Thrapston area)
Victim John the Smith's son
Undetected

John the Smith's son was killed by having his head smashed in with a stone. It was not known what Frankpledge he was in, so fines could not be levied at any specific Frankpledge of the Hundred. Englishry was not proved, so his death was recorded as murder.

This is a good example of the 'heads I win, tails you lose' legal trap of the time. Because the Crown could not extract a fine from any Frankpledge, it resorted to the system known as 'Englishry'.

After the Norman Conquest, a 'Murder Fine' was levied on any Hundred if a Norman was killed within that Hundred. So after every death, the Coroner would investigate to see whether the deceased was Norman or Saxon (English), with only direct evidence from next-of-kin being taken as good enough proof of the person being English. In the absence of any next-of-kin to prove his 'Englishry', the deceased was automatically assumed to be Norman, thus making the Hundred liable for the Murder Fine.

1202L Sometime during 1202. Somewhere in the Navisford Hundred

Victim Walter Wenge

Accused Robert the Piper; Peter, son of Robert the Piper; Turston.

Walter Wenge was murdered by Robert the Piper, his son Peter, and Turston, who have all since run away. Ailsworth, the Frankpledge they belonged to, failed to deliver them to Court, and is therefore fined. The murderer's goods have since been forfeited to the Crown and are worth a total of 3s 9d.

1202M Sometime during 1202. Somewhere in the Towcester Hundred

Victim An unnamed man, a messenger of the Earl of Leicester

Undetected

A messenger of the Earl of Leicester was murdered by persons unknown somewhere between Northampton and Brackley. No other details are known.

1202N Sometime during 1202. Somewhere in the Mawsley Hundred

Victim The husband of Amicia, daughter of Roger of Papcote

Accused Walter of Watford; Henry of Barrowby; William, son of Henry of Barrowby; Samson, son of Henry of Barrowby

Amicia accused Henry of Barrowby (which is in Leicestershire) and William and Samson his sons, of assaulting her husband, and holding him on the ground whilst Walter of Watford dealt him a blow to the head which killed him. Walter of Watford had since run away and had not yet been caught, so Amicia applied to the judge to have Walter outlawed. The Mawsley Hundred Jurors then said that they thought Walter was living with Henry of Barrowby.

1202P Sometime during 1202. Somewhere in Northamptonshire (Hundred not given)

Victim Henry Bret

Accused Osbert the Knight; Hugh Cracket; Serlo

Henry Bret was murdered by Osbert the Knight, having been accused by Henry's brother, Richard, who also named Hugh Cracket and Serlo as accomplices. But Richard Bret did not follow up his accusations at the Assizes, so he was fined. Englishry was not proved, therefore the Murder Fine had to be paid. But Hugh Cracket had since been captured, so he was remanded in custody until decisions were taken over Henry's murder.

A possible reason why Richard had not followed up his accusation and was thus not in court to prove his brother's Englishry is given in a margin note : 'Richard has since set out to Jerusalem'. He was probably therefore, a member of the Fourth Crusade which succeeded in capturing Constantinople from the Turks in 1204.

1202Q Sometime during 1202. Somewhere in the Cleyley Hundred (the Grafton Regis area)
Victim Robert, son of Ascelin
Accused Hugh, son of Wlric

Robert was murdered by Hugh and was outlawed for it. His Frankpledge, Ashton, did not present him, so they were fined. Hugh had no possessions, and Englishry was not proved.

1202R Sometime during 1202. Somewhere in the Cleyely Hundred
Victim Wimarc
Undetected

Wimarc was found murdered near to Watling Street. Englishry was not proved and so it was recorded as murder, and the usual fine was levied.

1202S Sometime during 1202. Somewhere in the Cleyley Hundred
Victim Roger Rumbaud
Accused Hugh, son of Walter the Priest

The Jurors of the Cleyley Hundred said that Hugh was outlawed for the murder of Roger Rumbaud, following the accusation of Robert Rumbaud, but had returned to court some time later with a King's Writ of Pardon. However, on the accusation of Geoffrey, son of Turston, Hugh was outlawed again. The Assize Judge therefore demanded an explanation as to why Hugh was outlawed twice for the same crime.

This case is very involved, but it illustrates the development of the law up to this date. Common Law was developing rapidly, but the ancient laws still held influence, with the system of Outlawry still being used, although by this date (the early thirteenth century) the days were long gone when an outlaw could safely be killed by anyone without fear of punishment.

Case 1202S is a very interesting Outlawry case. The Assize Court demanded an explanation why Hugh had been outlawed, then pardoned and then outlawed again for the same murder (of Roger Rumbaud). It was explained that in the time of King Richard (the 'Lionheart' - who had died three years earlier, in 1199) Hugh had been outlawed for the murder, on the accusation of Robert Rumbaud.

However, some time later, Hugh had returned to the Assizes with a Royal Pardon (which was easily obtainable by anyone after a certain period of service in the army) which also ordered the High Sheriff of the County to see that Hugh made peace with the family of the murdered man. Hugh was then sent away by the Court to see if he could find sureties for his future good behaviour.

Meanwhile, Roger Rumbaud's next-of-kin, on hearing that Hugh had returned, had presented Geoffrey, son of Turston to the Assizes, who promptly re-accused Hugh of the murder. But Hugh had never since re-appeared before the court, apparently finding sureties for his good behaviour hard to come by. He had therefore run away again because he feared for his own safety at the hands of Roger's next-of-kin, because the ancient law still applied which said that although the King could pardon the crime, he could not deprive the dead man's family of their right of vengeance.

Since Hugh had not re-appeared before the Court (after the customary three summonses) in an attempt to appease the opposing factions, he was therefore outlawed again, or in the words of the traditional sentence of the law quod gereretur lupinum capud sicut prius fecit - *'let him bear the wolf's head as he did before'.*

❀

(E1) **SEPTEMBER 1202**

HANGED FOR GANGSTERISM

Thomas the Baker

Until the appearance of the county constabularies in the early to mid nineteenth century, travelling criminal gangs were the scourge of the English countryside. When there is no organised police force to stop them, criminal gangs can go marauding about the place, plundering and pillaging at will.

The first such criminal gang recorded in Northamptonshire is mentioned in the surviving record of the 1202 Northamptonshire Assizes, which were held in September. Thomas the Baker had finally been captured after his gang had terrorised people from as far south as Bury Saint Edmunds, and as far north as Nottingham.

But Thomas was no Robin Hood figure robbing the rich to help the poor. His motive was purely greed - and self preservation.

No sooner had he been captured then he turned 'approver', in other words, 'grassing up' his gang members, hoping for a pardon. He named eighteen members of his gang, men and women, as well as others who had given them shelter. He confessed to crimes of burglary, theft and robbery, about twenty in all, but no doubt there were many, many more.

But it was all to no avail. Despite turning approver, Thomas was still hanged. And probably members of his gang were as well, although the Assize Roll is silent on this point.

AFTER THE 1202 ASSIZES, NO FURTHER WRITTEN RECORDS have survived until we get to the bulk of the Coroners' Rolls which started in the 1280s. However, the Northampton Jewish Massacre of 1277 is well known, appearing in several written documents :

1277

1277A Good Friday, 26 March 1277. Northampton
Victims 50 of Northampton's Jewish community
Undetected

Taking place on one of the great Christian festivals, the dreadful deaths of 50 Northampton Jews ranks as one of the more shameful episodes of the town's history. By their money lending habits, the Northampton Jews had gained ownership of virtually all the property within Northampton borough, thereby placing the other townspeople in the classic debtor's dilemma - they could only pay the interest on what they already owed by borrowing more money.

But this was the England of the reign of Edward I. Blatant anti-semitism was being actively encouraged, and which would, in 1290, lead to the expulsion of the whole of England's Jewish population. Taking advantage of this attitude, the Northampton townspeople saw a way of ridding themselves of their debts.

A rumour was circulated in the town that the Jews had stolen a Christian boy from his parents, and had killed him for use in their Passover Rites, by nailing him hand and foot to a wooden cross. Completely untrue of course, but this is the nature of 'the rumour', truth never enters into it.

So incensed did the Northampton people become that they dragged 50 of the leaders of the Jewish community into the street, beat them up, and put them 'on trial', with a priest perjuring himself in presenting the 'evidence'. Naturally, all 50 were sentenced to death, with the rest of the Jews being banished from the town immediately, not being allowed, of course, to take anything with them.

The 50 Jews were tied to the tails of great heavy cart-horses, some by their hands, some by their hair, others by their feet and waists. The terrified horses were then whipped to such a pitch that they stampeded up and down the road which is now called York Road, just outside the Derngate, dragging their screaming victims with them. Several times the horses were driven, getting more and more panic stricken as they trampled with their great iron-shod hooves over the screaming bodies, which were becoming increasingly mangled.

Eventually, the flushed and elated townspeople were satiated, but then all the bodies, both living and dead, were strung up in a row of trees where they were allowed to rot for months.

So, by the 'Good Friday Massacre', in just the one day, Northampton expelled all the Jews living in the borough. All their property was shared out equally, which was, of course, the whole point of the exercise. Despite the offenders obviously being well known, no person was ever tried for these murders.

WE NOW GET TO THE MAIN SOURCE OF INFORMATION ON medieval murders, the Coroners' Rolls. Those surviving for Northamptonshire are preserved at the National Archives at Kew, and they record inquests for 70 years, the first starting in 1288/89 and the last in 1420. In total, during those 70 years, there were 1307 cases of deaths investigated by the Coroners: 575 were criminal homicides; 716 were cases of misadventure/accident; and there were 16 suicides. So again, 575 homicides in 70 years, confirms that there was an average of eight murders every year in medieval Northamptonshire. The following cases are from the Coroners' Rolls, but only a selection of the most interesting ones will be given, as the description of all of them would make very boring (and repetitive) reading.

1288/1289

1288/1289A Sometime during 17 Edward 1. Northampton
Victim Henry, son of Richard le Vach of Northampton
Accused Robert de Cosewell

Robert de Cosewell struck Henry on the head with a stick, and killed him instantly. Robert immediately fled to the church of Saint Edmund in Northampton, confessed his crime and abjured the realm. His goods, forfeited to the Crown, were worth 9s 6d.

Sometimes in the Coroners' Rolls, as in this case, and in some of the following, the dating is done by the regnal year of the monarch. Henry III died on 16 November 1272, and therefore his son Edward, became king as

Edward I on that date. So Edward I's regnal year was 16 November until 15 November; and therefore 17 Edward I was anytime between 16 November 1288 and 15 November 1289.

1290

1290A Tuesday 5 December 1290. Brixworth
Victim Ralph le Blount of Brixworth
Accused Simon, son of Simon Avery of Brixworth

Simon killed Ralph and fled immediately to Brixworth church. He confessed his crime and abjured the realm. His goods were worth 1s 9d.

Because this murder occurred during daylight in the village of Brixworth, the village of Brixworth was fined because Simon was not captured before he gained the sanctuary of Brixworth church. A good example of the Crown extorting money by using any excuse.

1291/1292, 1305, 1323/1324

1291/1292A Sometime during 20 Edward I. Chipping Warden
Victim Geoffrey, son of Alexander Broun of Bradden

1305A Wednesday 8 September 1305. Woodford Halse
Victim William de Hynton, Clerk (priest) of Woodford

1323/1324A Sometime during 17 Edward II. Chipping Warden
Victim Geoffrey of Warden
Accused in all three Martin of Littlebury

These three murders are grouped together, because this is the case of Martin of Littlebury, who is Northamptonshire's first recorded serial killer.

One dark night, Martin of Littlebury met up with Geoffrey, son of Alexander Broun, on the banks of the River Cherwell, at a place called 'le Mede' in Chipping Warden. Martin then shot Geoffrey with a bow and arrow killing him instantly.

Martin fled, but before he could gain sanctuary, was captured and gaoled in Northampton Castle to await trial. In those days there was no difference between murder and manslaughter, and Martin, when found guilty of murder, was therefore imprisoned to await sentence by one of the King's justices at the next Assizes. All his goods were forfeited to the Crown, and amounted to £2 14s 6d. This would mean that Martin was a man of substantial means. However, he apparently escaped and managed to avoid capture for a number of years before he surfaced again.

On Wednesday 8 September 1305, Martin struck again. This time it was the parish priest of Woodford, William de Hynton. There are no exact details of this murder, but Martin fled to sanctuary in Chipping Warden church. He confessed his crime and abjured the realm. This time his goods were only worth 10½d. However, a piece of land worth £1 per year was found to be his in Chipping Warden, and this was sold for £37, a huge sum for those days. How Martin had acquired this land, or how he had kept it hidden from his previous brush with the law, it is best not to ask.

Eighteen years were to pass by before Martin of Littlebury came to light again. Presumably he had been abroad fighting for the king, because when he turned up he had a King's Pardon. But obviously he had come to settle a few old scores, and Martin finished up in a fight with Geoffrey of Warden, and in which Martin murdered Geoffrey by stabbing him with a knife.

Instead of seeking sanctuary this time, Martin fled, and eventually was declared an outlaw. There is no record of his subsequent career, and it is not known whether he was arrested or what. This is history's way of drawing a veil over one of Northamptonshire's less reputable sons - perhaps it is just as well.

1294

1294A Saturday 16 October 1294. Stoke Albany churchyard
Victim Richard Flaumauntevill, parson of Stoke Albany
Accused William Hanred

Sometimes history is not fair. The background for this incident would make fascinating reading - if we knew it. But we don't, and we are left to conjecture.

What was the nature of the dispute between the parson of Stoke Albany, Richard Flaumauntevill, and William Hanred? Was it related to money, or property? Or perhaps something more sinister. But whatever it was, the two men ended up fighting in Stoke Albany churchyard, and William stabbed the priest in the belly with a knife. Richard died in agony the next day.

Although William was captured, he managed to escape and fled for sanctuary to the nearest church, which, ironically enough, was Stoke Albany. William did not abjure the realm, but surrendered to the Sheriff of Northamptonshire to stand trial. This was the obvious course of action. He was not going to walk away and leave his immense fortune behind him, so he would take his chance and argue his case in court, which he was rich enough to do.

His gamble failed however. He stood trial for murder, and was found guilty, and was hanged. William Hanred must have been a very rich man indeed, because his goods amounted to £17 5s 8d, and his lands in Brampton Ash gave an income of £16 10s per year, which in today's terms, would make him a millionaire. Perhaps the dispute was over some portion of this immense wealth, who knows? But it is known that after his death, squabbles broke out over the ownership of the land, which needed a very lengthy and expensive court case to sort out.

1294/1295

1294/1295A Sometime during 23 Edward I. Daventry
Victim Philip de Montgomery
Accused Nicholas Golafre and Richard Keyne

Although Richard Keyne was captured after he and Nicholas Golafre had murdered Philip de Montgomery, Nicholas had escaped and had sought sanctuary in Daventry church. But before he could be assigned a port by the coroner, he had escaped and had apparently run away to join the king's army in France, which is what the majority of sanctuary seekers did anyway. If any man did this, then he could received the King's Pardon and return to

England. Nicholas Golafre had done this, but as soon as he had set foot in Northamptonshire again some 35 years later, he had been captured and thrown into gaol for the earlier murder. The Northamptonshire Eyre of 1329, had ordered Nicholas to be brought before them, but lo and behold, he had produced the King's pardon in writing, plus a certificate of service with the king's army in France. Nicholas was thus released and allowed to go on his way rejoicing and unharmed.

1294/1295B Sometime during 23 Edward I. Cottesbrooke
Victim Amice (aged 3) daughter of Henry Bonham
Accused John de Wylverton

Whilst getting in some practice with a crossbow, the parish priest of Cottesbrooke, John de Wylverton, was firing at a target. Unfortunately, the target was placed in front of Henry Bonham's house, and Henry's three year old daughter Amice, was standing quite innocently in her father's porch.

John's bolt missed the target and hit Amice in her chest. She died two days later. John immediately fled to his own church at Cottesbrooke, confessed his crime and abjured the realm.

This is a good example of the state of the English law at the time as regards homicide. At the start of the fourteenth century, every homicide (except in self defence) was punishable by death, whether done with malice aforethought or not. The medieval mind reasoned that every person was responsible for the consequences of every action they did, whether planned or not. In case 1294/1295B, there was obviously no evil intent, but John had to seek sanctuary for his crime. It was not for another hundred years, in 1390, that murders were separated from other homicides, or what we would now call manslaughter, by including the concept of malice aforethought.

1296

(E2) **SOMETIME DURING 1296**

HANGED FOR FELONY

William de Havering

There are two publications which give a list of executions within Northamptonshire. The first is *Executions in Northampton 1277-1893*, published in 1900, by the Dryden Press. The second list appeared in the *Northampton Daily Echo* of 3 April 1925, which was later reprinted as *Northamptonshire Executions* in an undated small booklet. These two lists differ slightly, and the hanging of William de Havering for a felony is only included in the latter booklet.

Despite research, no other information has come to light. So we are still in the dark about William de Havering and why he came to Northamptonshire (Havering-atte-Bower is in Essex) and what his felony was.

1297/1298

1297/1298A Sometime during 26 Edward I. Farthingstone
Victim William (aged 8), son of John le Hunte
Accused John, son of William le Clerk

William's age is given as eight, so presumably, John would be of a similar age, because the two were playfully wrestling in the way that young boys have done since time immemorial. But John threw William to the ground in such a manner as William died. He must have broken his neck as he fell, or something similar. John immediately took sanctuary in the church of Farthingstone, but later surrendered himself to the Sheriff.

Nothing is then recorded as to the fate of John. Perhaps even in those days there was enough compassion to forgive young children for childish horseplay, no matter how tragic the consequences.

1302

The next two cases are interesting. What makes the village of Yelvertoft have one parish priest murdered and another doing the murdering both within the space of nine years?

1302A Palm Sunday 15 April 1302. Yelvertoft
Victim Ralph de Hundele
Accused John Ruggele

Ralph de Hundele was parish priest of Yelvertoft, and when quarrelling with John Ruggele, John smashed a spade over the head of the parish priest. Ralph died as a direct result three days later.

John fled to Yelvertoft church, confessed and abjured the realm. During the assault, there were three other men present, and although they were not considered guilty of the murder, nevertheless, they were fined for not stopping the murderer or capturing him afterwards.

1305

1305A *See* **1291/1292A**

1311

1311A Saturday 7 November 1311. Yelvertoft
Victim John the Cobbler of Yelvertoft
Accused William of Wellington

William of Wellington was the parish chaplain of Yelvertoft, who on that Saturday evening was obviously needing light of the earthly kind, and so sent his clerk to the house of John the Cobbler in the village for a penny candle. But John, no doubt having been caught before, refused point blank to send the candle without the money.

This so enraged William, that seizing a stick, he stormed round to John's house, burst open the door, and set about John with an un-chaplain-like frenzy. So violently did William hit John's head, that the skull was burst open and John's brains were scattered on the floor. William fled immediately to his own church of Yelvertoft seeking sanctuary.

John's body was found by Juliana, daughter of William Craunford, who immediately called her horrified father and another man called Henry of Piddington. Eventually the Coroner was called, but the murderer's identity was never in doubt, as they knew full well by then that William was seeking sanctuary in Yelvertoft church. William came voluntarily before the Coroner, confessed to the murder, and was assigned to go to the port of Dover.

DURING THE REIGN OF EDWARD II (1307 - 1327), A NEW SYSTEM OF criminal law was tried, called the system of Supervisors, which has already been explained in the Introduction. In 1940, the Northamptonshire Record Society published the surviving Northamptonshire Supervisors' Rolls, of 1314, 1316 and 1320. An incredible 30 homicide cases appear in these three rolls, thereby confirming the extraordinary yearly average of criminal homicides in medieval Northamptonshire.

The scribe completing the original roll wrote very, very little detail, other than the bare facts of the people involved. But for the sake of completeness, and because of the historical interest concerning this evolutionary experiment to our court system, these are a few of the cases where just a bit more detail was added.

1314

On Tuesday 20 August 1314, a Supervisors' Court was held at Northampton before Henry Spigurnel, John le Peyvre, Walter de Molesworth and John de Wylughby. Amongst the complaints of criminal homicide made before the court, were these two

1314A Sometime during 1314. Geddington
Victim William the Tailor of Geddington
Accused Roger, the son of Richard the Glover of Geddington; and William, son of Martin Bode of Geddington

What lay behind this murder? Was it a dispute between village craftsmen? We shall never know, but the two accused were both ordered to be hunted and outlawed.

1314B Sometime during 1314. Rushmills, Northampton
Victim Amice of Piddington
Accused John de Piddington, of Great Houghton, husband of the said Amice; and Alice, daughter of Alice Harlewyn

Unfortunately we can guess only too well what lay behind this murder. The 'Eternal Triangle' was as much in evidence in fourteenth century Northamptonshire as it is now. Human nature is human nature, you cannot legislate against that.

1316

Another session of the court was held on Friday 23 April 1316. Before this court appeared Henry of Killingworth (1316A); William son of Peter Gosse (1316B); and William the Miller of Cropredy (1316C). All these were charged with murder. Unfortunately, absolutely no other detail is given, other than they were all found guilty of murder and hanged.

Also appearing on that day was John Cicaying of Hartwell (1316D), where there is a little bit more information in that he murdered his wife Agnes at Hartwell. But his fate was the same, he was also hanged.

✣✣ *Of the four Supervisors who sat in these Courts, only Henry Spigurnel was a qualified judge. The other three were what we would now call magistrates, having only minimal legal training, but sitting on a panel, and under the direction of the trained and qualified judge. As such, only Henry Spigurnel is listed in the standard work on judges' biographies.*

Spigurnel was the name given to the officer who put the seals on the Writs of Chancery, and only one family seemed to have been involved, the job being passed down from father to son. Gradually the name of the job came to be adopted as a surname by this family, which proceeded to build up large land holdings, especially in Northamptonshire. Henry Spigurnel was certainly a judge by the year 1297, when he was summoned to Parliament in that capacity. In 1308 he was Ambassador to Rome, and other places overseas. Obviously he was back in Northampton in 1314, and by 1323 was a judge in the Channel Islands. He was again summoned to Parliament in 1325, and he died in 1328, a very rich man, having extensive property in six of the Home Counties.

1316E Sometime during 1316. Either Gayton or Edgecote
Victim Thomas de Murdak
Accused Julianne de Murdak

Included in the *Victoria County History of Northamptonshire*, is this case, which is important because it is the first instance in the county of the offence of Petty Treason.

Julianne de Murdak, daughter and co-heir of Philip and Escholace de Gayton, married Thomas de Murdak of Edgecote. According to the *Victoria County History*, Julianne murdered her husband at the instigation of Sir John Vaux in 1316 and was convicted of the crime and burnt at the stake.

In Gayton parish church, there is a monumental effigy to Mabila de Murdak, daughter of Julianne and Thomas, who died about the year 1310. This diminutive freestone effigy measures only two feet two inches long and wears a veil and gown. It was discovered in 1830, built face inwards into the exterior of the east wall of the chapel. At the end, below the head, are two mutilated shields - a fess between six fleur-de-lis; and a fess in chief with three roundels.

On one side of the plinth is this inscription : HIC IACET IN TUMBA MABILA FILIA THOME DE...... The subsequent crime of her mother six years later, may account for this monument being mutilated, the name de Murdak not being thought fit to appear within a church.

Julianne de Murdak is the first instance in Northamptonshire of the offence of 'Petty Treason'. High Treason was for offences against the King and/or the State, but the offence of Petty Treason (from the French 'petit', meaning 'small') was committed when a master was murdered by his servant, or a clergyman by his inferior, or, as in this case, when a husband was murdered by his wife.

The punishment for a man found guilty of Petty Treason was hanging, but for reasons I have been unable to discover, the punishment for a woman was burning at the stake. Julianne de Murdak is the first of six burnings for Petty Treason to have occurred in Northamptonshire - all for wives murdering their husbands - the others being Mrs Lucas in 1631; two unknown women in 1645 and 1655; Elizabeth Tresler in 1715; and Elizabeth Fawson in 1735. Burning as a punishment was abolished in 1790 and the offence of Petty Treason in 1820. Thereafter these crimes were treated as murder, with hanging as the punishment.

1317

(E3) **WEDNESDAY 20 JULY 1317**

HANGED FOR HIGH TREASON

John Poydras

The reign of Edward II of England was probably one of the worst in English history. Although having started off in that most famous of ways by being the very first Prince of Wales in 1284, when Edward eventually came to the throne in 1307, the early years of his reign were bedevilled by continuous quarrels with the Barons, or large land-owners of the country. They wanted Edward to be a strong king like his father Edward I, but were faced with a man of little brain who wasted enormous sums of money on his favourites such as Piers Gaveston, who was probably his homosexual lover.

The murder of Gaveston in 1312, and the defeat by the Scottish at Bannockburn in 1314, forced Edward to accept the humiliation of the Barons' imposition of his cousin, Thomas of Lancaster, as the effective ruler of England instead of himself. In short, England was in a right mess. So is it any wonder that people wanted rid of him? And this is where John Poydras comes in.

John Poydras claimed that *he* was the son of Edward I, and therefore the rightful king of England, and that Edward II was no more than a changeling, being swapped at birth by a nurse. Poydras was brought to Northampton, where a Parliament was summoned to examine his claims.

It came to light that he was the son of a tanner from Exeter, so could produce no evidence whatsoever, for his claims. He had obviously been duped into being the stooge for others who wanted to draw attention to the worsening political state of the country. John Poydras was condemned to death for High Treason, and was hung, drawn and quartered on Northampton Market Square.

1323/1324

1323/1324A *See* **1291/1292A**

1323/1324B Sometime during 17 Edward II. Bozeat
Victim John of Rockingham
Accused John Bird of Barnwell

On Wednesday 7 March 1324, John Bird of Barnwell fled to sanctuary to the church of Saint Andrew in Luddington. With him was his partner in crime, one William of Grendon. Before the Coroner, John confessed to the murder of John of Rockingham at Bozeat; and William confessed to the murder of a man called John of Belgrave somewhere in Leicestershire.

These two must have been a right pair of charmers, obviously professional travelling criminals roaming the countryside, seeing what came their way, and living on their wits. So when they sought sanctuary and chose to leave the country, it must have been because they were cornered with no escape.

But the local Coroner, Henry of Titchmarsh, was also a wily old bird who had not learned a thing or two in his years of dealing with people of this sort. He realised that John Bird and William of Grendon would get up to more 'naughties' if they remained together. So in order to ensure that they were separated for good, Henry assigned John to go south west to Portsmouth, and William south east to Dover.

(1329)

AS EXPLAINED IN THE INTRODUCTION, THE MEDIEVAL KINGS REGARDED the legal system as one vast money-making machine. So when, in 1327, Edward III came to the throne needing money to wage his wars, a General Eyre was ordered, which reached Northamptonshire in 1329.

An Eyre, from the Old French, meant a Bench of Judges touring round the country with legal powers to examine records and impose fines. The official record of this Eyre has survived, and was published by the Selden Society in 1983, and when we read this, we can see that the judge in charge of the Eyre, Sir Geoffrey le Scrope, examined the Northamptonshire Coroners' Rolls for the previous thirty years. Therefore, some of the above criminal homicides appear again in the Eyre. But a few new ones will be given below, just for the sake of interest, and to illustrate exactly how the Eyre was viewed by the judge, who was trying to keep in favour with King Edward III, by screwing as much money as he could out of the good people of Northamptonshire, by whatever means he could think of. In this he succeeded admirably, see below. For the sake of interest, I tried to count the cases of criminal homicides reported to the Eyre. I got well into three figures, and gave up.

On a date unknown, in the town of Brackley, Geoffrey le Saltere of Yourlaston, and Agnes, wife of Richard le Saltere of Wouminton (all in Staffordshire) killed Richard le Saltere, in the house of Denise Crabbe in Brackley. Agnes and Denise were captured, but Geoffrey escaped. Later Agnes and Denise escaped. Therefore the Eyre fined the town of Brackley for letting them all escape.

Sometime during the year 1313 to 1314, Ralph fitz Philip Miller of Astrope killed Roger de la March in Brackley. Brackley was fined twice - for not raising the Hue and Cry in the first place, and then again, for having the audacity to let Ralph escape.

But for sheer brass-neck, the system of 'Deodand' could not be beaten for extorting cash, and Geoffrey le Scrope invoked this on at least two occasions during the Eyre. Deodand (from the Latin, 'that which must be given to God'), was where a personal chattel which had been the immediate accidental cause of the death of a human being, was forfeited to the Crown.

Geoffrey le Scrope came across a Coroner's report about an accident. A man riding a horse through a gate, struck against the gate, knocked himself off his horse and was killed. There was no other person involved. Because no *person* could be blamed, the judge blamed the horse, and declared it 'Deodand'. Because of the misdemeanour of nobody delivering the horse to the authorities, le Scrope promptly fined the town where the accident had occurred.

✣✣ *Sir Geoffrey le Scrope and his brother Henry, were from a Yorkshire family, and were both lawyers and judges. Geoffrey was a King's Sergeant (what we would call today either the Solicitor General or Attorney General) by 1316, and as such accompanied Edward II on his campaigns. He was made a Judge of Common Pleas in 1323, and Chief Justice of the King's Bench one year later. Being thus seen to be an ally of Edward II, le Scrope was quickly removed from office when Edward II was deposed in 1327. But he was soon reinstated when Edward III, on finding the country's coffers totally plundered by his father, ordered the General Eyre, and so needed all the judges he could get, Geoffrey le Scrope amongst them. By 1339, Geoffrey le Scrope had become Edward III's personal secretary, and so went with him to France in 1340 when Edward started pressing his claim to be King of France, thus starting off the Hundred Years' War. Military action obviously did not suit our Geoffrey, and he died a few months later in Ghent.*

1332

1332A Thursday 30 April 1332. Everdon

Victim Adam Waundevylle

Undetected

We will have just one more case from the Coroners' Rolls, but an interesting one it is. When the king was moving about his country, his army of retainers obviously went with him. This was not good news for the townships where the court was, because they had to supply the food. On 30 April 1332, King Edward III's court was travelling near to Everdon, when a dispute arose between the people of Everdon and the stewards of the king's household, no doubt over the provision of food for the court.

What happened during the dispute, whether blows were struck or punches thrown, is unknown, but we do know that many of the Everdon villagers fled to the churchyard, which was also considered Sanctuary, along with the actual church building. Whilst he was standing in the churchyard, and therefore in Sanctuary, Adam Waundevylle, was killed immediately by an unknown member of the king's household who shot at him with a bow and arrow.

Because a member of the king's court was the suspect, the Inquest had to be carried out by the King's Coroner rather than the local one. William de Valdon, therefore, as the King's Coroner, attended the scene, although he was accompanied by the local Coroner, John de Tew. William de Valdon was one of the special officers who always travelled with the king, and who were known as 'Coroners of the King's Household and Verge', the 'Verge' extending to a twelve mile radius around the king's residence for the time being.

What happened at the Inquest we do not know, only that the murderer was never named, let alone punished, even for the otherwise inexcusable crime of the violation of Sanctuary. Whether his social position with the king saved him, we can only now conjecture.

NO MORE CASES FROM THE CORONERS' ROLLS WILL BE GIVEN, AS THEY are tediously the same. However, to emphasise how much store was placed on the system of Sanctuary in ridding the country of its murderers, the following is a list of the murders from the remaining Coroners' Rolls, where the murderer chose exile under the Sanctuary scheme.

1364

1364A Wednesday 15 May 1364. Finedon.

Richard Body killed Richard Picke, by splitting his head open with a hammer. He sought Sanctuary at Finedon and was assigned to Dover.

1364B Saturday 9 November 1364. Kettering.

Hugh de Welborn stabbed Robert Sionges with a knife, sought Sanctuary and was assigned to King's Lynn.

1367

1367A Sunday 14 February 1367. Wellingborough.

Hugh Walsshman and David Walsshman made a frenzied attack on Thomas Walsshman, fatally stabbing him in the back and chest several times. Both sought Sanctuary, and Hugh was assigned to Sandwich, and David was sent to Southampton. Obviously Walsshman refers to the men's nationality rather than family surname; it is doubtful they were related.

1367B Saturday 22 May 1367. Oundle.

Robert Glover stabbed Stephen Derby in the heart with a knife. He sought Sanctuary, but the assigned port is not recorded.

1377

1377A Monday 26 October 1377. Rothwell.

William Thorewall murdered John Godale of Cranford by an unknown method. He was assigned to Dover.

1380

1380A Sunday 15 July 1380. Barnwell.

John Chesham sought Sanctuary in the church of Saint Andrew, Barnwell. He confessed that he had stabbed to death the Chaplain of Barnwell, John de Syreston. The port of Dover was assigned to him.

THUS ENDS THE BULK OF THE DOCUMENTS WHICH RECORD the criminal homicides of the medieval period. We are now left with a huge gap with hardly any accessible written legal records at all. However, the murder of William Tresham is well known, but is given again because of its historical importance - the murder of an Attorney General and Speaker of the House of Commons is not something which happens every day.

1450

1450A Wednesday 23 September 1450. Moulton

Victim William Tresham

Accused Evan ap Rice (never caught)

William Tresham was Attorney General to the Lancastrian king Henry V. He had been the Speaker of the House of Commons on four occasions, and in 1449 had been created the Chancellor to the Duchy of Lancaster. William Tresham was therefore an important and influential man in the Lancastrian hierarchy. So to have dealings with the Yorkist faction was, to say the least, not very clever of him.

William Tresham, for a reason history does not tell us, set out from his Sywell home, to meet the Duke of York on one fine September morning in 1450. But Lord Grey of Ruthyn, a staunch Lancastrian, got to hear, and not unnaturally wanted to stop him.

No direct evidence involves Lord Grey, but it was obviously his gang of 150 roughs who waylaid William Tresham in the vicinity of Thorplands in Moulton. William Tresham was run through with a lance and died instantly. It was an open secret that the murderer was the Welshman Evan ap Rice, who then stripped the body of valuables, and was seen riding Tresham's horse for some time afterwards.

Despite all this, all the appeals for justice by Tresham's widow, Isabel, came to nothing. For this was on the eve of the Wars of the Roses, when justice of any sort was the last thing on the minds of the rulers of the country.

1469

(E4) **THURSDAY 27 JULY 1469**

BEHEADED FOR HIGH TREASON

William Herbert, Earl of Pembroke
Sir Richard Herbert

Grafton Regis in Northamptonshire had been the family home of the Woodville family for generations, but the family had never risen above the social status of Lords of the Manor. However, on Tuesday 1 May 1464, Elizabeth Woodville became Queen of England when she had married King Edward IV. Within a year, she had arranged for most of her family to be married into the great noble families of England.

But all this empire building attracted powerful enemies, the most powerful being the old 'Kingmaker' himself, the Earl of

Warwick. Edward IV was a Yorkist, as was Warwick, but the Woodvilles were Lancastrian. Warwick found himself being increasingly 'sidelined' by these Lancastrian upstarts. Something had to be done.

Not wishing to have his own name involved, he engineered a rebellion in the north of England, led by Sir John Conyers, masquerading under the nickname of 'Robin of Redesdale'. Marching south with his army, Conyers headed straight for Grafton Regis, the home of the hated Woodvilles. On Wednesday 26 July 1469, a weak Royalist army, under the command of William Herbert, Earl of Pembroke, and his brother Sir Richard Herbert, met in battle with Robin of Redesdale at Edgecote, which is near to Culworth in the south of Northamptonshire.

By trickery, and treachery by some of their own men, the Herbert brothers were defeated and captured. Not even receiving the dignity of a trial, the Herbert brothers were beheaded on Northampton Market Square on Thursday 27 July 1469. It was common knowledge that these Northampton executions (as well as those of Earl Rivers and Sir John Woodville, the Queen's father and brother soon afterwards at Kenilworth) were the direct orders of the Earl of Warwick for his own political purposes.

THE TUDORS AND STUARTS

1501-1700

After the abundance of the material available in the Middle Ages, we now come to a very sparse period. No Assize records have survived, so we have to rely on other sources - and they are also scarce.

However, we do have a glimmer of hope. From the 1870s onwards, a Northampton firm called the Dryden Press published a series of booklets called the 'Northamptonshire Tracts', one of which is that most helpful publication *Executions in Northampton, 1277-1893* by an unacknowledged author, and which has provided many a reference for the book you are now reading.

The Dryden Press, owned by John Taylor and his son and having premises at 9 College Street, also published a magazine called *Northamptonshire Notes and Queries.* The *Northamptonshire Notes and Queries* magazines, containing many interesting 'snippets', were bound into books, and many volumes of these are still available in the county libraries. The majority of the following therefore come from these Dryden Press publications.

1559

(E5)

SEPTEMBER 1559

BURNT FOR HERESY

John Kurde

Heresy was both a civil crime, as well as an ecclesiastical one. In 1678 however, the civil criminal part of it was dropped, and it is only now punishable by the church authorities.

Burning was the normal punishment for heretics, and the only burning for heresy that has occurred in Northamptonshire, was that of John Kurde, in September 1557. And this of course was during the reign of Queen Mary I, the aptly nicknamed 'Bloody Mary'.

Being the daughter of the Spanish Catholic Catherine of Aragon, Henry VIII's first wife, she had been raised in the Catholic faith, and had been traumatised by her father's break with the Roman church in 1534. She had looked on when her half-brother, Edward VI, had continued with the Protestant church, but vowed that if she ever became queen, then she would reverse the Reformation. And queen she did become in 1553, at the age of 37, when Edward VI died aged sixteen. Easily brushing aside the nine day challenge of Lady Jane Grey, or her supporters, she ascended the throne determined to lead England back to Catholicism.

In her short reign of just five years, nearly 300 people - *one person every week for five years* - were burned as 'heretics', including John Kurde. Is it, therefore, any wonder that she earned the nickname of 'Bloody Mary'?

John Kurde was a shoemaker from Syresham who had been arrested for refusing to attend Catholic Holy Communion in his parish church, and for denying the doctrine of Transubstantiation. Transubstantiation is the belief that the bread and wine at the Communion *actually becomes* the body and blood of Jesus Christ, only the appearance of bread and wine remaining.

He was imprisoned in Northampton castle and stood 'trial' at All Saints Church in 1557. Not surprisingly, he was found guilty.

In September 1557 (the exact date is unknown), Kurde was led out of the town by the north gate (Barrack Road) to Kingsthorpe Hollow. There, in front, of thousands of people, whilst the bundles of sticks were still being piled about him, the Vicar of Saint Giles', John Roote, told him he would be pardoned if he recanted. John Kurde's answer was simple, 'I have had my pardon by Jesus Christ'. His martyrdom is included in Foxe's *Book of Martyrs*.

1587

(E6) **SUNDAY 8 FEBRUARY 1587**

BEHEADED FOR HIGH TREASON

Mary Stuart, Queen of Scotland

The story of Mary, Queen of Scots is so well known, and is far better told in other places, that it will not be repeated here. She had been brought to Fotheringhay Castle, near to Oundle, in 1586, there to stand trial for High Treason.

Her cousin, Elizabeth I of England, had not wanted to take such a drastic step. But faced with evidence of her involvement in the Babbington Plot, reluctantly (if we believe the history books) and only at the insistence of her ministers, had her put on trial. But having taken that irretrievable step however, the outcome was inevitable. It would have been difficult for the Protestant Elizabeth to allow the Catholic Mary to live, and thus be the centre of plots to usurp the throne.

At 8am on Sunday 8 February 1587, Mary Stuart entered the Great Hall of Fotheringhay Castle and mounted the newly erected platform. Despite crude attempts by the Dean of Peterborough, Richard Fletcher (later made Bishop of Bristol, Worcester and London by Elizabeth), to get her to renounce her Catholicism, Mary resisted and died a Catholic. After taking three blows of the axe to sever her head, the executioner, a man called Bull, seized her hair, but her famous auburn locks turned out to be a wig, and her head, with its prematurely greying hair (she was 44) fell to the ground. 'So perish all the Queen's enemies' yelled the Dean.

Mary's body was sealed in a lead coffin but was not buried for six months. Eventually she was given a (Protestant) burial in Peterborough Cathedral, but in 1612 her body was exhumed by her son, by then James I of England and VI of Scotland, and reburied in Westminster Abbey.

1599/1600

1599/1600A Alderton
Victim William Johnson
Accused John Simpson

In Volume 1 of *Northamptonshire Notes and Queries*, dated 1886, article 136, we get this :

> 'The following paragraph appears in a tract called *A Breviate of the Prelates intollerable usurpations, both upon the Kings Prerogative Royall, and the Subjects Liberties.* - Published by W. Huntley Esquier - Edition 3. much enlarged - In the year 1637.
>
> The extract is taken from a chapter entitled "Their Encroachments upon the Subjects Liberties....It is cited in support of the Author's charge against the Prelates who says that "Their (The Prelates') proces and proceedings are irregular, contrary to all the forecited statutes".

So what had happened by the year 1637 that was making the author rail against 'The Prelates' and their irregular proceedings contrary to all the laws of the land which had been passed previously and were still in force? For a start, who were The Prelates? And why should this interest us in a book about criminal homicides?

William Laud had been made Bishop of London in 1628 by King Charles I, and because he supported the king in his squabbles with Parliament, Charles then made him Archbishop of Canterbury in 1633. The problem was, Laud was extremely anti-Puritan, and was utterly intolerant of views other than his own. He saw his life's work as bringing other people round to his way of thinking, and would stop at nothing to do it.

And the way he attempted to do it was through the Court of High Commission. This had been set up by Queen Elizabeth I in 1559 to deal with ecclesiastical measures. The problem was, the bishops ('The Prelates') who ran it, went far beyond their original remit, and started interfering with other courts, much to the resentment of these. So by the time that William Laud came to be in charge of it, the Prelates of the High Commission, were committing outrageous acts in order to stamp out Puritanism.

It is this Court of High Commission that the author of the 1637 booklet is attacking and criticising, saying that that actions of the bishops are entirely illegal, and are way beyond the Commission's powers, and are encroaching on the liberties of the ordinary people. And to prove that the Commission's actions are illegal, he states the case of the homicide of William Johnson, in the village of Alderton, in the 42nd year of the reign of Elizabeth I, that is, between 17 November 1599 and 16 November 1600.

> 'In C.42 of Queene Elizabeth, the High Commissioners directed a warrant to one Richard Butler, Constable of Aldrington *(sic)* in the County of Northampton, for attaching and arresting the body of John Simpson of that Parish, and the bringing of him before them, for' (here follows the offence) 'the Constable hereupon with one William Johnson, Edward Fust's servant, came to a widdowes house at Aldrington, where Simpson was, at eight o'clock at night, and the doores being open, would have arrested Simpson...[who] not withstanding resisted, and in his own defence shot Johnson, who came in aide of the Constable, with a Pistoll so hee fell downe dead.'

John Simpson duly appeared at the next Northamptonshire Assizes charged with murder. But the question arose, was it murder or manslaughter? It was argued that it would only be murder if the warrant for his arrest was lawful. This question was then referred to the rest of the English judges, and their verdict was delivered at the next sessions of the Assizes.

The Judges' verdict was that the original statute which set up the High Commission in 1559, did not give any powers to issue arrest warrants, only powers to issue summonses. Therefore, the High Commission warrant was illegal - therefore the attempted service of it by the Parish Constable Richard Butler was also illegal - therefore John Simpson had the right to defend himself by whatever means - therefore he was found not guilty of murder - therefore he was acquitted.

It was this case that the 1637 author was citing to prove that the Prelates of the High Commission had no powers to arrest anyone, adding 'as they now dayly doe'. This pamphlet must have been one of many, but they obviously worked.

William Laud was himself arrested in 1640 by Parliament and condemned to The Tower, and that same Parliament abolished the High Commission the following year. All this was just one more step in the build-up to the Great English Civil War which started in 1642. William Laud was beheaded in 1645.

1607

(E7)

JULY 1607

HANGED FOR RIOTING

The Newton 'Rebels'

The disturbances of 1607 were the first of the so called Enclosure Riots, which were destined to last on and off, for the next 200 years. James VI of Scotland when he became James I of England in 1603 found his English coffers empty, and so had to do something about it fairly quickly. He hit upon the idea of selling off vast acres of land and royal forests to local landowners.

Because there was a greater profit in rearing sheep for wool, the landowners promptly started pulling up trees, and enclosing the land by planting hedgerows, and splitting it into fields, so as to keep sheep which were far more lucrative. This was bad news for the peasants, as they now faced starvation because the common land they had used for generations had suddenly became unavailable.

The only redress, therefore, was to make their feelings known to the landowners in the form of mass demonstrations, which for want of a better term, were called 'riots'. It is believed the first Enclosure Riots started in Northamptonshire and eventually spread to all the midland counties.

In this area, the main landowner against whom the peasants' ire was directed, was Sir Lewis Tresham, the latest squire of the Tresham family, which had been the local 'bigwigs' for over 200 years. The fact that his elder brother Francis, had been one of the Gunpowder Plotters, never seemed to have held him back, and he had just been made a Baronet.

On May Day Eve 1607, riots began in Northamptonshire, with known disturbances occurring at Thrapston, Rushton and Pytchley. The leader of the peasants was a man called John Reynolds, who called himself 'Captain Pouch', because of the large leather pouch which he hung from his belt. 'This pouch', he said, contained 'sufficient matter to defend against all comers'.

On Friday 8 June 1607, the rebels led by Pouch, were confronted by the local Militia (the contemporary equivalent to the Territorial Army) at Newton near to Geddington. The Militia were armed with muskets and the peasants with pikes, bows and axes. The result was inevitable.

An estimated 40 or 50 peasants were killed and many more injured. It can be assumed that Captain Pouch was killed on that day, as there are stories of his pouch being opened and found to contain just a bit of mouldy cheese.

The remaining ringleaders were rounded up and appeared at the Northamptonshire Summer Assizes of July 1607. Unfortunately, records of the Assize have been lost, so we have no knowledge of the number of the Newton 'Rebels' hanged - but hanged they were.

1611

(E8) SATURDAY 23 FEBRUARY 1611

HANGED FOR AN UNKNOWN OFFENCE

Thomas Sparrowe

As with the case of William de Havering in 1296, this execution is included in the booklet *Northamptonshire Executions*, published in the 1920s, but not in *Executions in Northampton 1277-1893*, published in 1900. It is now unlikely that any more information will ever come to light, and so the fog of ignorance will forever surround the demise of Thomas Sparrowe.

There are five more executions which only appear in *Northamptonshire Executions* : Stephen Preston in 1611; Alice Chadwick in 1622; John Hilliar in 1623; Arthur Bett in 1638; and the unnamed person in 1685.

❁

(E9) MONDAY 8 APRIL 1611

HANGED FOR AN UNKNOWN OFFENCE

Stephen Preston

This is one of the executions that appears in only one of the two books which provide the sources for Northamptonshire executions. No information whatsoever is known, except that the hanging took place at Wallbank, Kingsthorpe.

1612

(E10) **SUNDAY 22 JULY 1612**

HANGED FOR WITCHCRAFT

Agnes Brown
Joan Vaughan
Arthur Bill
Hellen Jenkinson
Mary Barber

Scholars are still arguing why, from the 1480s until the 1730s, the persecution of 'witches' became so common. In western Europe for instance, it has been estimated that during that period, about 40,000 people, the vast majority of them women, were executed as witches.

Why the two German scholars Jacobus Sprenger and Heinrich Kramer, wrote their book *Maleus Maleficarum* ('The Hammer of Witchcraft') in 1486, is not known. But it was certainly *Maleus Maleficarum* which produced the 'model' for the persecution of witches for the next 250-odd years.

In England, however, we were relatively 'mild' in our persecution, with an estimated figure of between 300 and 1,000. And in Northamptonshire, we contributed eight to that total, in three separate spates : these five in 1612; one in 1674; and two in 1705.

Agnes Brown and Joan Vaughan were mother and daughter from Guilsborough. They were accused of bewitching the Lord of the Manor, Dabridgecourt Belcher, and his sister Elizabeth. No doubt they were beaten before they started in trying to defend themselves against their socially superior accuser.

Arthur Bill was accused of bewitching to death a woman and some of her cattle at Raunds. He was clapped in irons after failing the 'Ordeal by Water', as did his mother, who cheated the hangman by cutting her own throat.

Nothing is known about Hellen Jenkinson of Thrapston who was accused of bewitching a child to death. Nor of Mary Barber of Stanwick was accused of doing the same to a grown man.

On Sunday (chosen deliberately?) 22 July 1612, all five were hanged together on the permanent gallows in Abington village.

1620

1620A 31 July 1620. Charwelton

Victim Sir Euseby Andrew

Amongst the 'Northamptonshire Tracts' *(see above)* is a booklet *The Poysoning of Sir Euseby Andrew* published in 1881. It is a straight reprint of a manuscript which is in the Isham collection at Lamport Hall, and gives the opinion of a Doctor John Cotta of Northampton as to the death of Sir Euseby Andrew.

It is all very curious, because Dr Cotta indicates that he appeared at the Northamptonshire Assizes, and gave his opinion that Sir Euseby was poisoned. In the manuscript he goes into great detail about the physical condition of Sir Euseby, all the bodily functions, and everything Sir Euseby said to him on his death bed. Apparently Sir Euseby suspected a woman called Mistress Moyle of giving him a poisoned 'gellie'.

However, that's all we have, the manuscript goes no further. So can we can assume that this Mistress Moyle was indicted for murder and tried at the Assizes?

No records survive, so we do not know one way or the other. Certainly no woman (or anyone else for that matter) was executed for the murder of Sir Euseby Andrew, and despite extensive research, no other information is forthcoming.

This case has been included, because it obviously happened. And you never know, information may suddenly spring to light one day.

1622

(E11) **THURSDAY 7 MARCH 1622**

HANGED FOR AN UNKNOWN OFFENCE

Alice Chadwick

This is one of the executions that appears in just one of the two books which provide the sources for Northamptonshire executions. No more information is known, not even the offence.

1623

(E12) **SATURDAY 19 JULY 1623**

HANGED FOR AN UNKNOWN OFFENCE

John Hilliar

This is also one of the executions that appears only in one of the two books which provide the sources for Northamptonshire executions. Nothing whatsoever is known.

1625

1625A In the *Northampton County Magazine*, Volume Two, of 1929, is this entry:

> 'Ann Hamblin wife to Addam he knockt her on the hed on 8 December and shee was buried on ye 11 December 1625 Nassington'

No further information can be gained about this, despite a perusal of the Nassington parish registers.

1630

(E13) SOMETIME DURING THE YEAR 1630

PRESSED TO DEATH FOR REFUSING TO PLEAD

'An Unknown Malefactor'

This is the only recorded incident of someone being 'pressed to death' in Northamptonshire. On an unknown date in 1630 'a malefactor' was pressed to death in the New Pastures, Northampton (now Spencer Parade). This means of torture (for such it was), was done for a very specific reason, and was reserved for those who on being charged with a felony, refused to enter a plea before the court. Pressing was done to force the prisoner to enter his plea of 'guilty' or 'not guilty', although in this case, the torture did not work, and the prisoner died. This is not so idiotic as it appears at first glance.

When a prisoner was found guilty and hanged, then all his property was confiscated. This meant that his next of kin would be left destitute, and so face possible starvation - there being no welfare state in those days. However, in refusing to plead, he could not have been placed on trial, and so could not have been found guilty, and so could not have been hanged as a convicted felon.

In this case, it is obvious that he thought the evidence against him was so great that he would not stand a snowball's chance of getting off with it. He thus reasoned that he would have been hanged anyway. In refusing to plead, therefore, he made sure that his surviving relatives inherited all his property and would not face destitution. Which when you come to reflect on it, is quite a brave and noble thing to do.

The actual mechanics of being pressed to death are simple. The naked prisoner was laid on his back on the bare floor so there could be placed upon his body 'so great a weight of iron as much as he could bear, and more'. In this position, the prisoner was given only a mouthful of bread on one day and three sips of water on the next. This alternating daily diet continued until either the prisoner died, or he pleaded to the charges against him. In this particular instance, it is not known how long the prisoner lasted - maybe days, or it could have been weeks.

1631

1631A Date unknown. Moulton
Victim Mr Lucas
Accused Mrs Lucas

The second of our ladies found guilty of 'Petty Treason'. Scant information is known about this, not even the Christian names of the two major players. All that is known is that Mrs Lucas poisoned her husband at Moulton, and that she was pulled on a wooden platform, or sledge, by a horse to Hunsbury Hill, tied to a stake - and burnt to death.

1636

1636A Date unknown. Pytchley?
Victim an illegitimate child
Accused **John Barker, a woman relative, and a servant.**

Not much is known about this, except that the child was the woman's, and the triple execution took place on the permanent gallows at Abington.

1638

(E14) **MONDAY 5 MARCH 1638**

HANGED FOR AN UNKNOWN OFFENCE

Arthur Bett

This is one of the executions that appears in only one of the two books which provide the sources for Northamptonshire executions. No information whatsoever is known, except that his execution was on the permanent gallows in Abington village.

1643

1643A Sunday 2 July 1643, Lois Weedon
Victim Reverend William Losse
Undetected

The wars of the seventeenth century saw many excesses, all done in the name of religion. Possibly the second martyrdom in the county (the first was John Kurde, executed during the reign of 'Bloody' Mary in 1559), William Losse was the Vicar of Lois Weedon, and had been since 1618.

This was his first living after having been ordained in 1616, whilst a Fellow of King's College, Cambridge. Before Cambridge, he had been to Eton, so it appears he may have been from the landed gentry. Which is possibly why he was described as a 'valiant royalist', and possibly why he was disliked by Cromwell's puritans.

On Sunday 2 July 1643, whilst conducting morning service, twelve roundhead soldiers entered the church. They demanded Losse should leave, which he did, walking into the churchyard. There, the soldiers tried to arrest him, but he broke away and rushed back into church, barring the door behind him.

The soldiers broke in, causing Losse to flee to the church tower. As the terrified congregation were too petrified to help, Losse climbed up through a trapdoor to the roof. The soldiers followed him, but fearing to climb through the trap door after him, they fired their guns through the trapdoor in an attempt to kill him. They failed, but then they thrust their swords through the trapdoor, and this time fatally wounded him, and his blood seeped through the roof.

Knowing that they had done what they had set out to do, the soldiers left. Not one of the soldiers was ever brought to trial, as the turbulence that the country was in at that time, stopped anyone being interested in justice.

1645

1645A Date and place unknown
Victim Husband
Accused Wife

Even less information is known for the third offence of 'Petty Treason' in the county. Not even surnames are known. All that is known is that is that the burning took place in Northampton, 'on the left hand side of the road leading to Queen's Cross, near the pits', which presumably would put it somewhere between the River Nene and Delapre Abbey.

1651

(E15) SOMETIME DURING THE YEAR 1651

HANGED FOR THEFT

Leonard Bland

Like Thomas the Baker (1202), Leonard Bland was a gangster. The only thing we know about him is that he was the mafioso of a 'knot of thieves who broke into Northampton'. Presumably this was at night when the town gates were locked.

Anyway, Leonard was caught and 'executed on a new gallows made for him'. These were not in Abington, where apparently there was a set of permanent gallows, but the exact location is unknown. And that is all that is known about Leonard Bland.

1655

1655A Date and place unknown
Victim Husband
Accused Wife

With the fourth offence of 'Petty Treason' in the county, we do know just a touch more. She was obviously tried and found guilty at the 1655 Summer Assizes, because, according to *Executions in Northampton* she

> 'was drawn on the sledge to Boughton Green, and there burnt on July 18th. It is probable that the executioner strangled her to insensibility before consigning her to the flames. The people were already getting more humane than the law. But whatever their humanity their credulity was rampant.'

1674

(E16) **SATURDAY 22 AUGUST 1674**

HANGED FOR WITCHCRAFT

Ann Foster

The fifth of the seven 'witches' of Northamptonshire, Ann Foster's only crime it seems, is that she was 'an old woman who had long been seen muttering to herself'. And when she was clapped in irons in Northampton Castle, her body swelled so much, that the gaolers had to release her time and time again. And then, the proof positive, the devil visited her in the form of a rat - a rat, in prison!

But it is easy to sneer at the prejudices of a substantially more gullible and unenlightened period of our history than our own times. We must not do that. We must not look at our ancestors' thoughts through our own modern eyes. We must accept that people at that time were genuinely frightened, and would infer far more from incidents which today, with our sophistication and understanding of the ageing process, bodily traumas and hygiene, we can see have a totally logical explanation.

Be that as it may, Ann Foster was tried for witchcraft at the 1674 Summer Assizes (of which no record remains) and found guilty. She was hanged at Northampton on Saturday 22 August 1674.

1685

1685A Friday 23 January 1685. Wappenham

Victim The 'Reverend' Theophilus Hart (65)

Accused George Tarry (Butcher)

The Wallop family were Lords of the Manor of the village of Wappenham, which is near to Towcester. When Sir Henry Wallop died, the Manor passed to his son Robert. This was during the English Commonwealth under Lord Protector Cromwell, and Robert Wallop, who was obviously a Royalist, then started falling on hard times.

Robert Wallop's chaplain was the 'Reverend' Theophilus Hart, although there is some doubt as to whether he was an ordained priest or not. These were religiously troubled times, and in 1646, the Westminster Assembly sequestered Hart to the parish of Wappenham. The Westminster Assembly was the Parliamentary arm of church reform, and had forced Hart onto the parish after the rightful incumbent, the Reverend Caesar Williamson, had been ejected because he had fought on the Royalist side at the Battle of Edgehill.

Ceasing his chance when Wallop was falling on hard times, Hart eventually bought all Wallop's property in Wappenham and declared himself the Lord of the Manor. In this position he made himself extremely unpopular with his parishioners by continually squabbling and litigating against them.

With the Restoration of the Monarchy in 1660, the inevitable backlash happened and all the incumbents who had been forced out of their livings by Parliament, were allowed to return. Hart, however, remained at Wappenham by the simple expedient of bribing the Bishop of Peterborough's secretary. And not only this, but he became the Vicar of Blakesley as well, and so had two salaries coming in. Because he could afford it therefore, he employed curates to do all the ecclesiastical work for him, thus disguising his lack of spirituality and vocation.

So the years ticked by, and Hart continued on his scandalous way. But his come-uppance was at hand.

On Tuesday 23 January 1685, the local Wappenham butcher, George Tarry, decided to call at Wappenham Rectory. Whether he knew what he would find, or whether he had been ignorant of such things, we can only now guess at. But in bed with the Rector, he found his own wife.

Showing much nimbleness for a man of 65, Theophilus Hart fled naked from the Rectory, being pursued over the fields by the irate George Tarry, equipped with the tools of his trade. Eventually the chase ended, and then Tarry proceeded to practise his trade on the unfortunate Rector. Theophilus Hart died instantly when his brains were expertly extracted by the raging and cuckolded husband.

Trial **1685 Lent Assizes. Presiding Judge unknown**

George Tarry's guilt was never in doubt, and even the mitigating circumstances did not help. George Tarry was hanged for murder at Northampton on Wednesday 27 May 1685, and buried in Saint Giles' the same day.

❁

(E17) WEDNESDAY 11 MARCH 1685

HANGED FOR AN UNKNOWN OFFENCE

'An unknown malefactor'

The fifth and last of the executions that only appears in *Northamptonshire Executions* and not in *Executions in Northampton*. The author of *Northamptonshire Executions* must have got his knowledge from somewhere, but unfortunately, no reference notes are given in the pamphlet. So we are left wondering.

1695

1695A In the *Northampton County Magazine* of 1928, page 269, appears this :

> 'Mary Crisy, a servant, was slain with a pistol at the Red Lion in this parish August ye 3rd day. She was buried at St Giles 1695'.

No details can be found despite searching of the register of Saint Giles. So again, we are left wondering.

THE EIGHTEENTH CENTURY

Part 1 : 1701 - 1750

With the founding of the *Northampton Mercury* in May 1720 - which is still being published, making it one of the world's oldest surviving newspapers - we should have, for the very first time, a relatively easily available record of the Northamptonshire Assizes.

However, in its early days the *Mercury* was more of a 'scissors and paste' newspaper, where national news stories were 'borrowed' from the London papers and regurgitated for local consumption. Consequently, local news took very much of a back seat, and so the reporting of the Northamptonshire Assizes was very sparse indeed. The popularity of the voyeurism of court reporting took a few years to dawn on the owners of the *Mercury*.

Thus, although we can deduce a complete record of all the homicides from 1720 onwards, we only have very brief details about the majority of them. But, in order to fulfil historical and criminological interest, *every* homicide appearing at the Assizes *will* be listed, together with a running total, which will be in brackets, above the yearly reference number; so we can see, for example, that in the 31 years from 1720 to 1750, there were 38 cases of criminal homicide.

But we need to remember one small point. As there were no Assizes between the Summer Assizes in July or August of one year and the Lent Assizes of February or March of the following year, then a lot of the cases appearing at the Lent Assizes, actually took place in the previous year. But as we have little, if any, information as to dates given to us by the *Northampton Mercury* reports, then we must accept that the figures for some years may not be quite accurate.

In the year 1741, history touches us. The United Kingdom is remarkable throughout Europe, by not starting organised police forces until very late in its history. The French, for example, had an armed gendarmerie mid-way during the seventeenth century; and even the quiescent Swiss had canton-wide forces by the 1740s.

Britain, however, persisted with its parish constable system, where each parish had only the one constable in it, who was entirely autonomous and totally separated from any other constable, and was beholden to no one except the local magistrate. The parish constable system had been designed for small country villages, and so when the big cities started growing up in the mid eighteenth century, is it any wonder that the system broke down? And nowhere more so of course, than in the biggest city of them all, London.

By the 1730s, lawlessness in London was epidemic. But the only response from central government was to pass Acts of Parliament increasing the number of capital offences (the so-called 'Bloody Code' - see the year 1722). At this time, the governing classes viewed organised police forces with suspicion, the thinking being, that the mere *threat* of the death sentence would provide the ultimate crime deterrent - therefore police forces wouldn't be needed - and so central government certainly wasn't going to spend money in providing something that wasn't needed!

But it was obvious to those individuals who were observing the situation, that without the certainty of being caught in the first place, the 'Bloody Code' would not actually work. Thus, with no lead from central government in providing this means of being caught (that is, a police force), it was left to interested private individuals to do something about it.

The most famous of these, of course, were the Fielding brothers, whose efforts at restoring some kind of law back to the streets resulted in that most famous of all private initiatives, the Bow Street Runners, founded in 1750. But the Fielding brothers were not the first. They readily acknowledged their debt to a certain Thomas de Veil.

Appointed in 1729, as Magistrate for Westminster and Middlesex, with an office in what is now Leicester Square, Thomas de Veil was unlike his contemporary magistrates, in that he did his own detective work. He had to. If he wanted to reduce the crime that he found around him, and having no organised and trained police force, then he had no option but to do it himself.

With an army background (he had been a Captain, and had seen action in Portugal), de Veil was made of stern stuff. He was not afraid of standing up to the criminal gangs that roamed London unchecked, and which had previously intimidated other magistrates.

It was his direct influence, despite attempts on his life, that two of the most notorious gangs of London, the Wreathcock Gang (named after its leader), and the Black Boy Alley Gang, were broken up and brought to justice. As such, he started making some inroads into the crime problem, and was eventually awarded a government salary and a knighthood.

De Veil was the first person to make some attempt to reduce the enormous amount of crime that was endemic in London at the time. Having moved his office to Bow Street in 1739 (which he would later hand over to the Fielding brothers), his influence stretched over what is now the Home Counties, and he was the first detective to give help to provincial authorities. It is surprising therefore, that no biography of him has been written, and that he is not even in the *Dictionary of National Biography.* He died in September 1746.

However, perhaps the reason that he does not appear in the *DNB*, is because of his personal habits, of which the prudish Victorian compilers of the *DNB* did not approve. If any female came to him for help, and she had no money to pay for his services, then de Veil would extract his fee in kind, for which purposes he had a bedroom next to his office. Consequently, the number of his illegitimate offspring is unknown, but has been estimated probably as many as thirty.

But despite of all this, Thomas de Veil remained a dedicated thief taker, and it was this same Thomas de Veil who came to Northampton in 1741, to figure highly in the conviction of Bryan Connell for the murder of Richard Bromley (1739A).

1705

(E18) SATURDAY 17 MARCH 1705

HANGED AND BURNT FOR WITCHCRAFT

Elinor Shaw
Mary Phillips

And the last two witches to be hanged in Northamptonshire, and indeed the whole of the country, are these two, both coming from Oundle. They were both charged with bewitching to death the wife of Robert Wise of Benefield; bewitching to death Elizabeth Gorham of Glapthorne aged four; and ditto Charles Ireland of Southwick. And not only humans were killed by them, but the horses, pigs and sheep of Matthew Gorham, father of Elizabeth.

The trial at the Northamptonshire Lent Assizes of 1705 was a foregone conclusion. The 'evidence' was their own confession, obtained by two Parish Constables by threatening them with death. Unsurprisingly, they were found guilty.

They were hanged on Saturday 17 March 1705, but before they were completely dead, their bodies were burned.

1713

1713A On a date unknown. Badby
Victim Richard Tresler
Accused Elizabeth Tresler

Elizabeth Tresler was the fifth of the six women to be burnt at the stake in Northamptonshire for the crime of 'Petty Treason' (*see* 1316A). And she nearly got away with it.

The Tresler family were affluent farmers in Badby, and their son, Richard, was thus regarded as the 'catch' of the district. Imagine the family's horror, therefore, when Richard started 'walking out' with Elizabeth Miller, who, as the saying goes, 'was no better than she should have been'. In other words, she was a gold-digger, and Richard's family knew it.

But Richard didn't, and the couple were married within a few months. However, the couple seemed to settle down well, and the Tresler family's fears subsided somewhat.

Because of the family wealth, Richard seemed not to have too much of an occupation, and he spent his time taking long walks in the country. On one summer afternoon, Richard, accompanied by Elizabeth, and a friend David Winters, went for a walk in the Badby countryside.

Richard had peculiar eating habits, and was fond of drinking sugar water. On nearing a stream, Elizabeth was seen to drop a tiny paper packet on the ground. Picking it up, Richard undid it, and saw what he thought were sugar crystals dropped for him by his loving wife. He mixed them with water from the stream and drank it.

What he did not know, was that the white crystals were the poisonous white mercury crystals. And he had just taken enough to kill him.

A few hours after returning home, Richard Tresler died in agony. The village doctor diagnosed natural causes because everyone knew of his peculiar eating habits. He was buried in Badby churchyard, and that appeared to be that.

But a couple of months later, Elizabeth disappeared. Searches were made for her, but came to nothing. Eventually, village gossip moved on, and the incident went into village folk lore. Richard's sister however, was not so easily put off. She was convinced that her brother's death was no accident, and that she would do something about it. It took her two years.

Making a social visit to London in 1715, who did she see walking down the street, but her sister-in-law. When she called out the name 'Elizabeth', Elizabeth on turning round saw who it was and immediately took to her heels.

But she was caught, and forced to come back to Northampton. On the way, Elizabeth made a full confession to her sister-in-law, and on arrival in Northampton was handed over to the authorities.

Trial **1715 Summer Assizes, date and presiding judge unknown**

Because she had made a full confession, Elizabeth Tresler was found guilty of Petty Treason by reason of murdering her husband.

She was burnt at the stake on Northampton Racecourse on an unknown date in the summer of 1715.

1714

1714A On an unknown date, and at a place unknown, but probably Spratton

Victim Mary Eyle

Accused 'Mr Knighton'

Absolutely nothing is known about this at all, as it only appears in one of the two lists of Northamptonshire executions that have survived. However, we do know that 'Mr Knighton' was hung on Friday 9 April 1714 for the murder of Mary Eyle.

And there the matter would have rested. But the research for this book has unearthed the following account in the *Northampton Mercury* of Monday 5 March 1722, when it was reporting upon Thomas Ratnett appearing before the 1722 Lent Assizes for the murder of his wife :

> 'The whole Discourse of People here is taken up with the lamentable Case of Mr Ratnett, who was condemn'd at the Assizes, held for this County on Thursday last, for the barbarous Murther *(sic)* of his Wife who was big with Child, and at down lying. As to the Particulars of his Trial, they being too long for Insertion here, we refer our Readers to the Trial itself, containing the Depositions of 24 Evidences *(witnesses)* against him, and sold by the Men that carry this News. In the mean time his behaviour since Condemnation is not to be parallel'd, unless in the Case of that Ignorant and vile Wretch K……n, formerly of Spratton: For this, as the latter did before he was hang'd, eats, sleeps and seems as unconcern'd as if his Crime and Death were insignificant, tho' for the inhuman Murder of a Wife with who he had a considerable Fortune, where the other only murder'd his Company-Keeper but with this Aggravation, that the loss of her precious and immortal Soul, he like the Fiend who provok'd him, hellishly

> attempted, by repeating his lascivious Embraces with her the instant before he murdered her, when she (Poor Soul!) was full of hopes that he was about to hide all Frailties by carrying her where she might be made his lawful Wife : This he confess'd before his death and many other surprising Truths, drawn up by an impartial Hand, and design'd for the Press, but for some extraordinary Reasons deferr'd.'

So, what's all that about? Let us examine this paragraph closely. First of all, it shows the development of written English over the past 280 years. Nowadays, we don't capitalise nouns, we don't replace the final 'e' with apostrophes, and we use less florid language. But that apart, what is the meaning?

It is contrasting the behaviour of Thomas Ratnett (see 1722A) after being sentenced to death, with the behaviour of the 'ignorant and vile Wretch K------n formerly of Spratton'. Could this be referring to our 'Mr Knighton'? It is only eight years since Knighton was hanged, and thus well within memory.

And the part about Ratnett murdering his wife, but the 'other only murdered his Company-Keeper'. Does that refer to Knighton murdering Mary, who with the surname Eyle, was obviously not his wife, but was his 'Company-Keeper' - his mistress, his partner?

This is speculation of course, on purely hearsay and flimsy evidence. However, it does seem 'to fit'. But what 'the Fiend who provok'd him' by 'repeating his lascivious Embraces' means, is now anyone's guess. I leave that to your fertile imaginations.

However, let us now permit ourselves a flight of fancy. Sensational stuff like this would have been printed in a broadsheet, and sold separately by the 'Men who sold the News' - the 'Chapmen'. A Chapman was a paper seller who not only sold the Mercury *around the streets, but also sold the 'Chapbooks' as well. Chapbooks were small pamphlets and broadsheets containing tracts, ballads or the latest sensational local news.*

By the last paragraph in the extract above we see that a broadsheet had been written 'by an impartial Hand, and design'd for the Press, but for some extraordinary Reasons, deferr'd'. So why was this broadsheet deferred, thus losing money for the printers/publishers?

If this man Knighton was a fellow from the common herd, then surely his full name would have been given, as with all the other men who have been hanged. But all we have is the 'Mr', which makes us think that perhaps this Mr Knighton was not a common working man, but from a higher level of society.

The only surname Knighton that I can find in all the history books of Northamptonshire, is in Northamptonshire and Rutland Clergy *by the Reverend Henry Longden. In that magnificent work, he gives the entry of a Reverend Doctor John Knighton, who was Vicar of Higham Ferrers between 1662 and 1671. He had two sons, Goddard Knighton and John Knighton, both born in the early 1670s, probably both at Higham Ferrers.*

Goddard took Holy Orders like his father, and moved away out of the district. John however, although he went to Christ's College, Cambridge, did not follow his father into the clergy

Can we now make an enormous leap of logic, totally unsupported by any evidence? Would it be possible that this John was the 'black sheep' of the family, and that he did wicked things, and that he was disowned by his despairing father, brother and family?

In 1714, John Knighton would only have been in his early 40s. Could it be possible, the murder of Mary Eyle by 'Mr Knighton' was deliberately hushed-up and obscured by his family, so as to spare them any blushes and scandal? Is this why the publication of a scandalous broadsheet was 'for some extraordinary Reasons, deferr'd'? Was pressure applied by the family on the printers? Did money change hands? Who knows? Your guess is as good as mine.

1720

As the *Northampton Mercury* did not start until May 1720, the Lent Assizes were therefore missed, so the only two homicides we know of for 1720 come from the Summer Assizes. These started on Tuesday 26 July, before either Mr Justice Tracy or Mr Chief Baron Bury.

(1)

1720A The first case is of Thomas Perkins, 'who unfortunately killed his Brother's Maid, and likewise his Brother's Child in her Arms by Accident.'

And that is all we know, because the *Mercury* says that Perkins was bailed until the next Assizes. But no mention at all is made of him in the 1721 Lent Assizes. So we lose all sight of him, we do not know either the place or date of this accident.

(2)

1720B Monday 2 May 1720. Northampton

Victim Mr Welch

Accused Mr Folliot

From the *Northampton Mercury* of Monday 9 May 1720, we get this :

> 'And on Tuesday last, Mr Folliot who rid *(sic)* in General Wade's Regiment was committed to the [County] Gaol for the Murder of one Welch his Camerade *(sic)*, the day before. The true Account of this Quarrel will be publish'd next Saturday and sold by the Men that carry the News. Mr Folliott served 3 Campaigns in Flanders, as Voluntier *(sic)*, under General Wynn; and was also in the last Expedition at Vigo, under Colonel Ligonier, in both which Posts he behav'd himself like a Gentleman and a Soldier.'

Again, because of the sparse newspaper report, all we know is that Mr Folliot was found guilty of manslaughter, although we do not know his punishment, as the *Mercury* did not say.

✣✣ *Thomas Bury had been made a Baron of the Exchequer in 1701, after being a Barrister of Gray's Inn for 25 years. He had been promoted to Chief Baron in 1716, and unusually, not knighted. But this would be his last visit to Northampton, as he would die in 1722 aged 67.*

✣✣ *Born in Ireland and the second son of Viscount Tracy, Robert Tracy had been made an Irish judge in 1699. The following year, he came to England and was made a Baron of the Exchequer. He was transferred to the Common Pleas in 1702, where he stopped until he died in 1735 aged 80.*

However, Mr Justice Tracy does have some niche in history. The 'Glorious Revolution' of 1688 had taken the Catholic James II off the throne, which then led to sixty years of him and his descendants trying to get it back again, in the attempts that history calls the Jacobite Rebellions. There were four such Rebellions : in 1708, 1715, 1719, and probably the best known, in 1745. All of them were crushed, and the inevitable government backlash after every one, saw many Jacobites tried and executed. And it was Mr Justice Tracy who sentenced to death numerous Jacobites in Carlisle in 1716, after the 1715 Rebellion.

1721

No homicides occurred in 1721

1722

(3)
1722A Thomas Ratnett appeared at the 1722 Lent Assizes on Tuesday 27 February, before either Mr Justice Tracy or Mr Baron Aland. From the newspaper reports (*see* 1714A), we can deduce that Thomas Ratnett murdered his pregnant wife, while she was 'down lying'. From the same report, we can also deduce that, 24 witnesses appeared against him, and that once convicted, Ratnett was totally unconcerned about his death sentence.

The hanging of Thomas Ratnett is not recorded in either of the two lists of executions for Northamptonshire, so this hanging is a new discovery. Thomas Ratnett was hanged on Northampton Racecourse on Friday 16 March 1722.

✣✣ *Not much is of interest in the life of Sir John Fortescue Aland, later Baron Fortescue of Credan. He had been Solicitor-General in 1714 and 1715, before being made a Baron of the Exchequer. He would transfer to the Court of Common Pleas in 1728, where he would remain until he died, aged 76 in 1746. These 1722 Lent Assizes were the third of only four visits to Northampton.*

❀

We now come to that hundred year period in British legal history where judicial execution reached its pinnacle. Britain was the only major country in Europe not to have a full time police - and very proud of it we were as well. The majority of people thought that a full time police would have been far too unconstitutional, and not at all what was wanted - having all those 'police spies' all over the place - much too continental!

So instead of an organised police force to combat crime, Britain relied on the parish constable system, backed up by the deterrent principle. And what bigger deterrent was there than death? Which is why in this country, the death sentence was looked upon with such favour.

This started in 1723, when some poachers who had blacked up their faces so as to make identification difficult, had been caught and hanged under powers given by a new Act of Parliament which had just been passed to discourage lawlessness. This legislation, which then came to be nicknamed 'The Black Act' after the poachers, is infamous for introducing that most notorious of penal codes in the entire history of this country, the 'Bloody Code'.

Lasting for just over 100 years, the 'Bloody Code' would eventually list nearly 230 offences as punishable by death - including 'crimes' such as impersonating a Chelsea Pensioner; writing a threatening letter; and consorting with gypsies - all these were capital offences under the 'Bloody Code'. And this is why, from 1723 onwards, judicial executions in Northamptonshire for non-homicide offences, increased dramatically - about 30 (the number of Newton rebels is not known precisely) in the previous 400 years, as opposed to 74 in the following 100 years.

❀

1723

(4)

1723A Tuesday 16 November 1723. Oundle

Victim Eleanor Snarey

Accused Richard Snarey (shoemaker)

Richard Snarey of Oundle, shoemaker, was committed to the County Gaol at Northampton charged on the Coroner's inquest with :

> 'the wilful murder of Eleanor Snarey his wife, by inhumanly beating and kicking her about the body on the 16th inst so that the rim of her belly and bladder were both broken, of which wounds she died on the 23rd day following.'

Trial 1724 Lent Assizes, Tuesday 3 March. *Either* Mr Justice Powys *or* Mr Baron Gilbert

No details of the trial have survived, but it can be surmised from report of the Coroner's inquest, that the case was 'open and shut'.

Richard Snarey was hanged on Northampton Racecourse on Friday 20 March 1724.

✣✣ *As far as can be ascertained, Sir Littleton Powys had been a regular visitor to the Northamptonshire Assizes, and would be, until he retired in 1726. He was no stranger to Northamptonshire, however, as his more famous brother, and fellow judge, Sir Thomas Powys had bought Lilford Hall, near to Oundle, and would become the ancestor of the Lords Lilford. It was Thomas Powys who was the prosecutor of the Seven Bishops in 1687, but that does not concern us here.*

Littleton Powys had been created a Baron of the Exchequer in 1695 before transferring to the King's Bench in 1700. He would die in 1732 aged 84.

1724

As well as the Snarey case, three more homicides appeared at the 1724 Lent Assizes. As the *Mercury* gives no details, the dates of the occurrence of these are unknown.

(5)
1724A Ann Hull, for murdering her illegitimate child at Little Houghton. She was acquitted, and that is all the information we have.

(6)
1724B Thomas Horsely for killing Matthew Billing an infant 'per infortunem' (*'by misfortune', which is taken to mean 'accidentally', or 'misadventure'*) at Oundle.

No details whatsoever on this case were given.

(7)
1724C And this one is a most tragic case. In the *Northampton Mercury* of Monday 2 March 1724 is this :

> 'Geoffrey Cowper, an Infant, was committed to this Gaol for shooting Richard Barnaby, an Infant, in the Belly, of which Wound he died'

And in the report of the trial, all we have is that Geoffrey Cowper, an Infant, was found 'guilty of Manslaughter by Misfortune and deliver'd.'

What story lies behind this, is now lost to history. How old were the two 'Infants'? Was it just a tragic accident whilst at play? What was the weapon? Presumably, the verdict 'deliver'd' means that Geoffrey was sent to someone or somewhere safe.

✣✣ *Sir Geoffrey Gilbert was a bit of a legal literary commentator, just like Sir William Blackstone (see 1773). Indeed Blackstone himself commentated very favourably on one of Gilbert's many legal tomes.*

Believed to be Irish born, Gilbert was a barrister of the Inner Temple, and was made a Baron of the Irish Exchequer in 1715, before coming to England to be made a Baron of the English Exchequer in 1722. Not for long though, as he died in 1726 aged 52.

1725

No homicides occurred in 1725

1726

No criminal homicides in 1726

1727

And none in 1727 either. Three years without a criminal homicide was a very rare occurrence. It would be another 40 years before this happened again (1767, 1768 and 1769), and then not again for another 60 years after that, when we managed an incredible four years in a row without a murder or manslaughter.

1728

Only two homicides occurred in 1728, and both at the Lent Assizes on Tuesday 19 March. Mr Baron Price and the extremely interesting Mr Justice Cowper graced Northampton with their presence.

(8)
1728A Frances Campion was acquitted of 'murdering her bastard child'.

(9)
1728B Sarah Butler was also acquitted of exactly the same charge. In neither of these cases is any more detail given.

✣✣ *Spencer Cowper could certainly sympathise with people who were charged with murder who were standing in the dock before him - because he had also been in exactly the same position himself. In 1699, at the age of 30, and having been a barrister for nine years, Spencer Cowper had been charged with the murder of Sarah Stout in Hertford.*

The Cowper family were the local 'bigwigs' in Hertford, and such attracted attention, including one young lady by the name of Sarah Stout, who had fallen in love with Cowper, although he was already married. When he shunned her advances, she became inconsolable.

Imagine the shock, therefore when she was found drowned in the River Lea. It came out that Cowper had been at the woman's house late on the evening before she was found drowned, along with three other men - make of that as you will.

An inquest was held which returned the verdict of suicide. But despite that, Cowper and the three others were placed on trial for murder at the Hertford Assizes in July 1699.

Very flimsy evidence was presented by the prosecution, who relied chiefly on the theory that as the body had floated, it must have been put in the water after death. Anyway, Cowper brought medical evidence to refute this, and because of his allegations that the prosecutions were the malicious work of his political enemies, all four defendants were acquitted.

This, however, seemed not to have harmed his career. He was elected to Parliament three times, and in 1727 was made a justice of the Common Pleas.

These 1728 Lent Assizes were destined to be his only visit to Northampton, as he died just a few months later, aged 59. His grandson, was the famous poet William Cowper of Olney, who wrote the famous poem concerning John Gilpin.

1729

(10)

1729A Tuesday 7 January 1729, Paulerspury

Victim Philip Bevins

Accused Edward Branson (never caught)
Samuel Adams

Edward Branson and Samuel Adams were partners in crime who supplemented their weekly wages by relieving lonely travellers of *their* wages - by violence if necessary.

It was on a cold winters afternoon, just after 5pm on Tuesday 7 January 1729 when Philip Bevins, a gardener by trade, started on his way home after having been to Towcester market. Walking his horse before him, he set off from Towcester along the Watling Street towards his home at Stony Stratford.

But unbeknown to him, he was being followed by Adams and Branson who saw easy pickings from this unaccompanied traveller. They had been hanging around at Lacy's Corner in Towcester for the sole purpose of watching out for a victim who was travelling alone, so presenting an easy target for robbery. Until recently, this used to be called 'loitering with intent'.*

Whether Bevins was known to Branson and Adams or whether he just happened to be the one who came along first, is unclear. But what is clear, is that Adams and Branson stalked Bevins as he walked his horse towards Paulerspury.

On reaching a lane in Paulerspury parish, Bevins stopped and prepared to mount his horse to ride the rest of the way home. This was the opportunity. As soon as Bevins was seated on his horse, Branson broke cover, rushed up to him and gave him three violent blows to the head with a stick, which he then used to push Bevin off his horse onto the ground.

It is doubtful whether Bevins even saw his attacker, and he was certainly not given the opportunity of recognition as he lay on the ground, because Branson continued smashing his head in with the stick. So violent was this attack (*the later post mortem would reveal no less than eight skull fractures*) that Bevins died immediately. The 'stick' used by Branson, and which he had just cut from the hedgerow, was 'over six feet long and very heavy'. This was discarded at the scene, but would be recovered later by the Towcester Parish Constable to be produced at the trial. The 26 shillings that Bevins had in his pockets was divided between Adams and Branson, who then split up to go their separate ways.

Although it was Branson and not Adams who had murdered Bevins, only Adams was to stand trial. And ironically, he would be arrested for a totally different crime, and before the Bevins murder was even known about.

The previous November, Adams and Branson had attacked, robbed, and left for dead, a certain farmer called Daniel Hix at Calverton in Buckinghamshire. Hix however recovered and reported the crime, and it was for this robbery that Adams was captured on the evening of the 7 January at his home in Towcester, just a couple of hours after the Bevins murder. It was only Adams' confession after arrest that caused the Towcester Parish Constable, Michael Rooker, to go to Paulerspury, where he would find the body of Bevins laying alongside the murder weapon.

Trial 1729 Lent Assizes, Tuesday 4 March. _Either_ Mr Baron Price _or_ Mr Justice Reynolds

Only Samuel Adams stood trial, because Branson, on hearing of Adams' arrest, disappeared and was never heard off again. As Adams had confessed to the murder in which he was implicated, the verdict was never in doubt.

Samuel Adams was hanged on Northampton Racecourse on Friday 21 March 1729 :

> 'At the place of Execution' reported the *Northampton Mercury* 'he behaved with a great deal of intrepidity and delivered a Paper to the Under Sheriff containing his confession of the Crime which he suffered'.

* *The offence of 'being a suspected person loitering with intent to commit a criminal offence' was subsequently made part of the Vagrancy Act 1824, and was otherwise known as the infamous 'sus' law. After a tremendous public campaign by 'racial monitoring groups', together with the usual ragbag of band-wagon-jumping politicians, alleging police misuse of this offence, the 'sus' law was repealed. Having achieved what they saw as a victory over the police, which was undoubtedly their intended aim, rather than protection of human rights, the campaigners then lost interest, enabling the replacement to the 'sus' law, the Criminal Attempts Act 1981, to be passed by Parliament without a whimper of dissent. But this new law, however, gave far greater powers to the police than the old 'sus' law ever did. Ah well, such is life.*

(11)

1729B At the same Lent Assizes, John Wright was acquitted of the murder of his wife. Absolutely no other details are given.

✣✣ *Sir Robert Price has the standard judges' biography. He had attended Saint John's College, Cambridge, before becoming a barrister of Lincoln's Inn. Politics then followed, when he was MP for Weobley (Herefordshire) on three occasions between 1685 and 1702. His 'reward' was to be made a Baron of the Exchequer in 1702. He died in 1733 aged 80.*

✣✣ *And James Reynolds can match this almost exactly : Queen's College, Cambridge; Barrister of Lincoln's Inn 1712; MP for Bury Saint Edmunds 1717; Judge of the King's Bench 1725; Lord Chief Baron 1730. He died in 1739 at the early age of 53, and unusually for that time, was never knighted.*

1730

(12)

1730A Saturday 25 July 1730. Saint James' Toll House, Northampton

Victim John Hall, Toll keeper

Accused William Walker
Thomas Parsons

Ten years after the founding of the *Northampton Mercury*, although the majority of local crimes were still reported sparsely, there were one or two that seemed to strike the local nerve, and were reported in full. This is amply illustrated by the murder of a local toll keeper, John Hall. The whole story can be gleaned purely from the newspaper reports - which are thus reproduced verbatim.

From the *Northampton Mercury*, Monday 27 July 1730 :

> '25 July this morning, John Hall, who kept the Toll House at Saint James End near this Town was barbarously murdered by William Walker and Thomas Parsons, belonging to Captain Roberts' Troop in the Right Honourable Lord Cobham's Regiment of Horse, now quartered here. The above William Walker who has since fled was born at Huntingdon is between 30 and 40 years of age, about 5'10½" high, of a darkish Complexion usually wearing, and had on when he went away, a brown frock Coat, a red Waistcoat and Breeches and a dark brown Wig. The friends of the deceased offer all charges to anyone that shall secure the said Walker, who was the person that gave the mortal wound. The other (Thomas Parsons) was this evening committed to the County Gaol and is doubly ironed.'

From the *Northampton Mercury* Monday 3 August 1730 :

> 'Last Thursday, William Walker was apprehended at his sister's house in Huntingdon in a Chamber over the

1732

(13)

1732A Thursday 24 August 1732. Pilsgate, Barnack

Victim The wife of William Allcock

Accused William Allcock

Trial **1733 Lent Assizes, Tuesday 27 February. *Either* Mr Baron Price *or* Mr Justice Probyn**

Although Barnack is in the Soke of Peterborough, which is now in Cambridgeshire, in 1732 the Soke was firmly inside Northamptonshire, which is why the trial was at the Northamptonshire Assizes.

The *Northampton Mercury*, Monday 5 March 1733, in reporting on the Assizes, goes into unusual lengths over this case. William Allcock was accused of the murder of his wife on the...

> '24th of August last on the Road (near Pilsgate in the parish of Barnack in this County) as he was carrying her to Colchester from Bourn in Lincolnshire, where he had left her for 15 years to be maintain'd by the Parish. She was found strangled with a small Cord round her Neck by the Country People going to Stamford Market. He denies the Fact, tho' the Evidence was strong and clear against him, and both on his Trial, and at receiving Sentence, he behaved with the greatest indifference and Unconcern ever known.'

William Allcock must have been quite a character, as we can judge from the report of his hanging on Friday 9 March 1733.

> 'On Friday last was executed her William Allcock for the Murder of his Wife, condemn'd on a clear and full Evidence. He never own'd the Fact, neither had he any concern on him on Account of his approaching Death, from the time of his Sentence to his last Moments, constantly affecting a Resolution, or as he call'd it, a Shew of Manhood, far beyond Words to express or Imagination to conceive : He would never suffer any Divines to discourse with him and always refus'd their or any other Personal Prayers, coveting Promiscuous Conversation and Company, continually craving after Liquor; and on the Morning of his Execution when he had drunk, by one Means or other, rather more than was

> sufficient for one in his Circumstances, privately sent and paid for a Pint of Wine, which being deny'd to him, he insisted upon the Hardship of the Usage he met with, and demand'd to have the Money return'd to him again, before he would enter the Cart. On his way to the fatal Tree he sung part of an old Song *Robin Hood*, with the Chorus, *Derry, derry down* &c, and swore, kick'd and spurn'd at every Person that laid hold of the Cart, and before he was turn'd off, he took off his Shoes, to avoid a well known Proverb, declar'd the Injustice of his Case from the Witnesses against him, as well as exclaiming against both Judge and Jury, all of whom he protested an utter Abhorrence as having so much as one single Thought of forgiving or dying in Peace with.'

How about that for sang froid - demanding your money back on your way to being hanged!

(14)

1732B Sometime during 1732 in Wellingborough

Victim Mary Viccars

Accused Robert Partridge

***Trial* 1734 Lent Assizes, Tuesday 5 March 1734. *Either* Mr Justice Probyn *or* Mr Baron Comyns**

This is a strange case. All we know is that at the 1734 Lent Assizes, Richard Partridge was accused of :

> 'being privy to, and on suspicion of being concerned in, the Murder of Mary Viccars of Wellingborough in this County, about two Years ago.'

Because this is so imprecise, it has been impossible to find any reference to a murder of Mary Viccars in Wellingborough about this time, despite a trawl through the *Northampton Mercury*. All we know is, that there appears to have been very little evidence, as the case was obviously held over until the 1734 Summer Assizes, and at them, Richard Partridge was acquitted.

❋

(E21) **FRIDAY 10 MARCH 1732**

HANGED FOR BURGLARY

Samuel Bayly

HANGED FOR SACRILEGE

John Cuthbert

Both John Cuthbert and Samuel Bayly appeared at the 1732 Lent Assizes on Tuesday 29 February, before either Mr Baron Price or Mr Justice Page. Not much information is given in the *Northampton Mercury*, but Samuel Bayly was charged with

> 'breaking open the House of James Harris of Finedon in this County and taking from thence a Pewter Cup, a Knife, a piece of Beef and a Quantity of Butter.'

John Cuthbert was charged with burglary and sacrilege by 'robbing Charlton Church'. Both Bayly and Cuthbert were found guilty, and were hanged together on Friday 10 March 1732. No report of this hanging appeared in the *Mercury*.

✣✣ *As the old saying goes, the pen is mightier than the sword. And perhaps the greatest proof of this is given by the life of Sir Francis Page, because in his lifetime he managed to upset not one, but three of the greatest literary figures of the age, who then absolutely vilified him in print, giving him a reputation that stayed with him for the rest of his life.*

But that was to come later. Before all that, his life had already been more than interesting. Having qualified as a barrister later than usual (he was 30, in 1690) his career was slow to take off. However in 1705 he was one of four barristers in the Ashby v White *case, the crux of which was that after some Aylesbury men had had the temerity to sue the Aylesbury Returning Officer for refusing to accept their votes, the House of Commons promptly gaoled them all. In applying for a grant of Habeus Corpus on the Aylesbury men, Page and his colleagues were immediately declared guilty of a breach of privilege by the House of Commons, who ordered the authorities to arrest them. Page managed to escape (others weren't so lucky - see 1737, Mr Justice Denton), and go into hiding for four months until Parliament was dissolved, and a General Election was called,*

All that was put behind him, however, and eventually he entered Parliament himself, as MP for Huntingdon after gaining the patronage of Edward Montagu, third Earl of Sandwich. The Montagus were a Northamptonshire family with a country seat at Barnwell, where the third Earl is buried; along with his grandson, the notorious fourth Earl of Sandwich - the 'inventor' of the sandwich.

Francis Page was made a Baron of the Exchequer in 1718, and after 1723, it was his unflinching application of 'The Black Act' (see *1722) which earned him the nickname of 'The Hanging Judge'. He was transferred to the King's Bench in 1727, just in time to try the poet Richard Savage for murder, and to pass the death sentence upon him. Apparently, though, Page's summing up was so biased against Savage, that eventually he was reprieved.*

But Savage was the leading poet of his day - in line to become Poet Laureate - and as such he had the friendship of the two great literati of the age, Alexander Pope and Doctor Samuel Johnson. And Pope, Johnson and Savage then turned the literary thumb-screw. Numerous of their works were published, all vilifying Page, thus ensuring, and continuing, his reputation as one of the most brutal judges of his time - 'The Hanging Judge'.

Page obviously knew of this, and maybe played on it. The story goes that at the very end of his life, when shuffling unsteadily away from court, someone asked about his health. 'Sir' he replied 'you see, I keep hanging *on,* hanging *on.' Francis Page died in December 1741, aged 80.*

1733

The only homicide to occur in 1733 appeared at the Lent Assizes on Tuesday 27 February, before either Mr Baron Price or Mr Justice Probyn.

(15)
1733A Mary Monsell was indicted for murdering 'her Bastard Child'. No details are given as to where or when this occurred. All that is given is that Mary Monsell was acquitted.

✣✣ *This was the first of only four visits made to Northampton by Sir Edmund Probyn, before dying in 1742 aged 64. Admitted as a barrister of the Middle Temple in 1702, he was made a judge of the King's Bench in 1726, and became the Lord Chief Baron in 1740.*

1734

No homicides occurred in 1734

1735

(16)
1735A Believed to be Friday 25 April 1735. Place unknown
Victim Unknown
Accused Thomas Winpress
Trial **1735 Summer Assizes, Thursday 17 July. Mr Justice Reeve**
All we are told about this one, is that Thomas Winpress was referred to trial because he had been 'found guilty on the Coroner's Inquest of Man-slaughter.' Obviously the judge and jury disagreed with the good coroner, because Thomas Winpress was acquitted.

(17)
1735B Friday 9 May 1735. Grendon
Victim Henry Wright
Accused William Clarke
Trial **1735 Summer Assizes, Thursday 17 July. Mr Justice Reeve**
No details of this are given in the *Mercury*. All we are told is that William Clarke was found guilty of manslaughter and burnt on the hand.

(18)

1735C Wednesday 18 June 1735. Weston-by-Weedon

Victim Thomas Fawson

Accused Elizabeth Fawson

The last of the six women of Northamptonshire to be found guilty of Petty Treason for murdering their husbands, Elizabeth Fawson was burnt at the stake on Friday 8 August 1735 on Northampton Racecourse. And the fact that she had only been married for barely five weeks, surely gives an indication of her character, and as to why she had got married in the first place.

Elizabeth Bull was the daughter of the landlord of the *Red Lion* at Helmdon. As was customary at that time, she was sent away 'in service', in other words as a housemaid/servant to a large house in the district.

However, once she was away from home and off the leash, her character changed. From being a polite young lady, she became aggressive, ill-mannered, and fond of the boys. So much so, that she was quickly dismissed from her job and sent back home, where she quickly took up with one of the local larrikins, one Edward Monks by name.

But her eye also fell on Thomas Fawson, son of a local farmer, and thus with a few bob in his pocket. And reading between the lines, as he was only seventeen years old, and probably completely innocent and naive in the ways of the world, to have a feisty female throw herself at you, he soon became totally besotted with her. Despite his family and friends warning him off, the couple were married on Sunday 18 May 1735.

It was obvious to all observers that Elizabeth was only after the money, and not Thomas, as she still continued to 'carry on' with Edward Monks, right under Thomas's nose. Whether Elizabeth and Edward hatched the plot together, or it was Elizabeth's alone is not known, but Elizabeth was determined to rid herself of Thomas, and thus inherit the money.

On Wednesday 18 June, Elizabeth prepared a meal for Thomas when he came home from working in the fields. The meal was a porridge of bread boiled with beer, a frequent meal amongst farm labourers of the time. But Elizabeth had doctored the porridge with crystals of white mercury, a deadly poison.

A few hours later, Thomas was in agony, and Elizabeth called a doctor. The doctor, however, knew poisoning when he saw it, and immediately suspected what had happened. But he told Elizabeth it was a virus about which he could do nothing, and so left. Thomas died in agony a few hours later.

Thinking about his intuition, the doctor went straight to Northampton, and reported his suspicions to the authorities. Elizabeth Fawson was arrested within two days.

Trial **1735 Summer Assizes, Thursday 17 July. Mr Justice Reeve**

During her month in prison awaiting trial, Elizabeth Fawson became very sullen, spoke to no one, and certainly never made any confession of her alleged crime. But at the Summer Assizes, her guilt was quite easy to prove anyway, even without her confession.

Accordingly, Mr Justice Reeve sentenced her to be burnt at the stake for Petty Treason. And that occurred at 3pm on Friday 8 August 1735 on Northampton Racecourse. The *Northampton Mercury* carried an eye witness account :

> 'Tis observable that she continued to her last moment inflexible in her sullen temper, and had all over her face a black hood, which she never suffered to be removed, nor would she make the last speech to the spectators about her crime or repentance, where it is but too well known may without injustice be attributed to the frequent visits and admonitions of a near relation, only when she was lifted out of the sledge, desired several times that they would soon despatch her, and one of the attending officers begged she might be quite dead before the fire was lighted'.

And we can deduce from the newspaper report, that the usual custom was carried out, in that she was strangled, either to death or to unconsciousness, before the bonfire was lit, thus ensuring no pain was felt during the burning. The crowd was estimated at between twelve-thousand and fifteen-thousand strong.

✣✣ These Summer Assizes were the only time that Sir Thomas Reeve came to Northampton, and it is not known what he thought of having three criminal homicides on the Calendar on one day, as well as Elizabeth Wilkinson. Nothing much is known of his life, except that he became a

barrister of the Middle Temple in 1713, was knighted on becoming a Judge of the Common Pleas in 1733, and became Chief Justice in 1736. He died only one year later, in 1737, aged 65.

❁

(E22) **FRIDAY 8 AUGUST 1735**

HANGED FOR THEFT (PICKPOCKETING)

Elizabeth Wilkinson

An interesting thought occurs in the case of Elizabeth Wilkinson. Appearing at the 1735 Summer Assizes, before Mr Justice Reeve, charged with 'Picking the Pocket of one William Hicks of One Pound Seventeen Shillings and Ten Pence', she was described as 'being an old Offender in her Practice'.

But if she was 'an old Offender', why had she not been hanged before under 'The Black Act', now some thirteen years old? Perhaps the judges of the time had some discretion after all.

Be that as it may, patience was obviously worn out, and the death penalty was invoked. Elizabeth Wilkinson was executed on the same day as Elizabeth Fawson, though not at the same time, Elizabeth Wilkinson meeting her maker at 8am.

1736

The Lent Assizes of 1736 began on Tuesday 16 March and lasted for three days, before Mr Baron Comyns or Mr Justice Lee. Two manslaughters appeared on the Calendar :

(19)

1736A Robert Bland was indicted after a Coroner's Inquest of the manslaughter of Susannah Jackson. Robert Bland was found not guilty and was discharged. No other details are known.

(20)
1736B David White was indicted, after a Coroner's Inquest, of the manslaughter of Samuel Earle. He was found guilty, and was burnt on the hand. No other details are known.

✣✣ *Sir John Comyns had been a Baron of the Exchequer since 1726, after 25 years as MP for Maldon in Essex. Although briefly transferred to the Common Pleas in 1736, he would finally become the Chief Baron of the Exchequer in 1738. He had first come to Northampton in 1730, although there were no homicides on the calendar, and he would make periodic visits until his death in 1740*

✣✣ *Sir William Lee, having entered the Middle Temple in 1703, became the Personal Secretary to both George I and George II, before becoming Attorney-General. Made a Justice of the King's Bench in 1730, he would finally become the Chief Justice of the King's Bench and Privy Councillor in 1737. He died in 1754 aged 66.*

But it was the Summer Assizes that made the headlines for 1736, with the infamous Mary Haddon case :

(21)
1736C Saturday 13 March 1736. Welton
Victim the mother of Mary Haddon (her Christian Name is unknown)
Accused Mary Haddon

As far as we can tell, the actual death occurred at Welton on Saturday 13 March 1736. The death was reported in the *Northampton Mercury* of Monday 29 March :

> 'On Monday last was committed to our County Gaol. Mary the Wife of John Hadden *(sic)* of Welton near Daventry, being charg'd on the Coroner's Inquest with poisoning her own Mother by giving her a Quantity of Ratsbane *(a poisonous plant, and a possible source of arsenic)* in some Victuals on the 13th Inst of which she languished about nine Hours and then died.'

Trial 1736 Summer Assizes, Thursday 5 August. Lord Chief Justice Hardwicke

No details whatsoever are known about the trial, but the verdict, obviously, was guilty. The *Northampton Mercury* of Monday 23 August, carried the report of her execution on Friday 20 August :

> 'some time before her execution she confessed the fact and a person who attended her wrote down in her own mouth every particular circumstance thereof, which is now in print'.

This Broadsheet would have had a tremendous circulation in the town. Unfortunately, no copy has survived.

✣✣ *Philip Yorke (Lord Hardwicke) was one of the 'greats' on the eighteenth century legal scene. Born in 1690, Philip Yorke remarkably never went either to public school nor to Oxbridge - then, as now, the standard entry qualifications for the Bar.*

Instead, he worked in a London solicitor's office when he was sixteen, and studied to be a barrister in his spare time. He was so good that he did become a barrister, of Lincoln's Inn, in 1715.

He was knighted and made Solicitor-General in 1720, and Attorney-General in 1724, prosecuting several of the important cases of the day, including Edmund Curll for publishing seditious and immoral books; Thomas Bambridge, warden of the Fleet prison on charges of murder and torture of prisoners, and the Reverend Thomas Woolston, who dared to publish pamphlets saying that some of the Bible was allegory and not fact. Because of his performances on these occasions, he was appointed Chief Justice and ennobled as Baron Hardwicke in 1733, becoming the Lord Chancellor in 1737.

Subsequently, his career also touched on the nation's history. He was responsible for passing the laws citing high treason against Bonnie Prince Charlie during the Jacobite Rebellion of 1745. Afterwards, he sat on the trials of the Jacobite rebels, and was responsible for the laws which caused the Highland Clearances, and the banning of the wearing of tartan. As his reward, he was promoted in the peerage, and thus became the 1st Earl of Hardwicke in 1754. He died ten years later.

1737

(22)

1737A Date and place unknown

Victim The daughter of John and Elizabeth Elliott (name unknown)

Accused John and Elizabeth Elliott

Nothing is known about this case either. John and Elizabeth Elliott appeared at the 1737 Summer Assizes, on Tuesday 19 July, before either Mr Justice Denton or Mr Baron Carter. But both were acquitted.

✣✣ *Also involved in the 'Men of Aylesbury' case in 1705, Alexander Denton was caught and sent to prison, not like Francis Page, who escaped (see 1732). However, when all that lot was sorted, Denton was elected as MP for Buckingham in 1708 until 1710, and again from 1715 until 1722. In that year he was appointed as a Justice of the Common Pleas, but such was his ambition, that he wanted to climb the ladder even higher.*

In 1729 he secured the position as Chancellor to the Prince of Wales, which meant many visits to the Royal Court. But he was continually agitating to get something better, and actually wrote to Lord Hardwicke, by then Lord Chancellor (see 1736), pushing himself forward to become Chief Justice of the Common Pleas.

Hardwicke told him to go away, and gave the job to Mr Justice Reeve (see 1735). On Reeve's death in 1737, Denton tried again, but was again rebuffed. The next year, Denton was offered the job of Chief Baron of the Exchequer, and in a fit of pique turned it down, but immediately regretted it, and tried to accept the offer, only to be told to go away again because the job had already gone to somebody else.

This continual pushing of himself did not endear himself to his fellow judges, and Mr Justice Abney (see 1747) wrote scathingly about him. But Denton was so disappointed at his perceived lack of progress that he sank into depression, and this, according to Mr Justice Abney 'sat so heavily on his spirits that they contributed much to shorten his days.' Alexander Denton died in March 1740 aged 61.

❃

(E23) **SATURDAY 6 AUGUST 1737**

HANGED FOR HIGHWAY ROBBERY

Henry Doggs
Jacob Medlicoate

Also appearing at the 1737 Summer Assizes were these two, together with their accomplices by the names of William Mabbit, and a gentleman known only to the *Mercury* as J--B--. Why the court reporter didn't know his name is a mystery, as it would have been clearly displayed on the Calendar. Or are we again faced with a deliberate cover-up to protect some local (and wealthy) family?

Anyway, the *Mercury* gives absolutely no information about this case, which probably adds credence to a cover-up going on. Why is information given in the case of Bayly and Cuthbert in 1732 (although admittedly not much), but none in this? All we have is that these four were tried for 'a Robbery on the Highway'. William Mabbit and J--B-- were acquitted, but Doggs and Medlicoate were found guilty. Both were hanged on Northampton Racecourse on Saturday 6 August 1737.

1738

(23)

1738A Sunday 9 April 1738. Moreton Pinckney
Victim John Humphreys
Accused Henry Clarke (Butcher)

Not much is known of this, except that Henry Clarke stabbed John Humphreys in the left side of the neck over the collar bone with a long clasp knife, which 'pricked him to the heart'. John Humpreys died within minutes.

Trial **1738 Summer Assizes, Tuesday 11 July.** ***Either*** **Mr Chief Baron Comyns** ***or*** **Mr Baron Parker**

Henry Clarke was found guilty of the murder, and was hanged on Saturday 29 July 1738.

✣✣ *Sir Thomas Parker had only just been made a Baron of the Exchequer a few weeks previously, at the age of 43. In an otherwise unremarkable career, he would transfer to the Common Pleas in 1740, before returning to the Exchequer Court as Chief Baron two years later. And in that capacity, he would be a frequent visitor to the Northamptonshire Assizes over the next thirty years. He would retire in 1772, and would die in 1784 aged 89.*

(24)

1738B Monday 4 December 1738, 7pm. Paulerspury

Victim Daughter of John and Frances Cotton (name unknown)

Accused John and Frances Cotton

By any stretch of the imagination, this is one of the most callous and horrifying murders that you will ever come across. And especially so, when the victim was only 27 months old, and the daughter of the accused.

The details in the *Northampton Mercury* are confused, but John Cotton murdered his daughter 'by taking [her] by the legs and dashing its (*sic*) brains out against a wall'. This apparently was in a stone pit in Paulerspury. He told nobody what he had done, and immediately fled the scene. When the crime was discovered Frances Cotton was arrested and clapped in Northampton gaol. John Cotton was finally captured at Ivinghoe in Buckinghamshire.

***Trial* 1739 Lent Assizes, Tuesday 6 March. *Either* Mr Justice Page *or* Mr Baron Thomson**

Frances Cotton, because she nothing of what had happened was acquitted. But John Cotton was found guilty.

He was hanged on Northampton Racecourse on Thursday 22 March 1739. But because his crime was so callous, and as a deterrent to others, his body was then hung in chains at Paulerspury, the scene of the crime, and then left there until it rotted. This ensured therefore, that he received the final humiliation in not receiving a proper burial.

1739

(25)

1739A Wednesday 4 April 1739. Weedon

Victim Richard Bromley, a butcher of Weedon

Accused Richard Fennell
Bryan Connell
FitzMorris (never captured)

Although Bryan Connell was Irish, he had lived in Northamptonshire for some time, at Weedon in fact, where, in the spring of 1739, his mother was still living. Which is why he knew Richard Bromley, who owned a butcher's shop in Weedon. Although it appears that his mother was relatively affluent, and had rich connections, Bryan had fallen in with a crowd of London villains, and was a member of a gang, alongside two others called Richard Fennell and a character by the name of FitzMorris.

This gang was suspected of assaults, robberies and murders in London. Which is probably why they came under the 'beady eye' of Thomas de Veil, the pioneering London crime fighting magistrate. And which also probably explains why Bryan Connell made regular excursions back to Northamptonshire, when it became too 'hot' in London with Thomas de Veil constantly breathing down his neck.

Richard Bromley owned the butcher's shop in Weedon, and thus was fairly prosperous and well-to-do. His body was discovered on Wednesday 4 April 1739 on Weedon Common. And here we resort to the report in the *Northampton Mercury* of Monday 9 April 1739 :

> 'On Wednesday last, between the Hours of Eight and Ten in the Evening was committed the most inhuman and barbarous Murder and Robbery that has been known to the Memory of Man on Richard Bromley, Butcher of Weedon, on his Return from Daventry Market, in the High Street Road, within a Quarter of a Mile of his own House, by some Ruffians, who, as supposed, having first knock'd him off his Horse, fractur'd his Skull, cut his Head almost off, cut and stabb'd him in the Body in 16 Places, out of which ten were declar'd by the Surgeons to be mortal; his Hands and Face were cut and wounded in a Miserable Manner, as we suppose, by endeavouring to save his Throat. 'Tis

believed to be done by some Neighbouring Villains that knew him, and that he was to have received a considerable Sum of Money, as well for a Note he had with him of 20L, to be paid that Day in Daventry, besides his Market Money, which was upward of 6L, and in a Hurry to come at the Money, they cut off with his Pocket a Part of his Thigh. How cautious therefore should People be of letting it be known when they go Abroad to receive Money, or of even travelling with Money late in the Evening.

NB. The Villains had the Assurance to bring and leave his Horse fasten'd to a Hook near his own House, before Ten o'Clock the same Evening.'

Immediately, the hunt started for his murderers, and notices appealing for witnesses and information appeared in virtually every newspaper in the country. But having no organised crime detecting agency (we would have to wait for another nine years before the Bow Street Runners came on the scene), only limited success was achieved.

Richard Fennell was captured first, because he was probably local as well. It was perhaps because he was local, that he knew Richard Bromley would be carrying a large amount of cash.

Appearing at the 1740 Lent Assizes, on Wednesday 2 April, before either Mr Justice Denton or Mr Baron Parker, Richard Fennell 'was try'd on suspicion of being concern'd in the

barbarous Murder of Richard Bromley, Butcher of Weedon on 4th April last'.

Obviously because of a lack of any direct evidence, Richard Fennell was acquitted. And there the matter would have rested, until Elizabeth Watson alias O'Neill turned King's Evidence,* and supplied the direct evidence that was needed.

Elizabeth Watson was Connell's girl friend, or perhaps we should call her his Moll. What made Elizabeth contact Thomas de Veil is not known, but contact him she did, and it was Elizabeth Watson's testimony, taken before Thomas de Veil, and naming names, that would eventually convict Connell of the murder of Richard Bromley.

All this took time of course. Which is why Connell was not arrested until September 1740, and his trial not held until the 1741 Northamptonshire Lent Assizes.

Trial **1741 Lent Assizes, Tuesday 10 March. Chief Justice Willes**

From the *Northampton Mercury* of Monday 16 March 1741, reporting on the Lent Assizes, we can glean that Bryan Connell was brought from Newgate prison to Northampton to stand trial. And coming with him was Thomas De Veil himself, to prove that Elizabeth Watson's testimony, taken before him, was true.

Elizabeth Watson said that on the day before the murder, she had come from London to Northamptonshire with Connell, and he told her to stay at a friend's house at Foster's Booth. At that time, Connell only had 1s 6d on him. The next morning, he came to collect her, but then had £5 on him, and was covered in blood. £5 was about two months wages for a farm labourer in the 1740s - today's equivalent would therefore be roughly £2,000, or thereabouts.

Some time later, they were again coming from London to Northamptonshire, when they arrived at a spot in Weedon parish. Connell killed a robin, and then said 'this is not the only life that has been lost here, on this very spot Bromley the butcher was killed'.

Elizabeth Watson then testified about a time the gang was all together in London. There was a fierce argument between Connell, FitzMorris and Fennel as to who had done what to Bromley. FitzMorris said that Fennell had told them that Bromley would have a lot of money on him that day; but there was an argument as to which one had actually knocked him down, and which one had cut his throat.

At his trial, Connell had contrived to bring ten of his Irish mates to come to the Assizes to give him an alibi. But because of the presence in the court of Thomas de Veil, all ten of them refused to appear. They knew full well, that de Veil would tear their own characters to shreds, as being London villains, they were all well known to him.

In the light of Elizabeth Watson's testimony, and faced with Thomas de Veil backing her up, the jury only took six minutes to find Connell guilty of the murder of Richard Bromley.

Bryan Connell, still protesting his innocence, was hanged on Northampton Racecourse on Friday 3 April 1741, in front of an enormous crowd. As with the body of John Cotton (1739A), his corpse was then hung in chains on Weedon Common - in fact, facing his mother's house - and left there until it rotted.

There are several little supplements to all of this. Because Connell appeared to be relatively well-to-do, and because Elizabeth Watson was 'an infamous woman who had lived with him in adultery for some years', well connected persons tried to get Connell reprieved.

This still goes on today. Comfortably brought up, affluent, well-to-do, upper class people, aristocrats, or 'celebrities', who have no idea of life 'down at the sharp end', seem incapable of seeing the whole picture, and are easily duped into championing characters that the rest of the world can see for what they are.

Thus it was that Doctor Philip Doddridge, Northampton's well known Minister of Religion, hymn writer, philanthropist and gullible soft touch, got involved, and believed implicitly everything Connell told him, with complete disregard for all the contradictory evidence.

Apparently Doddridge visited Connell in his cell after the verdict, and was convinced of Connell's innocence. At his own expense he sent friends to Whitchurch and Chester, who examined witnesses. The good Doctor of Divinity then came to the conclusion that Connell was in Chester on the day of the murder. Connell was still hanged.

And what of FitzMorris? Nothing is ever heard of him again, and so his name disappears from history. But with Elizabeth Watson, the saga continued.

In the *Northampton Mercury* of Monday 23 January 1749, in other words, eight years later, appears this :

> 'Friday last, at the Old Bailey. Elizabeth Watson who turned King's Evidence at Northamptonshire Lent Assizes 1741, received sentence of death for returning from transportation before her time. She pleaded her Belly, and a Jury of Matrons being impanell'd, she was found quick with child'.

So judging by that, was Elizabeth sentenced to transportation even though she turned King's Evidence? Surely not. But delving a bit deeper, we find the true story. In the *Northampton Mercury* of Monday 5 December 1748, we read :

> 'Elizabeth Watson transported for seven years for picking the pocket of Mrs Evered, a Cheesemonger's wife in Drury Lane, was taken at a public house in Gray's Inn on Sunday last for returning from transportation before her term of seven years expired'.

So it appears Elizabeth *was* let off for turning King's Evidence, but then started to be a naughty girl again, and was caught picking pockets. It is for this offence that she was transported, and for which she was caught and appeared at the Old Bailey, when she returned before the seven years were up. The mandatory sentence for returning from transportation was death by hanging. But as she was found to be pregnant, the sentence was commuted.

However, in the *Northampton Mercury* of Monday 12 March 1750, we read that 'Elizabeth Watson was deliver'd of her child, and was called down for her former sentence'.

But her former sentence was to be hanged. So was she hanged? Surely they wouldn't do that to a nursing mother, even in those days? No subsequent mention of her can be found, so it is possible that she may have escaped the ultimate sentence. And so, it is at this point, that we have, reluctantly, to say goodbye to Elizabeth Watson.

* *King's Evidence (and also Queen's Evidence, as it still goes on), is where an accused person confesses his or her guilt, and offers to give evidence for the prosecution against the other defendants. In return, they were normally acquitted of the charges against them.*

At the 1739 Summer Assizes, starting on Tuesday 31 July, before Chief Justice Willes or Mr Justice Probyn, only one homicide appeared on the Calendar :

(26)

1739B Robert Haseldine was indicted on suspicion of murdering Richard Lovet. No other detail was given, but Robert Haseldine was acquitted.

✣✣ *Sir John Willes had been Chief Justice of the Common Pleas since 1737, and would remain so until his death at the age of 76 in 1761. But he also had the standard judges' background : Trinity College, Oxford (MA in 1710 and Doctor of Civil Law in 1715); barrister of Lincoln's Inn 1713; MP for Launceston 1722-1726; MP for Weymouth 1726; MP for West Looe 1727-1737; Knighted, and Attorney General 1734-1737.*

1740

There were no criminal homicides in the year 1740

❁

(E24) **FRIDAY 25 APRIL 1740**

HANGED FOR BURGLARY

William Welford

Both William Welford and his criminal colleague, John Cheney, appeared at the 1740 Lent Assizes on Wednesday 2 April, before either Mr Baron Parker, or the sulky Mr Justice Denton. They were charged 'for taking a piece of Tammy out of the Shop of William Green'. Tammy, we are reliably informed, is a type of glazed woollen cloth.

No other details are given, such as the location of William Green's shop. All we do know is that John Cheney was acquitted, but William Welford wasn't. He was hanged on Northampton Racecourse on Friday 25 April 1740, and the *Northampton Mercury* did not think it important enough to print a report.

1741

The Lent Assizes of 1741 saw the trial of Bryan Connell (see 1739B). The Summer Assizes for that year began on Tuesday 14 July, before either Lord Chief Baron Probyn or Chief Justice Lee. On the Calendar was :

(27)
1741A Elizabeth Ward who was accused of the murder of her illegitimate child. Absolutely no other detail is known, not even the verdict.

1742

(28)
1742A This case appeared at the 1742 Lent Assizes, on Tuesday 9 March, before Chief Justice Willes or Mr Justice Abney. Absolutely nothing is known except that John Harlock was acquitted of the murder of his son.

(29)
1742B Tuesday 21 September 1742. Kettering
Victim Benjamin Meadows
Accused Timothy Cunningham
Richard Coulter
John McDowell
Adam Tate
William Porter
William Attleborough

By 1741, Britain knew that she would have to go to war on the continent of Europe, in what would become known to history as the War of the Austrian Succession. In enlarging the army to cope, no less than six new infantry regiments had to be formed during 1741 and 1742.

In those days, the regiments were called by their commanding officer's name. And it is to Brigadier Bragg's Regiment we must turn for our next piece of mayhem.

Throughout 1742, the British army was steadily being sent over to Flanders in support of the Austrians, and no doubt in September 1742, Brigadier Bragg's Regiment was the next to go. Which is probably why six soldiers of the regiment decided to have a genteel soirée to say 'au revoir'. And the hostelry they chose was the *Blackamoor's Head* in Kettering.

The result was unavoidable. Eventually, so much ale had been consumed, that when the landlord, Samuel Meadows, asked them to be good fellows, desist from blaspheming and riotous behaviour, and kindly leave his premises and go about their lawful business, that the inevitable fight broke out. During the commotion, Samuel Meadows had his hand almost severed, and his brother, Benjamin Meadows, was fatally stabbed with a bayonet.

Trial **1743 Lent Assizes, Tuesday 1 March. *Either* Mr Chief Baron Parker *or* Mr Justice Burnet**

All six soldiers appeared at the Assizes charged with the murder of Benjamin Meadows. Cunningham and Coulter were acquitted; McDowell and Tate were found guilty of a lesser charge and were burnt on the hand. But Porter and Attleborough, were found guilty.

Porter was hanged on Northampton Racecourse on Friday 11 March 1743. His execution was slightly unusual in that instead of riding on a horse drawn cart to the Racecourse, he walked there. And because he was walking, he was supplied with a pint of ale at the last inn on the way, the *Bantam Cock* on Abington Square.

Attleborough seemed to have wealthy connections in London, and so efforts were made by his family for a reprieve, which is why he was not hanged alongside Porter. But all it did was to postpone his fate. Attleborough was hanged on Northampton Racecourse on Saturday 26 March 1743.

> 'He behaved' said the *Northampton Mercury* 'with great Courage and Intrepidity, and was very penitent, but deny'd his being in any Shape guilty of the Murder'.

✣✣ *When compared to some of his contemporaries, Sir Thomas Burnet's life was relatively 'racy'. Thomas Burnet was the son of a famous Bishop of Salisbury, and by the age of fifteen when he entered the Middle Temple, had travelled extensively all over Europe. He was called to the Bar in 1715, but in 1719, was sent to Lisbon as the British Consul - at the grand old age of 25. He was appointed Judge of the Common Pleas in 1741, and knighted in 1745. He died in 1753 aged only 59.*

1743

Only one homicide occurred in 1743, and that was on the Calendar at the Summer Assizes, which started on Tuesday 19 July, before Lord Chief Justices Willes or Mr Justice Wright.

(30)
1743A Richard Hardin was accused of murder and was acquitted. Absolutely nothing else is known.

✣✣ *In 1730, Martin Wright, after being a barrister for twelve years, published his book* Introduction to the Law of Tenures. *This brought him to the notice of the powers-that-be, and he was promoted to be a serjeant-at-law, which was the highest order of barristers (this was abolished in 1873, being replaced with the rank of Queen's Counsel). In 1739 he was appointed a Baron of the Exchequer before transferring to the King's Bench one year later. He was knighted in 1745. Retiring in 1755 on the grounds of ill health, nevertheless he survived for another twelve years and died in 1767 aged 75.*

1744

And similarly during 1744, only the Lent Assizes, before Mr Justice Chappell or Mr Justice Abney, had a case of homicide :

(31)
1744A William Eyton and Ann Gilliam were acquitted of the murder of a child. Was it theirs? We don't know, as no detail is given.

✣✣ *Sir William Chappell had been the MP for Dorchester for fifteen years before becoming a Justice of the King's Bench in 1737. This was his second visit to Northampton, his first being the 1742 Summer Assizes where there were no criminal homicide cases. But these would be his last visit, as he would die the following year aged 68.*

1745

There were no criminal homicides in 1745

❁

(E25) **FRIDAY 9 AUGUST 1745**

HANGED FOR ROBBERY

Joseph Goodman

The owners of the *Northampton Mercury*, the Dicey family, were always on the look out to make more cash. So they hit upon an idea which they tried out first with the hanging of Joseph Goodman. Joseph Goodman had appeared at the 1745 Summer Assizes before either Mr Chief Baron Parker or Mr Justice Denison, and had been found guilty of 'Robbery on the Highway and Horse Stealing.'

Instead of printing the details of the case in the weekly newspaper, the owner/editor, printed all the details in a pamphlet or chapbook, which was sold separately. Thus, everybody who wanted to know all the details and who had bought the newspaper to read them, now found they had to fork out more money in order to buy the chapbook. Cunning or what? Hence the report in the *Northampton Mercury* of Monday 12 August 1745 :

> 'On Friday last Joseph Goodman was executed here for a Robbery on the Highway. He confess'd the Fact for which he had died, and many other Robberies committed by him and his Companions, which being in Print, we refer thereto.'

✣✣ *Not belonging to the establishment, indeed his father was 'in trade' in Leeds, Sir Thomas Denison did not have the standard background of a barrister. He did not go to public school, nor to Oxbridge, and had to go first to the Inner Temple, then move to Gray's Inn, before finally Lincoln's Inn called him to the bar in 1733.*

But so good did he prove, that just nine years later, he was made a Justice of the King's Bench. Very reluctantly, if we believe his epitaph, because Lord Mansfield (see 1763) wrote that he had 'been pressed, and at last prevailed upon' to accept this office. But once there 'discharged the important trust of that high office with unsuspected integrity and uncommon ability'.

Thomas Denison was knighted in 1745 in reward for being one of the judges who presented a loyal address to the king after the 1745 Jacobite Rebellion. A regular visitor to Northampton, Denison resigned in 1765 because of ill health and died just a few months later aged 66.

1746

The only homicide of 1746 appeared at the Northamptonshire Assizes, before Lord Chief Justice Willes or Mr Justice Birch, and which started on Saturday 13 September.

(32)
1746A Ann Holloway was accused of the murder of her bastard child. No other detail is given,

The reason why the Assizes were postponed from July to September in 1746 is not known. Perhaps the turmoil of the country during the last Jacobite Rebellion was the disrupting factor. The rebels, under 'Bonny Prince Charlie' had finally been defeated at the Battle of Culloden in April, which is when the organising of the Summer Assizes would normally have been taking place. Only after things had calmed down after Culloden, could things start being arranged.

✣✣ *Probably these 1746 Assizes were the very first that Sir Thomas Birch had attended, because he had only just been made a Justice of the Common Pleas in June of that year. He was also knighted at the same time, during that welter of congratulatory back-slapping that occurred after the 1745 Jacobite Rebellion. He had been called to the bar by the Inner Temple in 1715, and he would make regular visits to Northampton until his death in 1757 aged 67.*

1747

(33)

1747A An unknown date and place
Victim The wife of William Curtis
Accused William Curtis
***Trial* 1747 Summer Assizes, Thursday 30 July. *Either* Mr Chief Baron Parker *or* Mr Justice Abney**

The murder of his wife by William Curtis is a complete mystery. No detail is contained in the court report, so we do not know where, when or how it happened. All we know for certain is that William Curtis was hanged for murder on Northampton Racecourse on Friday 14 August 1747.

An interesting note is contained in the otherwise scant report in the *Mercury* of the 1747 Summer Assizes :

> 'Alexander Jacob being detected in picking pockets in the Sessions House while the Court was sitting, was tried, found guilty and order'd to be whipp'd.'

How's that for instant justice? *No* automatic bail, *no* inch thick crime files, *no* social worker's reports, *no* nine-to-five CPS lawyers then advising 'no further action' - none of that - all done and dusted there and then.

✣✣ Sir Thomas Abney had visited the Northamptonshire Assizes twice before, for the Lent Assizes of 1741 as a Baron of the Exchequer, and then again in 1744 as a Justice of the Common Pleas. But he knew Northamptonshire well, having married Frances Burton who came from Brackley.

He was called to the Bar by the Inner Temple in 1713. In the following years, he tried his hardest to be appointed a judge, and lobbied Lord Hardwicke (see 1736C) continually. Eventually he succeeded, and was appointed a Baron of the Exchequer in 1740, transferring to the Common Pleas in 1743. He remained there until, in 1750, his death came in very unusual circumstances.

The filthy state of the country's prisons in the eighteenth century left a lot to be desired, and as such, disease in them was rife and unchecked. In 1741, Abney tried to get out of being sent to Exeter because the disease there was said to be contagious, and he thought he might catch something from the prisoners. Again, in 1746, when he was sent north to try some Jacobite rebels, he tried to get out of it. But in 1750, he wasn't so lucky.

At the Summer Assizes at the Old Bailey, not only did he catch something, but Mr Baron Clarke did too, along with Sir Samuel Pennant, the Lord Mayor of London, and several others. All of them died from 'gaol distemper' (which is a disease now called typhus) nurtured by the unsanitary conditions of the prisons, and which they caught when the prisoners were brought before them. As such, the 1750 Old Bailey Summer Assizes are forever known to history as 'The Black Sessions'.

Mr Baron Clarke who also succumbed at 'The Black Sessions', had visited Northampton twice - for the 1745 and 1748 Lent Assizes - although there were no criminal homicides on either calendar. Charles Clarke, a barrister of Lincoln's Inn, had been the MP for Huntingdonshire and then Whitchurch, before becoming a Baron of the Exchequer in 1743.

1748

Two homicides occurred in 1748, and the first appeared at the Summer Assizes, which began on Tuesday 26 July, before either Lord Chief Baron Parker or Mr Justice Abney.

(34)
1748A Sarah Roberts was found guilty of the 'murder of her bastard child', and received the death penalty. However, she was 'repriev'd till the next Assizes'.

And at the next Assizes, the Lent Assizes of 1749, Sarah Roberts was transported for fourteen years. Again no detail is given, but to receive that amount of sentence, the murder must have been particularly callous or gruesome.

(35)

1748B Monday 7 November 1748. Byfield

Victim Herbert Venn

Accused Thomas Turner

A fight between Herbert Venn and Thomas Turner ended up with Herbert Venn losing his life. All the details have been lost, but the very same day, Thomas Turner was committed to the County Gaol by the Coroner, after being found guilty of manslaughter at the Inquest.

Trial **1749 Lent Assizes, Tuesday 28 February. *Either* Lord Chief Baron Parker *or* Mr Justice Birch.**

However, at the Assizes, the Jury disagreed. Thomas Turner was found not guilty, and released.

1749

(36)

1749A Sunday 10 September 1749. Croughton

Victim Zachariah Kersley

Accused Thomas Gregory

This all occurred in a public house - how novel. Thomas Gregory was fed up - fed up with having the 'mickey' taken out of him. A fight developed between Gregory and a few of his mockers, but was quickly broken up. However, Gregory was having no more of it, and drew a knife, saying that the next man who made fun of him would get a dose of this, brandishing the knife.

Kersley was standing in the crowd looking at Gregory, when someone pushed him forward. Gregory in his emotional state, obviously emboldened by the drink, immediately slashed out at Kersley. The knife sliced through Kersley's wrist, and almost severed the hand. But Gregory had not done. His next thrust with the knife entered Kersley's left chest, pierced the heart, and killed him instantly.

Trial **1750 Lent Assizes, Tuesday 13 March. *Either* Mr Justice Wright *or* Mr Baron Clive**

Thomas Gregory was found guilty of manslaughter. For his punishment, he was burnt on the hand.

✣✣ *These were Sir Edward Clive's first Northamptonshire Assizes, and he would be a fairly frequent visitor over the next nineteen years. Having been called to the Bar by Lincoln's Inn in 1725, he had been the MP for Saint Michael's Mount in Cornwall for four years before becoming a Baron of the Exchequer in 1745. In 1753 he would transfer to the Common Pleas where he would remain for seventeen years. He died in 1771 aged 67.*

✿

(E26) **FRIDAY 17 MARCH 1749**

HANGED FOR HIGHWAY ROBBERY

Joseph Elliott
William Lamb

Joseph Elliott and William Lamb were concerned together with the highway robbery of a Mr Fither at Deanshanger, on Sunday 19 February 1749. Although there are no more details of the crime itself, we do have a full description of the capture of these two, by courtesy of the *Northampton Mercury* of Monday 27 February 1749.

Elliott and Lamb were :

> 'drinking in a public house at Calverton near Stony Stratford, where abusing the landlord, they imagin'd they were known *(in other words, recognised)* and suddenly made off, leaving behind them a screw barrel'd gun, but a number of people went after them arm'd and took them in Wicken Field after some resistance. In the fray, a shepherd who began the attack, his gun missing fire, was shot in the back and is dangerously ill of the wound, notwithstanding which, he secur'd Lamb who is very much bruis'd about the head. They are supposed to belong to a gang who have long infest'd these parts.'

Both men appeared at the Lent Assizes, on Tuesday 28 February; and note how quickly the criminal justice system got them to court, just a few days. Both were found guilty and were sentenced to hang, which duly happened on Northampton Racecourse three weeks later.

1750

Two more cases of homicide appeared at the 1750 Lent Assizes, on the same calendar as Thomas Gregory (1749A).

(37)
1750A Elizabeth Tomson was indicted with the murder of her illegitimate child, by drowning it in a pool at Brixworth on Sunday 28 January 1750. That is the only information given, we do not even know whether the baby was a boy or a girl. Anyway, Elizabeth Tomson was found not guilty, and acquitted.

(38)
1750B Similarly, Isabell Lustwitt was acquitted of the murder of her illegitimate child on Thursday 8 March. There are no more details known, but notice how quickly the case came to court, Tuesday 13 March, less than one week later.

❁

(E27) **FRIDAY 23 MARCH 1750**

HANGED FOR ATTEMPTED MURDER

Thomas Wakelin

Thomas Wakelin was hanged for an attempted murder, which had occurred on Saturday 30 September 1749. This had resulted when he had been spurned by a young lady after he had obviously tried to force himself on her. There is no better way to describe this incident that in the original newspaper report of the time, taken from the *Northampton Mercury* of Monday 9 October 1749 :

'On Saturday last, between Six and Seven in the Evening a barbarous scene of Villainy was committed by one Thomas Wakelin, of which we have receiv'd the following Particulars:-
One Mary Groom of Denford in this County, going home from the Place of her Service at Thrapston, overtook the said Wakelin in her Way, who took a Bundle from her pretending he would carry it for her; they walk'd peaceably together for about Half a Mile, when he ask'd her, *If she would not rest herself?* which she answer'd in the Negative, and desir'd him to return her Bundle, that she might go forwards; on which he went up to her as if going to salute her, but she resisting, he threw her down, drew his Knife, and cut her in several Places on her Face, Hands and Throat, and threatn'd to kill her, which she prevented by her Struggling; at length She got from him, and ran several Yards but with the Loss of Blood issuing from her Wounds, she fell two or three times and got up again; at last slipping in to a Cart-Road by the River Side, she had not strength to rise before he overtook her, when he renew'd his Barbarity, by stabbing her Several times, and imagining She was dead, roll'd her into the River, and made off; But not being quite dead, she catch'd hold of some Rushes, which kept her above Water till some people came near the Place, who hearing her Groans, went to her Relief and drew her out, and she is now dangerously ill. We do not yet hear that the Villain is taken, but it is to be hop'd he will be brought to condign Punishment.'

And obviously he *was* caught, and brought to condign punishment, because he appeared before Mr Justice Wright at the 1750 Northamptonshire Lent Assizes. Thomas Wakelin was hanged on Northampton Racecourse on Friday 23 March 1750.

❁

(E28) **FRIDAY 24 AUGUST 1750**

HANGED FOR BURGLARY

Joseph Dobbs (22)

HANGED FOR ARSON

John Lavendar (17)

Both Joseph Dobbs and John Lavendar appeared at the 1750 Summer Assizes, on Tuesday 7 August, before either Lord Chief Justice Lee or Mr Baron Legge. There is no information whatsoever given in the *Northampton Mercury*.

All we know is, that John Lavendar was found guilty of arson at Kettering, for setting fire to the dwelling house of John Brooksby. And Joseph Dobbs was found guilty of housebreaking. They were both hanged on Northampton racecourse.

✣✣ *Heneage Legge was the second son of the first Earl of Dartmouth, the wealthy politician of Georgian England. A barrister of the Inner Temple, Legge was made a Baron of the Exchequer in 1747. Although he had visited Northampton once before, no homicide was on the calendar. He would come to Northampton for the next two years, before dying at the early age of 55 in 1759.*

THE EIGHTEENTH CENTURY

Part 2 : 1751 - 1800

Even though the *Northampton Mercury* had been going now for 30 years, local news still seems to be of secondary importance to what was happening in London and Europe. Now this raises two questions. Were the owners and editors of the paper ignoring local opinion and not giving local news because they thought it was of no importance; or was local news genuinely of no interest to the good people of Northamptonshire, and as such it was felt there was no need to report it?

Whatever the answer to that one is, it is a fact that from 1720, the Northamptonshire Assizes had only been given scant mention. However, as the eighteenth century progressed, and from about the 1760s, things do some to improve somewhat. But not much. There are still cases at the Assizes where detail given is tantalisingly miniscule, lilliputian and diminutive, but there are some cases which are given much wider and deeper coverage, and thus adds to our knowledge.

And by this time, the 'Bloody Code' was in full swing, no pun intended. Between 1751 and 1800, there were 42 hangings, only seven of which were for murder; the other 35 being for non-homicide offences. Included in this number is the hanging of William Love, at sixteen years of age, the youngest ever person to be hanged in Northamptonshire.

Of the homicides, in the 81 years between 1720 and 1800, there were 86 instances, an instantly calculated mean average of near-enough one per year. But the 50 years between 1751 and 1800 produced 48 instances of homicide, an even less mean average, no doubt influenced by the years 1766, 1767 and 1768 when there were both no homicides nor hangings. A noteworthy occurrence.

1751

Only one criminal homicide occurred in 1751, and that was on the calendar of the Lent Assizes, which began on Saturday 30 March, and lasted for three days. As the case load at these Assizes was not very heavy, only one Judge, Mr Baron Smythe, presided.

(39)

1751A Alice Eason stood trial for :

'ill treating and starving to death a female child she had under her care. The Jury were so particular in their Verdict, as to bring her in guilty of Beating and Starving to Death the Child, but observ'd to the Judge that they were sensible its Death did not proceed from any Wound given by an Instrument, as was imagined and reported.' (*Northampton Mercury*)

Alice Eason was found guilty and sentenced to death. However, just one week later she was reprieved. But at the Summer Assizes later that year, she received fourteen years transportation.

The child was probably not her own, as it was 'under her care', but we have absolutely no other details to go on. However, the later sentence of fourteen years transportation is possibly an indication of the opinion of the Judge on the severity of the case.

✣✣ *Only having been a judge for one year, these were the first Northamptonshire Assizes that Sir Sydney Stafford Smythe had attended, but he would be a frequent visitor over the next 26 years. He had been to Saint John's College, Cambridge; called to the bar by the Inner Temple in 1728; and was Member of Parliament for East Grinstead between 1747 and 1750. He would be appointed as Chief Baron in 1772, before retiring five years later. He died in 1778 aged 73.*

1752

Again, for the year 1752, only one homicide appears, and that is on the calendar for the Lent Assizes, which lasted for three days, between Monday 2 March and Wednesday 4 March. Mr Chief Justice Lee and Mr Baron Clive honoured the Assizes with their presence.

(40)
1752A Ann Ingman was acquitted of the murder of her son-in-law. And that is all the information that we have.

1753

Only one criminal homicide occurred in 1753, and appeared at the Summer Assizes of that year which started on Wednesday 1 August, before Mr Chief Justice Willes or Mr Baron Clive.

(41)
1753A Benjamin Wignall and Grace Robinson were acquitted for the murder of (their?) 'bastard child'. No other information is forthcoming.

1754

And similarly, only one homicide appeared at the Assizes during 1754, and that was at the Summer Assizes starting on Tuesday 30 July before Mr Justice Wright or Mr Justice Birch.

(42)
1754A Elizabeth Cawcutt was acquitted of the murder of her illegitimate child. And as with all these cases, that is all the information that the *Northampton Mercury* gives.

❁

(E29) **FRIDAY 16 AUGUST 1754**

HANGED FOR BURGLARY

William Love (16)

Precious little is known about the youngest person ever to be hanged in Northamptonshire. William Love was only 16 years old when he was hanged on Northampton Racecourse for Burglary. All we have to go on is the newspaper report from the *Northampton Mercury* reporting on the Summer Assizes of 1754, when William Love appeared before either Mr Justice Wright or Mr Justice Birch. The only thing we know is that he was convicted of 'stealing money out of a dwelling house at Wellingborough'.

At the same Assizes, John Maile and William Maile were found guilty of sheep stealing, and sentenced to death. But they were reprieved. Why William Love was not reprieved is unknown.

1755

No homicides occurred during 1755

❁

(E30) **FRIDAY 25 JULY 1755**

HANGED FOR BURGLARY

John Brown

Not much is known about the execution of John Brown. All that can be gleaned from the *Northampton Mercury*, is that he appeared at the 1755 Summer Assizes on Tuesday 8 July before either Mr Justice Denison or Mr Baron Legge.

All the newspaper report says is that 'John Brown was convicted of stealing £80 from the dwelling house at Alderton of Thomas Slater.'

1756

No homicides occurred during 1756

1757

And the only homicide to appear in 1757, was at the Summer Assizes on Tuesday 19 July, before Mr Chief Baron Parker or Mr Baron Legge.

(43)
1757A Hannah Stains was acquitted of the murder of her illegitimate child. Because she was acquitted, no details appeared in the *Northampton Mercury.*

1758

The one homicide of 1758 was on the calendar for the Summer Assizes, held on Tuesday 4 July before Mr Baron Legge or Mr Baron Adams.

(44)
1758A Mary Sheriffe, junior, and Mary Sheriffe, senior - presumably mother and daughter - were indicted for the murder of an illegitimate child; Mary junior, as the murderer, and Mary, senior, as an accessory. Both were acquitted. There are no more details.

It is interesting to note, that on the same calendar, a certain William Sheriffe was found guilty of stealing 'divers goods', and ordered to be publicly whipped. The fact that this was instant retribution, so that afterwards they could be sent on their way, leads to the conclusion, that the Sheriffe family belonged to what we would now call the gypsy or traveller community.

An intriguing aside, is that three brothers with the surname of Sheriffe, who definitely were *gypsies, were imprisoned for the bludgeoning to death of PC William Price of the Staffordshire County Constabulary at Stretton in January 1903.*

✣✣ *Yet another judge who succumbed to gaol fever* (see *Mr Justice Abney 1747), Sir Richard Adams died when he was on circuit at Bedford in March 1774, from the distemper he had caught at the Old Bailey. He was 64 years old and had been a Baron of the Exchequer since 1753. A barrister of the Inner Temple, he had been selected as the Recorder of London in 1748. And whilst holding that post, King George II had been so impressed with one of his speeches, that he was immediately promoted to be a Baron of the Exchequer.*

Always declining the opportunity to move to the Court of Common Pleas, Adams remained a Baron of the Exchequer until his death. Apparently, one of his contemporaries said of him 'I never saw him out of temper in my life.'

1759

The year 1759 was choc-a-bloc full. The Calendar for the Lent Assizes, which started on Tuesday 27 March before Mr Chief Justice Willes and Mr Baron Smythe, not only contained these three homicides, but also the cases of Richard Dove and William Smart for returning from transportation, Richard Alcock for theft, and John Forward for forgery.

(45)
1759A Elizabeth Stanton was indicted 'on suspicion of the murder of a bastard child or children'. The 'evidence' against her must have been very flimsy, or non-existent, as the Grand Jury found 'No True Bill' against her.

Up until 1933 when the practice was abolished, the Assizes used to have two juries. The Grand Jury used to examine every case to see if there was enough evidence to go into the Assizes. If the Grand Jury saw a prima facie case, then it would be sent into the Assizes to be tried before the second jury, the Petty Jury. If the Grand Jury saw no evidence, then the accused would be released as having 'No True Bill' against them.

For a better explanation of the two jury system, see my book Guilty M'Lud! The Criminal History of Northamptonshire.

(46)
1759B Elizabeth Wells was found not guilty of the murder of (her?) illegitimate child. No other details are given.

(47)
1759C An unknown date and place
Victim An unnamed child
Accused Ann Loale

No details of this case are given in the *Northampton Mercury*, which is not unusual. But what we do have, is a description of the hanging of Ann Loale, on Northampton Racecourse on Saturday 31 March 1759.

> 'She behaved with great Penitence and Contrition, and at the Place of Execution (where she died with the greatest Fortitude and Composure) that Green, whom she accused at her Tryal, was entirely innocent, but that her Master was present when she was delivered, which was about Three o'Clock in the Morning; and that immediately after the Birth he took the Child from her, stabb'd it, and put it in the Necessary House.'

Things don't add up here. Why didn't Ann Loale say this at her trial? Why was her Master (in other words her employer - she was a servant), not called for, or indicted, at the trial? Why did she try, and obviously fail, to involve the person Green, who we suspect is a man? Was she trying to protect her Master, who was probably the father of her murdered baby? These are questions that will never now be answered.

✿

(E31) **FRIDAY 6 APRIL 1759**

HANGED FOR HORSE THEFT

Richard Alcock

HANGED FOR FORGERY

John Forward

As is frustrating with the *Northampton Mercury*, the court reports are disappointingly brief. The only mention of these two is the all too brief report of the death sentence passed on :

> 'Richard Alcock for stealing two geldings [and] John Forward for uttering and publishing two forged Draughts, or Bills of Exchange, knowing them to be forged, with intent to defraud Jonathan Baker.'

❁

(E32) **SATURDAY 28 APRIL 1759**

HANGED FOR RETURNING FROM TRANSPORTATION

William Smart alias James Johnson alias James Smart

We have Mr Baron Thomson to thank for the idea of transporting criminals (*see* 1731), rather than hanging them, thus at least giving them a chance to mend their ways. However, if they refused to take that chance, and returned before the expiration of their term, then they found there was no *second* chance - they suffered the penalty which they would have received had they not been transported. In other words, they were hanged. Only two hangings have occurred in Northamptonshire for returning from transportation, and they occurred within four months of each other in the spring and summer of 1759.

The first of these was William Smart - the *Northampton Mercury* of Monday 30 April 1759 :

> 'Saturday last William Smart alias James Johnson who was condemn'd at our Summer Assizes 1755, by the Name of James Smart for robbing Mr Stapeyard of Rothwell, on the Highway of £48, was executed here, pursuant to the Sentence at the last Assizes, for returning from Transportation. He deny'd the fact for which he was first condemn'd, tho' he own'd he had been a very wicked Person; but would make no Confession of his Transactions. He was to have been executed with the two other Malefactors on Friday, the 6th Instant; but on his representing that he was press'd on board a Man of War from the place he was transported to, and forcibly brought to England, he was allow'd a Respite of three Weeks to make it appear.'

❃

(E33) **SATURDAY 11 AUGUST 1759**

HANGED FOR RETURNING FROM TRANSPORTATION

Richard Dove

The second of the hangings for returning from transportation, Richard Dove's story starts at the Summer Assizes on Wednesday 1 August 1753. Before Mr Chief Justice Willes or Mr Baron Clive, Richard Dove and Thomas Adkins were indicted for Highway Robbery. No details of the offence were given, but both were found guilty and sentenced to death.

However, just before the judges left Northampton, they commuted the death sentences to transportation. But the decision on the length of the transportation would have to wait until the next Assizes, which were the 1754 Lent Assizes. So in other words, Richard Dove and Thomas Adkins had to wait eight months in custody before they knew their sentences. And it was either Mr Chief Justice Lee or Mr Justice Birch at the 1754 Lent Assizes on Tuesday 5 March, who decided that Richard Dove and Thomas Adkins should be transported for fourteen years each.

Thomas Adkins must have accepted his fate, and stopped in America. Richard Dove, however, had other ideas. How he got back to England is unknown, and why he should come back to Northamptonshire, where he would be recognised, is also unknown. But he did, and someone must have seen him, because he was arrested again.

This time, there was no second chance, and he appeared before the 1759 Lent Assizes. However, his sentence was deferred until the Summer Assizes, but this was to be the end of the road. Either Mr Chief Baron Parker or Mr Baron Legge sentenced him to hang. The *Northampton Mercury* of Monday 30 August 1759 :

> 'Hanged here on Saturday last, Richard Dove. He confess'd his Committing the Robbery for which he was condemn'd at our Summer Assizes in 1753, acknowledg'd that he had deserted from several Regiments, and died very penitent.'

1760

No homicides occurred during 1760

1761

(48)

1761A The only homicide of 1761 appeared on the calendar for the Summer Assizes Tuesday 7 July before Mr Chief Baron Parker. Elizabeth Tack was acquitted of murder of an illegitimate baby. And that is all the information we have.

1762

(49)
1762A And similarly, no information is available when Ann Burton was acquitted of the murder of Margaret Burton when she appeared before Mr Justice Bathurst on Saturday 27 March at the Lent Assizes. There is no intimation what the relationship was, whether mother and daughter, or even where the deed took place.

✣✣ *For a more clear cut example of someone being born with a silver spoon, it is hard to beat the life of Mr Justice Bathurst. Firmly from the aristocratic English 'Establishment', Henry Bathurst, son of the first Earl Bathurst, was, like his father, a Member of Parliament when he was 21, and for the same seat, Cirencester, which was obviously a 'pocket borough' belonging to the Bathurst family.*

A 'pocket borough' was a parliamentary seat which was 'owned' by a family or group of patrons, and which could be given to anyone the patron wished. Election of the candidate was guaranteed, as the voters of the borough voted the way their patron told them to. Thankfully, this system was stopped by the great Parliamentary Reform Act of 1832.

Henry Bathurst remained the MP for Cirencester for nineteen years, until the age of 40, when he was advanced up the next step of the Establishment ladder, by being made a judge of the Common Pleas. These Assizes were his first visit to Northampton, but he would visit several more times before his next advancement arrived in 1771, when he was made Lord Apsley on being chosen as the Lord Chancellor.

In 1775, his father died and he became the second Earl Bathurst. He retired in 1782 aged 68, and died in 1794 aged 80.

1763

What would turn out to be by far the most awful murder of 1763, had yet to come to light, and would have to wait for another year before it hit the news. In the meantime, two cases appeared at the Lent Assizes, and one case before the Summer Assizes of that year.

However, again, the *Northampton Mercury* gives the minimum possible detail. Even after 43 years of publication, local news is still only considered of secondary importance, and only occupies half a column out of seven pages of (London and national) news of three columns each. The eighth page has all the adverts and notices.

(50)
1763A Martha Meals was acquitted of the murder of her illegitimate child. She had appeared at the Lent Assizes on Saturday 26 March before Mr Justice Bathurst.

(51)
1763B At the same Assizes, John Warner was found guilty of manslaughter. He was burnt on the hand.

(52)
1763C And a similar punishment was given to John Turner by Lord Chief Justice Mansfield himself at the Summer Assizes on Tuesday 12 July. John Turner was found guilty of the manslaughter of Thomas Harris, although this time, we do have a tiny bit more detail, in that the incident occurred at Kettering on Wednesday 8 June 1763.

✣✣ *William Murray, 1st Earl of Mansfield, was another of the 'greats' of Georgian England who came to the Northamptonshire Assizes; but these would be the only time he did. Born in Perth, he was called to the bar by Lincoln's Inn in 1730, and soon acquired an immense reputation. He entered parliament as MP for Boroughbridge in 1742, and was made Solicitor-General the same year. By 1747, he was effectively the leader of the House of Commons and as such, the rival of William Pitt the Elder.*

In 1756, he was made the Lord Chief Justice, and elevated to the peerage with the title of Lord Mansfield. Whilst in office, he strove to improve and rationalise the legal system, and in 1776 he was made the 1st Earl of Mansfield. Because of several cases where he upheld the rights of Roman Catholics, he became a target, and his house was actually burnt down during the anti-Catholic Gordon Riots in London in the summer of 1780.

Retiring in 1788 at the age of 83, he died five years later.

(53)

1763D Sometime between Thursday 29 September and Tuesday 18 October 1763. Guilsborough

Victim Thomas Corey

Accused Richard Butlin (Breeches maker)
John Croxford (Tailor)
Benjamin Deacon (Carpenter)
(Thomas Seamark - already executed)

This is one of the most callous murders in the annals of Northamptonshire criminal history. And it is the only one where public revulsion was so great, that the prisoners required an armed escort when they were driven from the county gaol to the place of execution.

Butlin, Croxford, Deacon and Seamark, a shepherd, formed a band of villains living in the Guilsborough area. They were addicted to gambling and drinking, and rather than do an honest day's work, would turn to crime, which soon would include murder.

Sometime during 1763, the exact date is unknown, a travelling Scottish pedlar, Thomas Corey, called on Seamark's house in Guilsborough. Inside the house drinking, were the four ruffians. They refused to buy any of his wares and sent him away. But they followed him, overpowered him and dragged him back to Seamark's house where Croxford murdered him by slitting his throat.

The four then shared out the pedlar's goods and clothes, and buried the naked body in a plot of disused land. But a few days later, they learnt that the land was to be ploughed up. Fearing that their crime would be discovered, they were then faced with ridding themselves of the decomposing body.

The body was duly dug up, and the entrails and brains were fed to the pigs and the dogs. The flesh was burnt off in the household fires, and hammers were used to smash the bones into dust and tiny pieces, which were then buried in the garden. The whole grisly deed took them three days to complete.

And because the pedlar was unknown in those parts, nobody missed him, so the four thought they had got away with it. But they hadn't, they had been witnessed.

The day after the actual murder, one of Seamark's children said to his brother 'If you give me a marble, I will show you the place where daddy and Croxford killed the man and buried him near the cucumber patch'. Kids will be kids, of course, and this story soon circulated on the village grapevine and reached the ears of Croxford, who then threatened Seamark's wife, Ann, with death if this story ever leaked out. And eventually, of course, it also came to the ears of John Bateman, the local squire and magistrate.

But here we have a subtle twist. On Thursday 8 March 1764, Thomas Seamark was, according to the *Northampton Mercury*:

> 'committed [to the County Gaol] for robbing on the highway Tuesday last Mr Thomas Quartley of Wicken near Stoney Stratford of between 20 and 30 Shillings in Silver and a Silver Watch. He is supposed to belong to a desperate Gang of Villains, who for a long time have visited this Neighbourhood and committed divers Robberies and Outrages therein'.

Thomas Seamark appeared at the 1764 Lent Assizes, and not surprisingly was found guilty. He was hanged on Northampton Racecourse on Monday 23 April, and remarkably did not 'grass up' his cronies.

But of course, in the Guilsborough area, his cronies were well known anyway. Two and two were put together, and on Friday 27 April :

> 'John Croxford was committed to our County Gaol on suspicion of having committed divers Felonies and Robberies in the Counties of Northamptonshire and Leicestershire and other Parts of this Kingdom'.

And the very next day, Benjamin Deacon was also captured.

Meanwhile, taking a very keen interest in the rumours circulating in Guilsborough, John Bateman, the Squire of Guilsborough, who was also a magistrate, started his own enquiries. Not unnaturally, he questioned Ann Seamark. By then a widow, she obviously thought she had nothing to lose, and she confessed the whole sad, sorry saga. Under her direction, John Bateman dug up the ashes and bone splinters of the unfortunate victim, as well as his walking cane.

By then, of course, Croxford and Deacon were already in the county gaol on robbery charges. The arrest of Butlin at Brackley came just a couple of days later.

Trial **1764 Summer Assizes, Thursday 2 July. Mr Chief Baron Parker**

Whether it was by luck or design, the trial judge was Mr Chief Baron Parker, who, having sentenced Thomas Seamark to death just three months earlier, knew all about this little bunch of bandits. Ann Seamark gave prosecution evidence, and her son testified that he had spied on all four men through a crack in the floorboards from the room above, and had actually seen a human hand hanging out of the oven, and a human leg burning in the fire.

A little grisly digression. At the trial, John Bateman gave all the members of the Grand Jury a little packet of the charred and splintered bones of the victim, Thomas Corey. In 1871, John Bateman's great-granddaughter, Grace Bateman, married Thomas Orde Hastings Lees, who was Chief Constable of Northamptonshire from 1875 until 1881, when he resigned to return to practice as a barrister. Apparently, he and his wife still possessed a little packet of these charred bones, which they showed to anyone who asked to see them.

Despite trying to prove that they were elsewhere at the time, Butlin, Croxford and Deacon were all found guilty, and the execution date was fixed for Saturday 4 August 1764 on Northampton Racecourse. Because this case caused so much public revulsion, this is the only time that any prisoners received an armed escort from the County Gaol (in George Row, Northampton) to the Racecourse, to stop them from being lynched before they were hanged. The *Northampton Mercury*:

> 'They were guarded from the Gaol to the Place of Execution by a Party of General Howard's Regiment of Dragoons, with their bayonets fix'd to their Musquets, which were loaded with Powder and Ball. The body of Croxford is to be hung in Chains on Hollowell Heath, in the Parish of Guilsborough, and the Bodies of Deacon and Butlin are to be disected'.

But that is not the last that was heard from John Croxford. Soon after he was hanged, a pamphlet was printed in Northampton written by an anonymous clergyman who claimed that he had had a meeting with Croxford's ghost on Sunday 12 August.

Appearing to the reverend gentleman whilst he was alone in his study after Sunday Evensong, the ghost confessed to the murder but explained their continued protestations of innocence by saying that 'while the blood still reeked', all four had entered into 'a sacramental obligation with dipping their fingers into the blood of the deceased and licking the same : by which they bound themselves in the penalty of eternal damnation never to betray the fact themselves; or confess if condemned to die for it on the evidence of others'.

The ghost also stated that there was no motive, they only murdered 'out of continued habit of wickedness' rather than for necessity, as they were in no need of money at the time. The ghost explained that the clergyman had been chosen deliberately so as to acquaint the world with this deterrent to others.

The clergyman was then told of the pedlar's ring. It had been buried by Croxford because he was afraid of the inscription on the ring which said 'Hang'd he'll be who steals me 1745'

The ghost disappeared as quickly as he had come. The very next day, the clergyman went to the indicated spot, and unearthed the gold ring, exactly as the ghost said he would.

1764

(54)

1764A This is one of the instances where the lack of information in the *Mercury* is maddening. Elizabeth Clarke and Ann Clarke were both acquitted at the 1764 Lent Assizes, of the poisoning of Richard Cross at Little Houghton.

How old were the Clarkes? Were they mother and daughter, sisters, aunt and niece, or what? Who was Richard Cross? Was he the boyfriend of one of them? Was he their employer? Why did they poison him? Was it for his money? Was he 'trying it on' with one of them, and they got even?

❀

❁

(E34) **MONDAY 23 APRIL 1764**

HANGED FOR ROBBERY

Thomas Seamark

Had not Thomas Seamark been hanged for this robbery, then undoubtedly he *would have been* for the murder of Thomas Corey, together with his partners in crime Butlin, Croxford and Deacon. But he had decided to go solo on the robbery of Thomas Quartley, and it is for this offence that he was captured in March 1764.

The Lent Assizes of that year were late, on Tuesday 10 April. Normally Northampton was the first date on the Assize circuit, but for some reason this year, Northampton was the last Assize of the circuit, which had first visited Oakham, Lincoln, Nottingham, Derby, Leicester, Coventry and Warwick. Which is why his capture was in time to appear before the Lent Assizes of 1764, before Mr Chief Baron Parker.

His guilt on this single-handed effort was indisputable, and he was sentenced to hang. But the *Northampton Mercury* of Monday 23 April contains a little teaser :

> 'He made no Confession of his Confederates being almost dead before he was carried to the Place of Execution.'

What had happened to make him 'almost dead' before he was hanged? Had somebody got to him? Had he tried to commit suicide? The questions are many, the answers, none.

❁

(E35) **SATURDAY 5 MAY 1764**

HANGED FOR ROBBERY

Russell Rowledge

Why, do you think, in what was supposed to be the Age of Enlightenment, can two men be hanged within three months of each other, and the local newspaper hardly comment on it? This is what happened to Russell Rowledge and John Kilsby in 1764.

Russell Rowledge was indicted at the 1764 Lent Assizes with :

> 'robbing Thomas Goer*(?)* on the road leading from Brixworth to Scaldwell of his watch and money.'

He was found guilty and sentenced to death, and the date for his execution fixed for Monday 23 April, alongside Thomas Seamark. But for some unknown reason, Russell Rowledge obtains a respite. But whatever caused the postponement, postponement it was and not a cancellation. Only two weeks later, Russell Rowledge was hanged on Northampton Racecourse. The *Northampton Mercury*, Monday 7 May 1764 :

> 'On Saturday last was hanged Russell Rowledge. He persisted in his Ignorance of the Fact for which he suffer'd to his last Moments.'

❁

(E36) **FRIDAY 10 AUGUST 1764**

HANGED FOR ROBBERY

John Kilsby

And for John Kilsby, we have even less news. Appearing at the 1764 Summer Assizes on Tuesday 31 July, before either Mr Chief Baron Parker or Mr Justice Clive, he was found guilty of the 'robbery of Samuel Haines on the Highway'. All the *Northampton Mercury* recorded, was that he was hanged on Friday 10 August.

1765

Only one criminal homicide occurred in 1765, and appeared on the calendar of the Lent Assizes on Tuesday 2 April before Mr Chief Baron Parker or Mr Justice Gould.

(55)
1765A Robert Holland was acquitted of the manslaughter of William Abbott at Great Addington. No other details are known.

✣✣ *This was the first time Mr Justice Gould had come to Northampton; and his next visit would be thirteen years later. As his father was also Henry Gould, our Henry Gould was called 'Junior', to differentiate himself from his father, another judge, Henry Gould, 'Senior'. There is nothing of much note in his career : barrister of the Middle Temple in 1734; Baron of the Exchequer in 1761; and Justice of the Common Pleas in 1763. He would die in 1794 aged 84.*

1766

No criminal homicides occurred in 1766

1767

No criminal homicides occurred in 1767

1768

And no criminal homicides occurred in 1768 either. These three consecutive years with no homicides (and no hangings, either - was this the 'deterrent' system working?) constitute a remarkable record. This had happened only once, 40 years before in 1725, 1726 and 1727, and would not happen again for another 60 years, when we managed the astonishing feat of four years without a murder or manslaughter - 1827, 1828, 1829 and 1830.

1769

(56)

1769A On Monday 3 July, Elizabeth Bradshaw was indicted at the Summer Assizes before Mr Justice Clive for the murder of her illegitimate child. However, Elizabeth Bradshaw 'was discharg'd; no Person appearing against her'.

1770

No criminal homicides occurred in 1770

❀

(E37) **SATURDAY 14 APRIL 1770**

HANGED FOR HIGHWAY ROBBERY

William Craddock
Anthony Harwood

Forget any romanticised notion about Highwaymen. Do not regard as 'gallant heroes' the likes of Dick Turpin riding from London to York on Black Bess, or 'Gentleman' Claude Duval, who kissed the ladies whilst he was robbing them. The reality is totally and brutally different - robbery is stealing by using violence or threats of violence, which William Craddock and Anthony Harwood did, and quite rightly got their 'come-uppance'.

The *Northampton Mercury* of Monday 18 September 1769 :

> 'Between the Hours of nine and ten on Wednesday night last as Mr William Walker the Younger of Kingsthorpe...Farmer, was going from this Town to Kingsthorpe...he was stopped at a place called Wallbank, in a little three cornered Close in the Footway, by a Footpad, who on a sudden came up to him, and without speaking to him, immediately fired a

large Horse Regimental Pistol at him, but missing him. Mr Walker immediately struck the Fellow with his Fist upon the Head or Face, and knocked him down, and seized him, but the Fellow, imagining himself overpower'd, immediately cried out for help, when one, if not two, other Fellows, who were lurking just by, instantly came up to his assistance, and beat Mr Walker about the Head and Face with their Pistols, and other Weapons in a very inhuman Manner, and after robbing him of a canvas Purse and about Three or Four Shillings in Money, they made off leaving Mr Walker insensible upon the Ground wallowing in his Blood; who after some little time so far recovered himself as to be able with very great difficulty to get to the Cock Inn at Kingsthorpe, where a Surgeon was immediately sent for, who dressed his Wounds. He now lies dangerously ill, but there are Hopes for his recovery.'

Both Craddock and Harwood appeared at the 1770 Lent Assizes before either Mr Chief Baron Parker or Mr Justice Aston. Craddock was charged :'on Suspicion of most cruelly wounding William Walker, jun, of Kingsthorpe'; and Anthony Harwood of 'being concerned with the above Craddock in wounding the said William Walker, firing a Pistol at him, and robbing him of a purse with Three Shillings.'

Both were given the death sentence. 'At the Place of Execution' said the *Mercury*, 'they acknowledged the latter part of the Crime

for which they suffered, but denied the Robbery. Craddock declared that he was the Man who so inhumanly wounded Mr Walker, and that Harwood was ready to assist him in case of his being overpowered. By their own Confession, their Intent was to proceed in those desperate Acts, and to have murdered all those who opposed them.-Harwood was born at Barnard Castle in the County of Durham, and was aged 26, ten of which he had been in the Army.-Craddock was born at Wellingborough in this County, was aged about 21 Years, and by Trade a Weaver.

1771

(57)

1771A Mary Cavendish, alias Bateman, was charged on a Coroner's Inquest with the wilful murder of Mary Cavendish junior. Her case appeared at the Lent Assizes on Tuesday 26 March before Mr Justice Aston, where she was acquitted. No other details are known.

✣✣ *Not much is known about Sir Richard Aston. He was born in 1717, and was called to the bar by Lincoln's Inn, before becoming the Lord Chief Justice of the Common Pleas in Ireland. But in 1765, he was brought over to England and made a Justice of the King's Bench. He visited Northampton only twice more, before dying in 1778.*

1772

(58)

1772A Only this homicide occurred during 1772, and it appeared on the calendar of the Lent Assizes held on Tuesday 22 March, before either Mr Chief Baron Parker or Mr Justice Willes. William Morris was acquitted of the manslaughter of Thomas Bryan of Kingsthorpe. Nothing else whatsoever is known.

✣✣ *Edward Willes was the son of a judge, Chief Justice Sir John Willes. The rest is inevitable. Oxford and Lincoln's Inn followed, with a lucrative practice, helped by father. Two stints as an MP saw him as Attorney-General in 1766, and a judge of the King's Bench in 1768. A frequent visitor to Northampton, he died in 1787, aged 64.*

1773

(59)

1773A Again, nothing much is known of the only homicide of 1773. Nathaniel Tinsley was found guilty of the manslaughter of John Blundell at Welton after a Coroner's Inquest. He was burnt on the hand and received six months in prison.

Nathaniel Tinsley appeared at the Lent Assizes held on Saturday 20 March. Mr Chief Baron Smythe was there, together with a judge on his first visit to Northampton, a certain William Blackstone.

✣✣ *Of all the judges who visited Northampton, arguably the best known would be Sir William Blackstone. And all because of one thing.*

After being called to the bar by the Middle Temple in 1741, he started practising, but only achieved mediocre success. He was made Recorder of Wallingford, Berkshire in 1749, but a couple of years later was invited to give a few lectures to the law students at Oxford. In 1758, a certain Mr Viner left £12,000 in his will to endow a Professorship of English Law at Oxford, and William Blackstone thus became the first Vinerian Professor of English Law at Oxford, a position he held until 1766.

His duties appeared not to be too heavy though, as at the same time he was elected as the MP for Hindon in Wiltshire and became Solicitor-General. However, it was during this time that he wrote the work that would ensure his eternal fame.

Blackstone's Commentaries on the Laws of England *in four volumes was published between 1765 and 1769. Despite some criticism, these were an immediate success, made him a very rich man, were very influential, and went into edition after edition. Blackstone's* Commentaries... *are still being published today, and are readily available, and it is a good bet that a copy of them will be found on the bookshelf of every solicitor and barrister in the land.*

After that success, is it any wonder that he was appointed a Justice of the Common Pleas in 1770? William Blackstone died on Saint Valentine's Day 1780. These Assizes were the first of three visits he made to Northampton.

1774

No homicides occurred during 1774

1775

(60)
1775A On the calendar for the Summer Assizes of 1775 appeared this : 'James Gill for homicide in casually killing Samuel Dickson by drowning him in the River within the Liberties of this Town'.

What story would lay behind this, if we only knew? But we don't, again no detail is forthcoming. All we know that James Gill appeared before either Mr Justice Blackstone or Mr Justice Aston on Tuesday 25 July - and was acquitted!

❁

(E38) **TUESDAY 11 APRIL 1775**

HANGED FOR BURGLARY

Samuel Paine

Nothing is known of Samuel Paine, whether he was local or not, or even how old he was. All we know is that he appeared in front of Mr Baron Eyre at the 1775 Lent Assizes on Saturday 25 March. He was 'charg'd on suspicion of breaking open the House of Henry Lucas, Gent, at Guilsborough and stealing thereout 22 Guineas'.

Today, 22 guineas would be about £3,000.

At the scene of his execution 'he made an Indirect Confession of a Part of the Crime for which he suffered, but strongly denied a Circumstance that led chiefly to convict him, which was, a Piece of a Knife that he had had from Mr Lucas's being found in a Box which he had broken open.'

❁

(E39) **FRIDAY 11 AUGUST 1775**

HANGED FOR FORGERY

William Barker

Only three people have been hanged in Northamptonshire for forgery. William Barker was the second of them, and his speciality was the forging and uttering (which is the actual passing into circulation of the forgeries) of £10 notes.

Apparently he had eleven of them, and actually managed to utter seven. Eleven £10 notes is obviously £110, which is the equivalent today of £14,000; and the £70 he actually managed to get into circulation would today be worth £9,100.

William Barker was born in Uttoxeter, but had obviously got mixed up with some London villains who had introduced him to forgery, and sent him around the country uttering his forgeries. But his luck ran out when he came to Northampton.

In late April 1775, Barker went into the shop of Henry Clarke, who sold hats. He selected a hat to buy, which cost five shillings, and then offered the £10 note. Mr Clarke immediately became suspicious. Today's equivalent would be like offering £1,275 to pay for goods worth about £30.

However, he kept Barker in his shop by saying that he had to get some change, and then sent his daughter out of the shop, ostensibly on the errand, but obviously to get help. A few minutes later, Barker saw her returning along the street, accompanied by a man. This was too much. He panicked, and mumbled something about coming back for his change later and ran off. But he was caught.

Appearing before the legendary Mr Justice Blackstone at the 1775 Summer Assizes, William Barker was sentenced to death, and hanged on Northampton Racecourse.

1776

(61)

1776A William Snow was indicted for the murder of his brother-in-law, Thomas Palmer, at Little Bowden. He appeared at the Summer Assizes on Tuesday 16 July, before Mr Justice Willes.

And this case would be a little bit controversial. Although we do have a fairly lengthy report in the *Northampton Mercury*, this gives no details of the actual murder (time, date, circumstances and so on) - only the court proceedings.

It appears that the jury thought the evidence so strong, that they brought in a verdict of guilty to murder. But Mr Justice Willes disagreed, and instructed them to reduce the verdict to manslaughter.

The jury were having none of this, and re-affirmed that it *was* murder, *not* manslaughter. The judge had no option therefore but to pronounce sentence of death.

However, he really did have the last say, when just before the Assizes finished, he postponed the sentence of death, saying that he wished to get the opinion of his colleagues. William Snow then languished in prison, while Willes J sought the advice of his fellow twelve judges.

England was split up into six 'Assize Circuits' *(Home, Oxford, Midland, Norfolk, Northern, Western - Northampton was on the Midland Circuit)* each having the two judges assigned to them, thus making twelve. Evidently, Willes J took the opinion of his colleagues and they all agreed on manslaughter rather than murder.

When the *Northampton Mercury* published the calendar of prisoners for the 1777 Lent Assizes, the week before they started, it included :

> 'William Snow convicted of murder at the last Summer Assizes but (by the opinion of the twelve Judges) being guilty of Manslaughter only, Sentence still remains to be pronounced against him'.

William Snow duly appeared before the 1777 Lent Assizes on Tuesday 4 March before Mr Chief Baron Smythe - *not,* you notice, before Mr Justice Willes. 'He was branded on the hand and imprisoned until 16 July next, making twelve months from the time of his first sentence'.

William Snow was thus, in effect, tried again by twelve judges, eleven of whom had not heard any evidence. What the original jury thought, was deemed to be irrelevant. The question remains. If judges could over-rule juries so easily, why bother to have juries at all?

1777

No homicides occurred during 1777

1778

Nor during 1778 either

1779

Four homicides occurred in 1779. Two appeared at the Lent Assizes of that year, on Tuesday 2 March, before Mr Chief Baron Skynner or Mr Baron Eyre.

(62)
1779A Charles Barker and Elizabeth Freeman were charged on the Coroner's Inquest of the wilful murder of a female illegitimate child (theirs?) at Mears Ashby. No details or date is given. They were both discharged by proclamation, in other words, 'No True Bill' was found against them.

(63)
1779B Esau Liston ('out on bail') was charged on the Coroner's Inquest with manslaughter. Absolutely no other detail is given. However, he was found guilty, branded on the hand, and discharged.

✣✣ *Sir James Eyre knew some 'interesting' people - or at least, one in particular - James Wilkes (see also Mr Chief Justice Mansfield in case 1806A). After being called to the bar by Gray's Inn, Eyre became Recorder of London in 1763. That same year, he defended Wilkes in one of his many court cases. However, when Wilkes was sued by King George III for libel soon afterwards, he was expelled from parliament, which caused enormous controversy. James Eyre, as Recorder for London, then refused to present to the king, the objection (or 'Remonstrance') of the City of London to Wilke's exclusion.*

No doubt because of this, in 1772, Eyre was made a Baron of the Exchequer, and eventually Chief Baron, before becoming Chief Justice of the Common Pleas in 1793. He made several visits to Northampton, before dying in 1799 aged 65.

The third and fourth homicides of 1779 appeared at the Summer Assizes on Tuesday 13 July before either Mr Justice Gould or Mr Baron Hotham.

(64)
1779C Mary White and Alice Garner were charged with the wilful murder of an illegitimate male child at Pattishall.

(65)
1779D Hannah Bull was charged with the wilful murder of her illegitimate female child at Hardingstone

✣✣ *Beaumont Hotham, was the 2nd Baron Hotham of the Irish peerage, after succeeding his brother. He was called to the bar by the Middle Temple in 1758. Between 1768 and 1775 he was the MP for Wigan, before being made a Baron of the Exchequer, a position he would hold for 30 years. This was the first of eight visits to Northampton over the next thirteen years. He died in 1814 aged 77.*

His grandson, another Beaumont Hotham, fought in the Peninsular War, and also at the Battle of Waterloo.

1780

The year 1780 gives us two murders. Both cases appeared at the Lent Assizes on Tuesday 29 February before Mr Chief Baron Skynner, and both resulted in the death penalty, neither of which is mentioned in the lists of executions previously published.

(66)
1780A Thomas Pool was charged by Coroner's Inquest with the wilful murder of William Luck at Moulton by giving him two wounds with a knife. Absolutely nothing else is known, except that Thomas Pool was found guilty, and received the death penalty.

(67)
1780B Catherine Parker was charged by a Coroner's Inquest of the wilful murder of Thomas Cottingham at Kettering, in February

1780. This is a most distressing case, and is best told in the words of the *Northampton Mercury*:

> 'On Thursday 24 February last another Inquisition was held before the said Mr Dexter at Kettering; at View the Body of Thomas Cottingham, an Apprentice-Boy, not 11 Years of Age, put out by the Parish of Weldon. The Jury, after sitting Three days, and examining a vast Number of Witnesses, with great Care and Attention, brought in their Verdict Unanimously, that William Parker of Kettering, aforesaid, Weaver, and Catherine his Wife, were guilty of the wilful Murder of the said Thomas Cottingham, their Apprentice; by beating, starving, confining, chaining, imprisoning and for Want of necessary Meat, Drink, Sustenance and Support - The said William Parker has absconded; but Catherine his Wife, is committed to the County Gaol'.

Catherine Parker was found guilty of murder, and received the death penalty. Both Catherine Parker and Thomas Pool were hanged together on Northampton Racecourse on Saturday 4 March 1780, these two executions being omitted from the two published lists of Northamptonshire executions (see 1296). However, the *Northampton Mercury*:

> 'Their Behaviour was very decent and becoming. Parker said she had been a very wicked Woman, and declared that her Husband was innocent of the Murder for which she Justly suffered'.

✣✣ *Sir John Skynner had been the Chief Baron of the Exchequer since 1777. He would retire in 1786, dying in 1805 aged 79. His career had been the standard progression of public school, Oxford, barrister, politician and judge. This was his third visit to Northampton, and he would visit several more times before retiring.*

1781

No homicides occurred during 1781

1782

And none during 1782 either

1783

(68)

1783A And only the one homicide occurred during 1783, and it appeared on the calendar of the Summer Assizes held on Tuesday 29 July, before either Mr Chief Baron Skynner or Mr Justice Willes.

Thomas Dunkley was indicted 'for feloniously slaying William Roddis at the *Saracen's Head*, Northampton'; and Samuel Dunkley

> 'for unlawfully striking the late William Roddis whilst he was fighting with the said Thomas Dunkley, whereby he instantly fell to the ground and expired'.

And that is all we have. Whether Thomas and Samuel Dunkley were related is not known; and what lay behind this pub brawl is also not known. But what *is* known, is that Samuel Dunkley was acquitted, and that Thomas Dunkley was found guilty of manslaughter, and fined £10.

1784

(69)

1784A Elizabeth Nokes appeared at the 1784 Lent Assizes, on Tuesday 2 March before either Mr Chief Baron Skynner or Mr Baron Eyre, charged on the Coroner's Inquest of the murder of her female bastard child at Sulgrave.

The date of the deed, and the circumstances, are not recorded in the *Northampton Mercury*. But what is recorded in the same newspaper one week later, is the report of the execution of Elizabeth Nokes, on Monday 8 March 1784, and the fact that her 'Body was afterwards delivered to the Surgeons to be dissected and anatomised

❁

(E40) **FRIDAY 26 MARCH 1784**

HANGED FOR WOUNDING AND ATTEMPTED HIGHWAY ROBBERY

Richard Wilson

Richard Wilson was convicted at the 1784 Lent Assizes before either Mr Chief Baron Skynner or Mr Baron Eyre, of firing a pistol loaded with powder and ball at John Daniel in the Lordship of Drayton, whereby the said John Daniel was dangerously wounded in the right arm. But the *Northampton Mercury* of Monday 29 March tells us far more :

> 'Before he left the Gaol [Wilson] delivered a Paper to the Clergyman who attended him containing an Account his Life; from which it appears that he was under 18 Years of Age - was born and educated at Daventry - that he had frequently robbed *(Wilson always uses the term 'robbed', which is incorrect, what he had committed was theft and not robbery)* his Father (who kept a Toll-Gate) of trifling Sums - He was put out Apprentice, at about the Age of 14, to a Shoe-Maker at Badby; but behaving very ill upon the Death of his Father, his Master gave up his Indentures. A short time after which he went to work with Mr Sleath a Shoe-Maker at Kilsby, whom he robbed of about Thirty Shillings; but his Master discovering the Theft, he turned him away: He then went to live with his Mother (who kept on the Toll-Gate) and robbed her of Money, Plate, &c to the amount of about 10l *(£10)*, but returned all again, except about 4l in money with Part of which he brought a Brace of Pistols at Daventry, on the 18th October last. On the Monday of the 20th, he bought some Lead which he cast into Bullets at Wardentown, and returned from there in the Afternoon to go to Daventry; and on his Way thither, between Byfield and Charwelton, he met with the above-mentioned John Daniel, who was then employed in burning Twitch by the Road Side: He offered Daniel a Shilling to bear him Company to Daventry, or a Mile further (which he accepted) and they walked together very

sociably till they got about two Miles beyond Daventry; when he took hold of the poor Man's Collar and bid him deliver his Watch and Money, threatening to blow his Brains out if he refused. Daniel attempted to disengage himself and begged of him for Christ's Sake not to kill him, and in the Struggle the Pistol went off, which Wilson said frightened him very much. He immediately ran away and hid himself among some Bushes where he was apprehended the next Morning - At the Place of Execution, his Behaviour was very penitent and becoming; Tears of Contrition poured plentifully down his Cheeks. He repeatedly admonished the surrounding Spectators (particularly the younger Sort) to take Warning by his untimely End, which he said he deserved Years ago, and about a Quarter before One o'Clock was launched into Eternity.'

1785

There were no criminal homicides in 1785, but the following six men surely made up for it.

❁

(E41) **SATURDAY 5 MARCH 1785**

HANGED FOR ROBBERY OF THE ROYAL MAIL

John Roberts

John Roberts and his brother William, were both indicted before the 1785 Lent Assizes, before Mr Chief Baron Skynner, with 'feloniously assaulting Rice Humphries on the King's Highway, in the parish of Boughton, on the 12th October last; and feloniously taking from him one Leather Portmanteau, and divers Leather Bags, containing Letters sent by the Post'. John Roberts was found guilty, but the *Northampton Mercury* fails to tell us if William was acquitted, or found guilty of a lesser charge, although it is a fact that William Roberts was not hanged alongside his brother.

And John Roberts' hanging occurred on Saturday 5 March, not on Northampton Racecourse as was usual, but at the scene of the crime, Boughton Green Lane, which was the fashion in those days, if the crime was considered repulsive, or if it was desired to make an example of the criminal. And robbing an officer of the Royal Mail *was* considered serious. The irony of the fact that some people, who had been convicted of *killing other people*, only got fined or branded, never seems to have entered the equation.

Anyway, John Roberts was hanged in Boughton Green Lane, and (the *Northampton Mercury*)...

> At the Place of Execution he admonished the numerous Spectators to take Warning by his untimely Fate, and particularly desired them not to reflect on his Brother, who was Charged with being his Accomplice declaring that he was entirely innocent.'

❀

(E42) FRIDAY 18 MARCH 1785

HANGED FOR HORSE THEFT

Thomas Skelcher alias Thomas Bates
John Bull alias Robert Lewin

Also appearing at the 1784 Lent Assizes, were these two, both charged with horse theft, in separate incidents. Thomas Skelcher alias Thomas Bates was accused of stealing a brown mare, the property of John Bird of Everdon, and also another mare belonging to William Shepherd of Blakesley. John Bull alias Robert Lewin was indicted for stealing two cart horses, the property of Jonathan Abbot of Irthlingborough. Both were found guilty and both sentenced to death.

At the place of execution, said the *Northampton Mercury*, Thomas Skelcher, who was under twenty years of age, made a full confession, and attributed his untimely fate to the 'undutiful

> manner he had behaved to his Mother, whom he once

> threatened to murder; he also acknowledged having been guilty of many petty Crimes, such as robbing Orchards, Hen-Roosts &c, and said that he had, at different times, stolen four Horses.'

John Bull declared to the clergyman who attended him, that he *really had* bought the two horses from Irthlingborough, but he found that these were not sufficient to bring in his harvest. So he *did* steal a horse - but from a farmer in Leicestershire! He said on the gallows that he had led a bad life, and left a wife and two children. The unhappy convicts, said the *Mercury*, met their fate with great resolution and they seemed to die very penitent.

❁

(E43) **FRIDAY 22 JULY 1785**

HANGED FOR HIGHWAY ROBBERY

James Tarry

Three highwaymen appeared at the 1785 Summer Assizes, which started on Tuesday 5 July, before either Mr Justice Willes or Mr Justice Gould. The first was James Tarry who was indicted 'for assaulting William Adams, of Brackley, on the Highway, in the Parish of Chipping Warden, on the 1st of June, about Midnight, in Company with another Person, not yet taken, and robbing him of 12£ 17s 10d'.

Note that only five weeks separated crime and trial, and subsequently only seven or so weeks will separate crime and hanging. No information about how James Tarry was caught, nor any details of the trial, nor any more information about the partner-in-crime, is forthcoming in the *Mercury*. Suffice it to say, it was obviously and open and shut case, with Tarry receiving the death penalty.

The *Northampton Mercury* of Monday 25 July 1785 describes the scene at the Racecourse :

> 'From the time of his Condemnation, he uniformly persisted in denying the Charge, and both before and after

receiving the Sacrament, made a Solemn Declaration to the same Purpose to the Clergyman who attended him.

His behaviour at the Place of Execution was very decent and becoming, he declared that he freely forgave his Prosecutor, and that he was composed and happy - he never was observed to change Countenance, nor did he discover the smallest Mark of Fear, but met Death with the Greatest Fortitude. In short, the whole Tenor of his Conduct through this trying Scene was such as impressed the Spectators with the Strongest Conviction of his Innocence - He has left a wife and three Children.'

❁

(E44) **FRIDAY 5 AUGUST 1785**

HANGED FOR HIGHWAY ROBBERY

John Smith
Richard Kelly alias John Hall

The second and third highway robbery merchants appearing at the 1785 Summer Assizes, were these two partners in crime. On the face of it, these seem a rum pair of coves. But look a bit deeper, and we discover that one could actually be described as a war hero.

John Smith was charged 'on the oath of Joseph Johnson of Newnham, with stopping him on the High Road, and robbing him of an Handkerchief, a Knife, and Four-Pence. And John Hall, a Mariner, for seizing and holding the said Joseph Johnson while the above John Smith robbed him'.

Absolutely no details of the crime or trial are printed in the *Mercury*, except that they were both condemned to hang.

However, in the *Mercury* of Monday 8 August 1785, which gives the description of the hanging, we read that Smith was between 30 and 40 years old, born at Quorndon in Leicestershire and apprenticed to a tailor. He then enlisted in the Leicestershire

Militia and on discharge joined the 6th Foot *(later to become the Warwickshire Regiment)*, but deserted from there and enlisted into the Guards *(it is not known which regiment, as the Grenadier, Coldstream and Scots were all in existence by that time, 1785).* But he had also deserted from them just one week before the crime. He had a wife and two small children.

But it gets more interesting as we read on. By this time, it had been discovered that John Hall's real name was Richard Kelly, who was :

> 'about 24 and from London, and had been two years a Fisherman at Wandsworth. At the Commencement of the War, he was impressed into the Navy, in which he served until the Peace was concluded, and was on board the *Namur* during Admiral Rodney's Engagement in the West-Indies on the 12th April. Upon discharge from the Navy, he got acquainted with a gang of thieves in London - two of whom were executed in the Old Bailey during his Confinement in Gaol.
>
> They both acknowledged the Justness of their Sentence, and behaved in a very penitent and becoming Manner. Great Intercession was made to save the Lives of these unfortunate men, but without Effect, the melancholy Situation which the County is in at present from the frequent Depredations of every Description that are committed having rendered it indispensably necessary that all Applications for an Extension of the Royal Mercy should be discountenanced'.

An explanation is needed about Richard Kelly's career, and why he can be described as a war hero. And the war being referred to, is the American War of Independence.

The thirteen American states who declared their independence from Britain in July 1776, obviously started it all off, and the war was ended by the disastrous British defeat at the Battle of Yorktown in October 1781. The British collapse at Yorktown, was exacerbated by the army not being supplied from the sea. This was because the Royal Navy had, in effect, lost control of the Atlantic by failing to drive off the French fleet after the 'drawn' Battle of Chesapeake Bay.

The French had entered the war on the American side, in an attempt to strike a blow against its old enemy of Britain. And after the British had been sent packing after Yorktown, the French, with Spanish help, wanting to rub salt into the British wounds, sent a large navy to wrest the Caribbean out of British hands.

But if the British had lost the American colonies, they were certainly in no mood to lose the Caribbean as well. In December 1781, the Prime Minister, Lord North, sent out a bigger British fleet under Admiral Sir George Rodney.

Locating the French fleet under Admiral de Grasse at the Iles des Saintes near Dominica on 12 April 1782, Rodney, by superior tactics, simply took the French fleet apart. Five French ships, including the flagship Ville de Paris, *together with Admiral de Grasse himself, were captured, in what is known to history as The Battle of The Saintes. So decisive was this victory, that it ended for ever the French threat to the Caribbean, which remained British from thereon in.*

The Battle of the Saintes was the longest, bloodiest and biggest naval engagement of the eighteenth century. It was essential to win it, and the British victory was as decisive as Trafalgar was to be, 23 years later. And Richard Kelly was there, in HMS Namur. *Purely surviving the battle was a miracle, yet three years later, he was hanged at Northampton.*

1786

(70)

1786A William Howell was found guilty of the wilful murder of Thomas Mee at the Lent Assizes on Tuesday 7 March, before either Mr Chief Baron Skynner or Mr Justice Heath. And that, is all we know. No other details are known, not even the date or place. All we know is that William Howell was sentenced to death and was hanged on Saturday 11 March 1786. But we do have an eye witness account of his execution from the *Northampton Mercury* of that same day :

> 'His behaviour was very decent but he did not seem to feel that important Sense of his Situation which we have often observed on similar Occasions. On his way to the Gallows,

he more than once desired the Cart might be drove faster, observing the Weather was very cold - Before he was turned off, he acknowledged giving Mee the unfortunate Blow which caused his Death, but declared he had no Intention of killing him. After hanging the usual Time, his Body was cut down and delivered to the Surgeons in Order to be dissected and anatomised, pursuant to the Statute.'

✣✣ *John Heath, born 1736, after taking his law degree from Christ Church College, Oxford, was called straight to the bar, entering the Inner Temple in 1762. The only thing of note in an otherwise unremarkable career, was that he was the Recorder for Exeter in 1775, before becoming a Judge of the Common Pleas in 1780. These 1785 Lent Assizes were the first time he had visited Northampton, and he would make intermittent visits until the 1815 Summer Assizes, but those would be his last because he would die the year after, in 1816, aged 80.*

❁

(E45) **FRIDAY 24 MARCH 1786**

HANGED FOR HORSE THEFT

Thomas Allen

The Lent Assizes of 1786 saw not only William Howell condemned to death for the murder of Thomas Mee (1786A), but also Thomas Allen for horse theft. The best way of describing Thomas Allen's crime, is to let the *Northampton Mercury* of Saturday 11 March tell it in its own way :

'Thomas Allen, removed by Habeus Corpus from Newgate, charged on the Oath of Clarke Page Barber, with feloniously stealing and riding away with a Mare, the property of Clarke Page Barber at Moulton and also with burglariously breaking into the Dwelling House of the said Clarke Page Barber at Moulton aforesaid in the night of the 2nd September 1785 and feloniously

> stealing a silver Cup, a Saddle, a Bridle and several other Things.'

And from the *Northampton Mercury* of Saturday 25 March :

> 'Yesterday, Thomas Allen was hanged in compliance with the Sentence at our last Assizes. His behaviour at the Place of Execution was very becoming a person in his unhappy Circumstances - And he earnestly exhorted the Spectators to take Warning by his untimely End, and to avoid Sabbath-breaking and Drunkenness which he said had been the first Steps to his Ruin.'

Reading between the lines, it can be guessed that Thomas Allen was employed by Clarke Barber, who on discovering the theft and burglary, knew exactly who had done it, and where he had fled to - London. Although there were six months between crime and trial, it is not known exactly how long it had taken to capture Thomas Allen in London, and therefore how long he had been 'on remand' in Newgate Prison. But by the year 1785, the Bow Street Runners had been in operation for over 40 years, and knew their stuff, and it was more than likely that Thomas Allen had been captured within days of the Runners being notified in September 1785.

Also now note that the Northampton Mercury *was being published on a Saturday rather than a Monday. The edition of Monday 15 August 1785 had been the last of the Monday editions, and the edition of Saturday 20 August 1785 had been the first of the Saturday editions, where it would remain from now on.*

1787

(71)

1787A Only this one homicide occurred in 1787, and that was on the calendar of the Lent Assizes, held on Tuesday 6 March before either Mr Chief Baron Eyre or Mr Justice Heath.

Ann Checkley was found guilty of the manslaughter of her husband John, at Woodford. She received one month imprisonment. No other details are known.

❀

(E46) **FRIDAY 3 AUGUST 1787**

HANGED FOR SACRILEGE AND BURGLARY

David Coe
John Hulbert

HANGED FOR ROBBERIES, ASSAULTS AND BURGLARIES

John Smith
William Bowers
Richard Law
William Pettipher
(The Culworth Gang)

Undoubtedly, the 'stars' of the 1787 Summer Assizes, which started on Tuesday 17 July before Mr Justice Ashurst, were the four members of 'The Culworth Gang'. But also appearing, were David Coe, Alexander Coe and John Hulbert.

David Coe and Alexander Coe (It is not stated what the relationship was - were they brothers?) were jointly charged with feloniously entering the parish church of Desborough on the night of 6/7 June, and stealing one tablecloth, two napkins, two pewter flagons, one silver cup and cover and one silver salver, one pewter salver and two pewter plates. In other words, all the church communion plate.

Now sacrilege is one of those crimes which is looked upon a little bit differently to 'ordinary' burglary. Stealing from a dwelling house is one thing, but stealing from a church is entirely another kettle of fish. As we do not know what happened in this trial (all the newspaper reports are taken up with the Culworth Gang's antics) we do not know how Alexander Coe got off with it, but David Coe did not. He was found guilty.

And perhaps because he was charged jointly with David Coe, John Hulbert was beat before he started. They were accused of the burglary of John Loakes' house in Desborough on 6 April, and stealing a flitch of bacon, a quantity of pork, and 30 shillings in cash. They were both found guilty and sentenced to death.

Enough has already been written about the Culworth Gang. For nearly ten years, the Gang, centred on the village of Culworth, committed robberies and burglaries throughout south Northamptonshire and north Oxfordshire, amassing a large amount of cash and property.

Fearing violent reprisals, no one stood up to them - until the early months of 1787. Law and Pettipher, when stopping overnight at an inn, had their baggage searched, and were caught with stolen property on them. As soon as it was seen that someone had the courage to stand up to them, the end for the Culworth Gang followed quickly. Law and Pettipher 'sang' like the proverbial canaries.

Together they implicated John Smith, his two sons, William and John junior; William Bowers; William Tervill; William Abbott and Richard Jack. All were quickly caught, except Richard Jack who escaped and was never heard of again.

So, eight members of the Culworth Gang stood trial at the 1787 Summer Assizes before Mr Justice Ashurst. Tervill and the two younger Smiths were acquitted, Abbott was transported for life, but the other four were sentenced to death.

Smith, Bowers, Law and Pettipher, together with Coe and Hulbert, were all hanged together on Northampton Racecourse on Friday 3 August 1787, before one of the largest crowds ever. Six is the largest number of men hanged at the same time in Northamptonshire. It would not be until 1819, with the arrival of the 'New Drop', that anywhere near that number would suffer the same fate.

✣✣ *William Henry Ashurst had been a Justice of the King's Bench since 1770. Again, he has the standard biography of public school, barrister and judge. He was however, sufficiently well thought of to be entrusted with the Great Seal of the Realm in 1783 and 1792. He had made several visits to Northampton previously, but had had no criminal homicides to deal with; and he would visit several more times until his death in 1807 aged 82.*

1788

The years 1788 and 1789 were dominated by the Gordon/Linnell case. A point of law was thrown up by it, which then necessitated a conclave of judges to get together and make a decision.

(72)

1788A Thursday 24 July 1788. Pattishall

Victim George Linnell, Parish Constable of Pattishall

Accused Thomas Gordon (19)

Winifred Gordon

George Linnell was of a well known Whittlebury family, but he had moved to Pattishall where he became the Parish Constable in 1788. Virtually at the same time, into the village of Pattishall moved Doctor Francis Gordon, his wife Winifred, and their son, Thomas.

Doctor Gordon started practising medicine in the district, but being of a violent temperament, soon got into several affrays with the locals. A complaint was made to George Linnell about a physical assault by Doctor Gordon, and a warrant was procured for his arrest.

On Thursday 24 July 1788, Linnell approached the Gordon house with a view to serving the warrant and arresting Doctor Gordon. On approaching the front door, he was confronted with Winifred Gordon, apparently as rancorous and aggressive as her husband, who told Linnell in no uncertain terms that her husband was not there. Linnell retreated, as obviously the situation was volatile, and it was equally obvious that Winifred Gordon was lying.

About an hour went by, and Linnell tried again, backed up by reinforcements from the village. They were met by Winifred again, but this time her nineteen year old son, Thomas, was also there. And Thomas was armed with a loaded shotgun.

The Gordons refused Linnell entry. This provoked the villagers to hurl sticks and stones at the Gordon house, resulting in broken windows and broken tempers. Winifred slammed the door, and going upstairs was heard to scream 'Fire! Fire at them!' Thomas did just that, killing George Linnell instantly.

Trial **1789 Spring Assizes, Monday 9 March. Mr Baron Thomson**

Thomas Linnell was found guilty of the murder of George Linnell. He had to be, he had done the deed before several witnesses. However, because of what followed, sentencing was postponed until the next Assizes.

Winifred Gordon was also found guilty of being an accessory to murder before the fact. But Thomson B differed from the jury. He argued that a person could not be charged both with being a principal to murder and at the same time, being an accessory before the fact. It was either one or the other, not both, as had happened in this case.

Because of this, a Writ of Certiorari was issued by the Court of King's Bench. A Writ of Certiorari is an order from a superior court to a lesser one for the case to be passed up to them because of some discrepancy.

The twelve judges of the King's Bench deliberated on 24 June 1789. Their decision was made known at the Summer Assizes, which started on Tuesday 21 July. Thomas Gordon's sentence was to stand, but his mother was to be re-tried, not as a principal to murder, but as an accessory.

Thomas Gordon's sentence was ordered to be carried out on Monday 3 August, but at 3am on the very morning, a messenger who had been riding all night, delivered a stay of execution for fourteen days. Thomas had been appealing against his sentence.

All to no avail, however, several witnesses had seen him do it, so he couldn't not be not guilty. His execution finally took place on Northampton Racecourse on Tuesday 18 August 1789. The *Northampton Mercury* reported his last words :

> 'I am now going to suffer for the Murder of this Man; and my Mother is shortly to be tried again for the same Offence. I declare in the Presence of God before whom I am now going to appear, that she never ordered me to fire, nor was she in the Room with me at this Time - That's all I have to say.'

Winifred Gordon was tried again, found guilty and received a term of imprisonment. George Linnell was buried in Whittlebury churchyard, where his headstone, although much weathered, can still be seen.

It is difficult to fathom what the fuss was about in this case. Winifred Gordon was obviously guilty of incitement and thus of being an accessory before the fact, as there were witnesses who heard her say what she did. But, that is what happened, make of it as you will.

✣✣ *Nicknamed 'Staymaker' by his fellow Judges, because he had the habit of slowing down witnesses who he thought were talking too fast, Alexander Thomson, was considered one of the great port drinkers and wits of his age. 'I also think my Lord' said a barrister to him once 'that after a good dinner a certain quantity of wine does a man no harm'. 'Oh no' said the learned Judge 'it is the* uncertain *quantity that does the mischief'.*

Born in 1744, Alexander Thomson was appointed Master of the Court of Chancery in 1782, and in 1787 was knighted and made a Baron of the Exchequer. He was a Baron for 27 years before being made Chief Baron in 1814. Despite his prodigious intake of port, he managed 73 years of life, dying at Bath in 1817.

❁

(E47) **SATURDAY 22 MARCH 1788**

HANGED FOR SHEEP THEFT

John Bateman

In an agricultural county such as Northamptonshire, threats to a farmer's livelihood are looked upon more seriously perhaps than other offences. John Bateman was the first person in the county to be hanged specifically for sheep stealing.

John Bateman was charged with stealing eighteen whether sheep, the property of Matthew Horwood of Steane and Hinton-in-the-Hedges, the previous June. He had then sent them to Smithfield Market in London where they were sold.

At his trial, at the 1788 Lent Assizes before Mr Chief Baron Eyre, he had said that he had stolen the sheep to pay for his wife's medical bills during her long illness. He also stated that his wife was far advanced in pregnancy with their third child. All this made no difference, he was hanged for sheep theft on Saturday 22 March 1788.

What is ironic, is that at the same Assizes, a certain John Gamble was also found guilty of stealing and killing one sheep the property of John Vials of Rothwell. Although he was sentenced to death, he was reprieved. Why *he* should be and John Bateman not, remains a mystery.

1789

The Lent Assizes, starting on Monday 9 March before Mr Chief Baron Eyre and Mr Baron Thomson, turned up three homicides, plus a burglary which resulted in the death sentence. There were no homicides at the Summer Assizes

(73)
1789A John Middleton was acquitted of the 'murder of a female bastard child' at Lamport. No details are given.

(74)
1789B Although William Baker and John Lay had accused William Byfield of murdering John Knighton of Titchmarsh Lodge, 'no true bill' was returned by the Grand Jury. William Byfield was therefore released. No other details are known.

(75)
1789C Mental illness was far from understood in the olden days, and so of the many homicides in the county, not many have been attributed to psychiatric causes. It is perhaps easy to say that only those people displaying the most obvious and unmistakeable symptoms of mental distress, had their crimes looked upon sympathetically.

Thus it was with John Sibley who appeared before the Lent Assizes charged with the murder of John Morris at Cogenhoe. No detail is given, but the *Northampton Mercury* states that John Sibley was examined by the Grand Jury, who finding him 'to be of unsound mind', caused him to be remanded until the next Assizes.

At the Summer Assizes, Mr Baron Hotham found him to be insane, not responsible for his actions, and discharged to secure accommodation.

❁

(E48) **FRIDAY 27 MARCH 1789**

HANGED FOR BURGLARY

Thomas Underwood

We only have the bare bones of this case to mull over. All we have to goggle at, is the size of the haul. Thomas Underwood, Thomas Andrew and Ann Smith were jointly charged with breaking into the house of Jonathan Nethercoat at Braybrook and stealing bank notes and money to the vale of £1,000, together with promissory notes to the value of another £500. Thomas Andrew was also accused of stealing two hemp sacks. Leaving the value of the two sacks aside, £1,500 in 1789, would be equivalent to an unbelievable £85,000 in today's money.

No details of the trial at the 1789 Lent Assizes or evidence are reported in the *Northampton Mercury*, only the fact that all three were found guilty and sentenced to death. Andrew and Smith however, were reprieved, but Underwood was not, and his sentenced was ordered to be carried out.

On the day before his execution day, Underwood was being shaved by the prison barber. Being distracted over something, the barber looked away, and quick as a flash, Underwood grabbed the razor (obviously one of the old open type, ironically called a 'cut-throat') and tried to cut his own throat with it. He was pounced on before he could do much damage, and his life 'saved' so that he could be fit enough to be hanged the next day.

1790

There were no criminal homicides during 1790

1791

Three homicides occurred in 1791. The first appeared at the Lent Assizes on Monday 28 February before either Mr Chief Baron Eyre or Mr Justice Grose.

(76)
1791A Elizabeth Craddock from West Haddon was acquitted of the murder of a female child at Guilsborough. No other details are known.

And the second and third homicides appeared at the Summer Assizes on Tuesday 2 August before either Mr Baron Hotham or Mr Baron Perryn.

(77)
1791B Henry Haycock of Dodford was found guilty of killing James Wilson in Dodford. He was fined the princely sum of sixpence and discharged. It would be nice to know the evidence and circumstances of this - but we don't.

(78)
1791C Frances Beal was found guilty of the murder of Eliza Beal. What relationship the two were is unknown. All that is known is that Frances Beal was acquitted because of insanity, but committed to secure accommodation.

✣✣ *Mr Justice Grose had the wonderfully evocative first name of Nash. Although visiting Northampton for the Summer Assizes in 1789, no homicides were on the Calendar, and these 1791 Lent Assizes were his second visit. After Trinity Hall, Cambridge he had entered Lincoln's Inn in 1766. He was knighted and made a Judge of the King's Bench in 1787. He retired in 1813, just one year before he died aged 74.*

1792

There were no criminal homicides in 1792

❁

(E49) **FRIDAY 23 MARCH 1792**

HANGED FOR ROBBERY

James Cross
Thomas Smith

Both Cross and Smith were aged 21, Cross coming from Harlestone, and Smith from Long Buckby. As is often the way, the two met after a drinking bout in a local hostelry, in this case, during the previous November of 1791, in Hanwell, which is just north west of Banbury. On the way home, Smith easily persuaded Cross to steal a goose from a local farmyard.

One thing led to another, and in the following three months, the pair escalated to robbery. The seventh robbery they committed was to Richard Manning at Long Buckby, when they robbed him of three one-guinea coins and two half-guinea coins (about £240 at today's prices), and was the one for which they were caught.

Mr Baron Thomson at the 1792 Lent Assizes, heard the men's confessions, and sentenced them both to death. The report of this double hanging appears in the *Northampton Mercury* of Saturday 24 March 1792, that is, the day after the hanging. The reporter, obviously struck either by the youthfulness of the two, or of their penitent behaviour, must have regarded himself as on a par with Milton or Dryden, and really let the prose flow.

> 'At the place of execution their exhortations to the populace were uncommonly fervid, earnestly entreating them to avoid drunkenness and Sabbath breaking, to which they attributed their ruin.
>
> There is an amiable trait in the human heart, that when a fellow creature comes to lay down his life as a forfeiture for his crimes, we are apt to forget his offences however enormous, and to view him with an eye of sympathy; in short, resentment is superseded by pity; so it was in this instance, the feelings of the multitude appearing to be interested to a high degree.

Thus perish the mortal parts of men, who but for the fatal bias of inordinate passions and depraved habits might have added to the general stock of usefulness in society, and have been a comfort to their connections.'

1793

(79)

1793A Though not the youngest persons to be tried for homicide in the county (that 'honour' belongs to Arthur Pittam in 1897, who was aged seven), Christopher Jefferies at fifteen, and William Harrison aged twelve, were certainly the next youngest. At the 1793 Summer Assizes on day 9 July, they appeared before either Mr Baron Hotham or Mr Justice Wilson.

Both were charged with the wilful murder of William Selland, a waterman's boy. Unfortunately, we do not have any more details, the *Mercury* not condescending to tell us, not even the place, or age of William Selland.

All we are told is that William Harrison was acquitted, but Christopher Jefferies was found guilty of manslaughter, and received one year's imprisonment. For a fifteen year old to receive a year in the 'slammer', his crime must have been particularly appalling. But that is guesswork, we do not know for certain.

✣✣ *These were the last Assizes that Sir John Wilson was to take, because he died a few weeks later aged 52. After Cambridge, he had been a barrister of the Middle Temple, and had only been a Judge of the Common Pleas for seven years.*

1794

A very full Calendar greeted Mr Chief Baron Macdonald and Mr Baron Thomson when they both arrived in Northampton for the 1794 Lent Assizes. Not only did they have the case of Thomas Gleeds for murder (1794A), but the cases of Pearce, Higgins and Brawn.

(80)
1794A Thomas Gleeds, alias Leeds, was charged with the murder of five year old Thomas Gill, somewhere within the parish of Saint Sepulchre, Northampton. No detail of the actual mechanics of the crime is given - which is perhaps just as well. But, unusually, the *Mercury* does give us a fairly full description of the court proceedings :

> 'Thomas Gleeds alias Leeds was ordered to remain in prison, till due order made concerning him by two justices as a dangerous lunatic. Upon his trial he acknowledged the truth of every circumstance concerning the murder alleged against him. It was, however, proved upon the oath of a sergeant of marines, into which corps he inlisted in the year 1790, and remained therein for about eight months, that he was generally considered *non compos mentis*, and on that account discharged from the said regiment, which also his discharge, produced in court, fully stated; and his unhappy weakness of intellect likewise corroborated by other circumstances, he was (tho' every charge in the indictment was fully proved) acquitted of the murder in the eye of the law.'

The case of John Sibley (1789C) and Frances Beal (1791C) and now this one, all in the space of five years, suggests that psychiatric disturbance is now being taken more seriously, and an understanding that it may 'excuse' individuals in the action they have taken. Perhaps George III's second attack of 'madness' which started in 1788 may have focused attention of the thinking professions on this subject, and may have caused a more sympathetic view of those accused of serious offences.

✣✣ *Archibald Macdonald was a lineal descendant of the Macdonald clan, the old Lords of the Isles. Educated at Christ Church, Oxford, he became a Barrister of Lincoln's Inn, and a KC in 1778. He was MP for Hindon in 1777, and for Newcastle under Lyme 1780 to 1793, Solicitor General 1784 to 1788, then knighted and made Attorney General in 1788. Created Chief Baron in 1793, he retired in 1813 with a Baronetcy. Macdonald CB would be a regular visitor to the county until his last appearance for the 1802 Lent Assizes. He died in 1826 aged 79.*

❁

(E50) **FRIDAY 21 MARCH 1794**

HANGED FOR BURGLARY

Benjamin Pearce

Benjamin Pearce, aged 26, was charged with the burglary of the shop of John Bartrums, a cordwainer (cobbler) of Stoke Bruerne. He was accused of stealing a number of lasts, women's shoes and slippers, and a quantity of leather and sundry other articles, belonging to John Bartrums; as well as some working tools, the property of Thomas Jones, journeyman shoemaker.

At his trial, it emerged that Benjamin Pearce was the youngest of eleven children of a Sulgrave family. His mother had died when he was nine, and his father when he was thirteen. Never having any education, Benjamin resorted to tramping the countryside picking up work as a chimney sweep. He was apparently heavily influenced by his father and elder brother Edward, both of whom were extremely brutal towards him. Edward would often skin mice alive and impale them on thorn bushes and revel in the creature's agony, as well as skinning frogs alive.

On the way to his execution, Benjamin was very fearful, cried incessantly, and at the scene denounced his father and brother. He left a pregnant widow and a three year old child.

❁

(E51) **FRIDAY 28 MARCH 1794**

HANGED FOR HORSE THEFT

John Higgins

HANGED FOR ROBBERY

Thomas Brawn

Due to appear at the 1794 Lent Assizes, were John Higgins and William James. John Higgins was charged, on the oath (accusation) of Thomas Gingell of Hardwick in the county of Gloucestershire, yeoman, on violent suspicion of feloniously stealing, in company with one William James, a certain mare, the property of the said Thomas Gingell, and exposing her for sale at Northampton Fair. And William James was accused of doing the same to a horse belonging to Thomas Copner of Quedgeley in Gloucestershire.

However, all is not as it seems. The *Northampton Mercury*, in its edition the week before the Assizes, on giving the Calendar of prisoners, added this :

> 'One of the above named prisoners for horse stealing committed by the name of William James proves to be a female; she is but 16 years of age, and says her real name is Mary James. Higgins her accomplice is about 45.'

However, be that as it may, she was still charged with horse theft, and thus appeared alongside John Higgins at the Lent Assizes. They had no defence against the charges, and so were both found guilty, and so both sentenced to death.

But the judge did hear that Mary James was completely under the influence of John Higgins. So although she was still guilty of the crime, because of the circumstances, her sentence was commuted to transportation for seven years.

John Higgins, however, was hanged on Northampton Racecourse. The *Northampton Mercury* added this :

> 'The day before the execution, Higgins wrote to his wife in which he expressed strong compunction for having been the means of bringing the poor girl into such a

> dreadful situation. Her parents died when she was young and Higgins and his wife took her in as a servant. She was entirely under the influence of Higgins, and he hoped that she would be pardoned before being transported.'

Thomas Brawn, aged 26 of Cottingham, was charged on the oath of William Bamford of Cottingham, with having assaulted him, in company with someone else, upon the King's highway and robbed him of ten guineas and some silver. Thomas Brawn protested his innocence. The story that unfolded was the same old familiar one, which has been repeated time and time again since time began.

Brawn was drinking in a public house with others. At 1pm Bamford came in. After some time, the drink started talking and Bamford and Brawn were soon resorting to fisticuffs.

At 10pm (nine hours later!) Bamford and a man called Taylor left the pub, and Brawn, with another man, followed them out, to 'settle the score'. The inevitable fight ensued, with Brawn knocking Taylor to the ground, who then got up and ran away.

Turning to Bamford, Brawn and his mate then started 'settling the score'. And so well did they 'settle the score' that Bamford was knocked senseless, and was unconscious for an hour or more. However, Brawn denied that he took any money, or ever had any intention to, his only motive being revenge for the 'ill usage' he had received.

Despite this, Brawn was found guilty of robbery and was sentenced to hang. What happened to his accomplice is not known. But perhaps we can feel some shred of sympathy, as whilst he was in prison, his wife died leaving an infant child. And as the *Mercury* said Brawn 'was a poor ignorant wretch and appeared to be an object of great commiseration.'

Thomas Brawn was hanged alongside John Higgins on Northampton Racecourse. 'They both died very penitent' said the *Mercury,*

> 'and Higgins, who acknowledged the fact for which he suffered, met death with great resolution.'

1795

No criminal homicides occurred in 1795, but it is interesting to note that now the *Northampton Mercury* starts printing some details of the civil cases appearing in the Nisi Prius Court, which it had never done before.

1796

There were no criminal homicides during 1796

1797

(81)

1797A The only criminal homicide of 1797 appeared at the Summer Assizes on Tuesday 25 July before either Mr Justice Ashurst or Mr Baron Hotham. Martha Dexter was charged that 'on

> Sunday 16 April 1797 at Thorpe Achurch, she unlawfully, wickedly and knowingly poisoned Jane Small the wife of Thomas Small, and Thomas Dexter son of the said Martha Dexter, by mixing a quantity of poison, called white arsenic with some flour, of which a pudding was made and of which the said Jane Small and Thomas Dexter did eat, and were thereby poisoned and died.'

Now, what lies behind all this, is anybody's guess - but the imagination runs riot. Her own son and another man's wife? Were they 'carrying on'? Did Thomas Small know? Didn't Martha approve? And then we have the practicalities. Surely Martha must have known that her own son would also eat the poisoned pud? Did she care? Did she also want rid of her son as well as 'the other woman'?

Lots of questions like these will never be answered, as the report in the Mercury tells us nothing. All we have is that Martha was acquitted and released. Why this should be so is never disclosed.

1798

All the five criminal homicides of 1798 appeared at the Lent Assizes, starting on Monday 12 March, before either Mr Chief Baron Macdonald or Mr Justice Grose.

(82)

1798A This was an unusual case to start of with. It appeared on the Assize Calendar thus :

> 'Christopher Chesterton charged on his own voluntary confession of having about 13 years ago, in the parish of St Martins in this county feloniously killed and murdered a person by the name of Burbridge by striking him a blow on the head with a stick of which blow the said Burbridge instantly died and then throwing his body into the river adjoining the said parish of St Martins.'

So what are we to make of all this? Well, for a start, the place must by Stamford, or to be more precise, Stamford Saint Martin otherwise called Stamford Baron, which in those days, because it was south of the River Welland, was in Northamptonshire, or again, to be more precise, the Soke of Peterborough, which was in Northamptonshire. And of course, the river was the River Welland.

So what did the court make of it? Nothing. How could it? There was absolutely no evidence that a crime had been committed, despite the 'confession' after thirteen years. No doubt records had been searched for a note of a missing man called Burbridge in 1785 or thereabouts, and obviously none had been found.

The Grand Jury therefore had no option but to find No True Bill against Christopher Chesterton, and he was sent on his way, no doubt pleased that his conscience had been appeased from the mental agonies that had made him confess in the first place. Or, as the saying has it today, he had achieved 'closure'.

(83)

1798B 'John Wareing and Samuel Johnson together with Thomas Gammage, not yet surrendered, feloniously stand charged on the Coroner's Inquest with having by

> misadventure beat and wounded Thomas Harris labourer, so that he died on the 3rd day of January following, of such hurt and wounding.'

Such was the indictment against Wareing, Johnson and Gammage. But the Grand Jury disagreed with the Coroner, and they brought in a verdict of 'No True Bill', so in other words, the case was thrown out before it even got into court.

This is a strange case, surely? Why did the Coroner's Jury think there was enough evidence for criminal homicide, and yet at the Assizes, the Grand Jury disagreed? What made Thomas Gammage not surrender to his Bail? Did he secretly know that the Coroner was right, and that if he had turned up at the Assizes, he would have risked being found guilty, with all that that entailed? Anyway, in the event, the case never even got into court, which must a been very impressive to the family of Thomas Harris, who, you remember, had lost his life.

(84)
1798C Samuel Herritage was found guilty of the manslaughter of John Rolfe at Kislingbury on an unknown date. He was fined 1 shilling and discharged. No other details are forthcoming.

(85)
1798D Both John Blunt and William Stanton were charged with the murder of Ann Carvell, in a scenario which is all to familiar. They were both charged with giving her a quantity of white mercury which she took in order to procure an abortion, at Grafton Regis. After a trial of nearly fours hours, both men were acquitted.

(86)
1798E As with the case of Thomas Gleeds (1794A), Elizabeth Dixon was acquitted of murder because of her psychiatric health. She had been charged with the murder of her daughter Alice at King's Cliffe, but was acquitted and was 'ordered to remain in

> prison till due order made concerning her as a dangerous lunatic by two Justices of the Peace.'

No further mention is made of Elizabeth Dixon. Let us hope she gained the treatment she needed, for what was probably some acute form of post-natal depression.

1799

There were no criminal homicides in 1799

❁

(E52) **FRIDAY 19 JULY 1799**

HANGED FOR HORSE THEFT

Thomas Hanger

Thomas Saunders appeared before Mr Chief Baron Macdonald at the 1799 Lent Assizes. He was convicted of horse theft and sentenced to death. But his sentenced was reprieved. Thomas Hanger, on the other hand, must have felt aggrieved when he was found guilty of horse theft at the Summer Assizes before either Mr Baron Perryn or Mr Justice Heath, was sentenced to death, but did not have his sentence altered. Why this should be so is a mystery.

Thomas Hanger was indicted 'on suspicion of stealing a horse belonging to John Worters of Broughton', and was found guilty. Why his sentence was not commuted is unknown, although perhaps we can glean a reason in the report of his hanging, where it implies that he was a constant offender. Perhaps he had been given several chances previously to mend his ways, but obviously had not. Perhaps this was the last straw. The *Northampton Mercury* of Saturday 20 July 1799 :

> 'Yesterday was executed here...Thomas Hanger, aged 43, for stealing a gelding, the property of John Worters of Broughton near Kettering - He was a native of Old Weston in Huntingdonshire, but resided a short time at Weldon in this county - Though known to be an old offender (exclusive of lesser crimes) supposed to have stolen several

horses, besides that for which he forfeited his life, particularly a pony belonging to Mrs Buck at the George Inn, Thrapston, which after cutting the knees in order to make it appear of less value, he sold it to a whitawer (*sic - presumably a knacker's yard*) to be slaughtered, yet he refused to make any particular confession though strongly pressed by the clergyman who attended him - His behaviour in prison since his trial, as well as at the place of execution, was suitable to a person in his unhappy situation and he appeared to die very penitent - He has left a wife and three small children at Brampton in Huntingdonshire, and we understand he has also another child living by a former wife.'

1800

And to round off the century, there were no criminal homicides in 1800 either

1801-1810

We still have to rely on the *Northampton Mercury* for information, as there are not too many Assize Calendars preserved at the Northamptonshire Record Office. But the *Mercury* is not yet printing full reports of the court proceedings, and is still not differentiating which of the two attending judges is sitting in which court. Thus both judges' names still have to be given. Full reports did not appear in the *Mercury* until its rival, the *Northampton Herald*, appeared on the scene in 1834. So although we can piece together an accurate list of the homicides, we still have no exact details of them.

For the years 1801 to 1810 therefore, hard information is sparse. The most we can do is to list all the cases appearing before each Assize, together with the result. If any details are required about any one individual case, more research will have to be done elsewhere. There may be Assize papers secreted about somewhere and which may suddenly be discovered. No Assize papers are kept either at the Northamptonshire Record Office, or the National Archives at Kew.

However, from what little information we have got, we can say that the first decade of the nineteenth century was indeed remarkable. Only nine cases of criminal homicide were tried before the Northamptonshire Assizes, and not one received the death penalty. This is an impressively low number. Compare this with the 1970s and 1980s, where sometimes nine homicides occurred in one year. Thus, in the 91 years from 1720 to 1810, 93 cases of homicide occurred, and therefore continues the mean average of about one homicide per year.

And there were only three executions for non-homicide offences, as well. Why this number is so low in comparison to the decades before and after, can only be conjecture.

Of the Assize judges who visited Northampton during the decade, only two stand out as having more than the standard judges' background - of public school - Oxbridge - practising barrister - knighthood - judge. Both James Mansfield and Edward Law had careers in which they seemed to give far more to the society of their time, than did the majority of their colleagues.

1801

(87)

1801A Date and place unknown

Victim Unknown

Accused A man called Nutt

***Trial* 1801 Lent Assizes, Monday 2 March. *Either* Mr Chief Baron Macdonald *or* Mr Baron Graham**

All we know of this, is that a man of the surname of Nutt was found guilty of manslaughter. No other details are known.

✥✥ *Sir Robert Graham was a Barrister of the Inner Temple, and in 1793 had been made a KC when becoming Attorney-General to the Prince of Wales, the Prince Regent. He became a Baron of the Exchequer in 1799, and was knighted in 1800. He died, aged 92, in 1836.*

(E53) **FRIDAY 31 JULY 1801**

HANGED FOR HORSE THEFT

William Walters, alias Waters, alias Blueskin

HANGED FOR SHEEP THEFT

William Higgerson

The Summer Assizes of 1801 were a riotous affair. Starting on Tuesday 14 July, Mister Justice Heath and Mr Justice Rooke, were faced with 26 separate criminal cases, producing 35 prisoners, as well as all the civil cases. Included in that lot, were two cases of sodomy (which until 1967 was a criminal offence in this country), and one case of rape. Also on the Calendar were these two.

William Walters, alias Waters, alias Blueskin, was charged with stealing a bay gelding, the property of John Wright of Northampton. William Higgerson, who had been arrested in Buckinghamshire and kept in Aylesbury Gaol until wanted at Northampton, was charged with stealing eleven sheep out of Hartwell Field, the property of Thomas Barker of Roade.

As is usual, no court report was given in the *Mercury*, all we have is the report of the double hanging. The *Northampton Mercury* of Saturday 1 August, however, now spells Higgerson as Higgason, which has been kept to preserve authenticity.

We can also reflect on the nickname of 'Blueskin' for William Walters. Could he have been of mixed race parentage, which would have given an unusual skin tone? Only conjecture.

> 'They were taken in a mourning coach to the place of execution where their behaviour was such as became persons in their unhappy situation, and they were launched into eternity amid a large concourse of spectators. Higgason *(sic)* left in his cell a written paper (which he desired might be published) in which he acknowledged his own guilt but solemnly protested that John Webb who was suspected of having been concerned with him in this and similar offences, was perfectly innocent of the same.
>
> Walters did not make any particular confession but acknowledged that he had been guilty of many offences against the laws of his country. Walters was a native of Staffordshire and Higgason of Hanslope, Buckinghamshire.'

❖❖ *Giles Rooke was educated at Harrow, and Saint John's College, Oxford. Being made a barrister by Lincoln's Inn in 1766 aged 23, he became a Fellow of Merton College, Oxford for nineteen years. He was knighted and made a Judge of the Common Pleas in 1793. He had visited Northampton twice before, in 1795 and 1800, but had no homicides to deal with. He would attend three more Northamptonshire Assizes before dying in 1808.*

1802

(88)

1802A Date unknown. Ringstead
Victim Matthew Teat
Accused William Roberts
Trial **1802 Lent Assizes, Tuesday 2 March. *Either* Mr Chief Baron Macdonald *or* Mr Baron Graham**

William Roberts was found guilty of criminal homicide and fined 1s with two months imprisonment. It is unknown why such a seemingly insufficient sentence was given for an incident in which, when all said and done, a man had lost his life. However, we are not in possession of all the facts, which the judge was.

It is rather gratuitous to add, that with the surname of Roberts and coming from Ringstead, William Roberts is of the same family as Margaret, Lady Thatcher (née Roberts), who was a memorable Prime Minister of this country, and whose father, Alfred Roberts, was born in Ringstead. The author feels sympathy, two of his relatives having been convicted of homicide in 1860 and 1886 (but wait for Volume 2 to learn about them).

(89)

1802B Date unknown. Middleton Cheney
Victim James Nevill
Accused John Holmer
Trial **1802 Lent Assizes, Tuesday 2 March. *Either* Lord Chief Baron Macdonald *or* Mr Baron Graham**

John Holmer was found guilty of criminal homicide and received one month imprisonment.

(90)

1802C Date unknown. Chalcombe
Victim Jonathan Muddling
Accused George Archer
Trial **1802 Summer Assizes, Tuesday 27 July. *Either* Mr Justice Heath *or* Mr Baron Thomson**

George Archer was found guilty of criminal homicide. He was fined 1s and discharged. As with cases 1802A and 1803A, it is not known why such a lenient sentence was given. The *Northampton Mercury* supplies no explanation, and we must therefore be left to conjecture.

1803

(91)

1803A Date unknown. Towcester

Victim Thomas Wilcox, junior

Accused William Smith

Trial **1803 Summer Assizes, Tuesday 19 July. *Either* Mr Justice Grose *or* Mr Justice Rooke**

William Smith was found guilty, and was fined 1s and three months imprisonment.

1804

There were no criminal homicide cases in 1804

1805

(92)

1805A Date unknown. Boddington

Victim Mary Haynes

Accused William Haynes

Trial **1805 Summer Assizes, Saturday 22 July. *Either* Mr Baron Thomson *or* Mr Justice Rooke**

William Haynes was found not guilty of the murder of his wife. Again, no information is forthcoming from any source.

1806

(93)

1806A Date unknown. Preston Deanery

Victim Unnamed baby boy

Accused Ann Coe

Trial **1806 Lent Assizes, Monday 3 March.** ***Either*** **Mr Chief Justice Mansfield** ***or*** **Mr Baron Graham**

Ann Coe was found not guilty of criminal homicide (of her illegitimate baby son?) and acquitted.

❖❖ *Not to be confused with William Murray, 1st Earl of Mansfield (see case 1763C), James Mansfield, before being knighted and becoming the Chief Justice in 1804, certainly knew how to mix with the, what shall we say, the 'live-wires' of English society. After Cambridge, he was admitted to the bar by the Middle Temple in 1758, and eventually became legal advisor to John Wilkes and the 'Duchess of Kingston'.*

You can guess the inclinations of John Wilkes, when you learn that he was a member of Sir Francis Dashwood's 'Hell Fire Club'. Wilkes' many digressions started with him libelling King George III - being outlawed and expelled from the House of Commons - publishing obscene literature - being exiled to Paris - returning to be locked up in prison - being released and elected an MP again, before being expelled from the Commons yet again for libel - being re-elected to Parliament three more times, but having elections annulled each time before finally getting back in on the fourth attempt. And yet after all that, he actually became Lord Mayor of London in 1774.

Elizabeth Chudleigh, who called herself the 'Duchess of Kingston', was never free from scandal throughout her life either, mainly brought on by her sexual pecadillos. Elizabeth Chudleigh in her time was the mistress to many of the ruling aristocracy, and even at one time to the king himself, George II. Many marriages and divorces followed until she settled for the Duke of Kingston in March 1773, which no doubt hastened his death the following September, leaving Elizabeth the beneficiary of all his property.

But she then had to face yet another onslaught, this time from the Duke's brother, who accused her of bigamy, of which she was found guilty by the House of Lords. Discreetly exiling herself to France, she endeavoured to have one of her previous marriages declared valid. She succeeded, and so the became the Countess of Bristol. Yet despite all that, Elizabeth actually managed to be received by the Pope when visiting Rome; and by Catherine the Great when visiting Russia.

So it was with all that behind him, that Mansfield CJ made his first visit to Northampton for the 1806 Lent Assizes. What he thought of Northampton is not recorded, but he only came to Northampton once more, for the 1809 Lent Assizes.

(94)

1806B Date unknown. Northampton

Victim An unnamed baby girl

Accused Robert Adams

***Trial* 1806 Summer Assizes, Monday 21 July. *Either* Lord Chief Justice Ellenborough *or* Mr Justice Rooke**

Robert Adams was found not guilty and acquitted

✤✤ *With a surname like his, Edward Law (Lord Ellenborough) was obviously going to be a barrister. Having the usual social background, Edward Law was educated at Charterhouse School and Peterhouse College, Cambridge before being admitted to the bar by Lincoln's Inn in 1780. Just seven years later he was retained by Warren Hastings as his defence counsel.*

Warren Hastings had been Governor of Bengal since 1772, where another member of the governing council was one Philip Francis. Hastings and Francis never saw eye-to-eye, and for the next eight years a constant 'battle' was fought between the two. Accusations of corruption, 'bending' the law, illegal executions of corrupt officials, coupled with immense financial chicanery, were made on both sides, eventually culminating with Hastings wounding Francis in a duel.

Although hanging on to the governorship for four more years, Hastings was finally recalled back to London to face impeachment charges for all the mayhem that had been going on. Lasting an incredible seven years, Hastings' trial began in February 1788, with Edward Law opening for the defence. Eventually Hastings was found not guilty of all charges, but the trial financially ruined him, costing him £80,000, which in today's prices would be £4,000,000.

Edward Law must really have impressed in the right circles, however, because he then became what we would now call a 'high-flyer'. Engaged as Counsel for the Crown in several important state trials, he eventually became Attorney-General in 1801. The following year he was elected to Parliament as the MP for Newtown, on the Isle of Wight, and was knighted; and in 1803, he was ennobled as the 1st Lord Ellenborough, made a Privy Councillor, and became the Lord Chief Justice of England.

By 1805, he was Speaker of the House of Lords, and so, as befitted his obvious talents, in 1806 he was admitted to the so-called 'Ministry of All the Talents'. Following fears of a Napoleonic invasion, William Pitt the Younger had taken over as Prime Minister from the ineffective Henry Addington in May 1804. But Pitt had died suddenly in January 1806 at the age of 46, still with Napoleon posing a threat despite his defeat at Trafalgar.

Reluctantly agreeing to be Prime Minister, Lord Grenville formed a kind of coalition government nicknamed the 'Ministry of All the Talents'. Lord Ellenborough was asked to serve, which he did, in the capacity of what we would now call a Minister without Portfolio.

Lasting just thirteen months, the 'Ministry of All the Talents' fell because of King George III's refusal to accept Catholic emancipation. Yet for all Grenville's shortcomings, he and his Ministry passed what is perhaps one of the greatest pieces of British legislation ever, the Abolition of Slavery Act in 1807.

So it was, whilst still a member of the 'Ministry of all the Talents', that Lord Ellenborough presided over these 1806 Northamptonshire Summer Assizes, his first visit to the county. Five more years would pass before he would visit Northampton again, for the 1811 Lent Assizes. Edward Law, 1st Lord Ellenborough, died in 1818 at the age of 68.

1807

There were no criminal homicides in 1807

❃

(E54) **FRIDAY 20 MARCH 1807**

HANGED FOR ATTEMPTED MURDER

Robert Stafford

The case of Robert Stafford is an all too familiar one. The 'Eternal Triangle' happened then, and unfortunately, it happens now. At the 1807 Lent Assizes, before Chief Justice Mansfield, Robert Stafford was charged with mixing poison in a quantity of tea and flour with intent to murder his wife. And everything drops into place when we find that also appearing, was Hannah Seaton, charged with aiding and abetting Robert Stafford.

Again, no details are forthcoming in the *Mercury*, all it says is that 'Robert Stafford for feloniously and maliciously

> administering poison with intent to murder his wife, was found guilty after a trial which lasted eight hours, was capitally convicted and is left for execution. Hannah Seaton was delivered by proclamation.'

So Hannah Seaton got away with it - at least in the eyes of the law - as 'delivered by proclamation' means that the Grand Jury examined the evidence against her, found it wanting ('No True Bill'), and did not allow her case to go before the court. But was she left with something more tangible? Consider the report of the hanging in the *Northampton Mercury* of Saturday 21 March :

> 'Robert Stafford who was convicted at out last assizes of administering poison to his wife in flour, tea etc with intent to murder her, was executed here yesterday pursuant to his sentence. He appeared to be about 26 years of age, was born in the parish of Yelvertoft where he followed the occupation of a labourer, and had two or three children by his wife, with whom he lived in good harmony, but unfortunately getting acquainted with a young woman who lived in the same place and who it appears is now pregnant by him; he formed the horrid resolution in poisoning his wife that he might the more readily carry on his criminal intercourse with the object of

> his misguided passion. The means he employed for this purpose were, by mixing arsenic in the flour which he knew his wife intended to make into bread, also in the tea etc by which means the lives of several other persons were likewise greatly endangered; but providentially none of them have died; though the poor woman who was the immediate object of his guilt, remains still in a very distressed state - Since his trial, his behaviour has been penitent, and such as became a person in his unhappy situation. At the place of execution he acknowledged the justness of his sentence and exhorted the spectators to take warning by his fate, and to avoid sabbath breaking, vicious habits and vicious connexions which had been the means of bringing him to an inglorious end. A very large concourse of spectators attended the execution.'

So was Hannah Seaton the object of Robert Stafford's 'misguided passion'? If it was indeed Hannah Seaton, then having to bring up Robert Stafford's child would be a far more burdensome, lifelong, reminder than any gaol sentence would have been.

1808

No criminal homicides in 1808 either

1809

(95)

1809A Date unknown. Weedon Bec

Victim An unnamed baby girl

Accused Elizabeth Smith

Trial 1809 Lent Assizes, Monday 6 March. *Either* Mr Chief Justice Mansfield *or* Mr Justice Bayley

Elizabeth Smith was found not guilty of criminal homicide (of her illegitimate baby daughter?) and acquitted.

✤✤ *Sir John Bayley had only been a judge for a few months before coming to Northampton for the 1809 Lent Assizes, and he would only visit twice more, for the 1817 Summer Assizes, and 1832 Lent Assizes. He had been made a Judge of the King's Bench, but would transfer to the Exchequer Court in 1830. Educated at Eton, he was called to the bar by Gray's Inn. He would retire in 1834 with a Baronetcy, dying seven years later in 1841 aged 78. He was also an author of some note on legal and religious matters.*

1810

And no criminal homicides in 1810

1811-1820

The *Northampton Mercury* remains the most important source of information for this decade, as there are still not many Assize Calendars for this period preserved in the official papers at the county record office. However, by one of those curious quirks of fate beloved by historians, help comes in an entirely unforeseen way.

Preserved at the Northamptonshire County Record Office is the Memo Book of Thomas Horner of Broughton (NRO Reference ZB68/1). Pasting into his book anything that took his fancy, Thomas Horner, God bless him, not only preserved a complete set of Assize Calendars for the years 1818 to 1840, but also a complete set of the lurid, sensationalist posters of his day, advertising all the public executions for the same period. So again, we are still able to build up a complete list of the criminal homicides of the period, although exact detail is still a bit sparse.

Only twelve homicides occurred during this decade. However, two of them attracted the death penalty, as they were obviously pre-meditated, with one being particularly gruesome. But even so, 107 homicides in the 101 years since 1720, is still maintaining, near enough, the one homicide per year trend.

Eleven other judicial executions took place, but it was this decade which saw a drastic, and more humane, change in the actual mechanics of the death penalty. With the introduction of the 'New Drop' in 1819, gone were the days of the rabble following the tumbrells up to the Racecourse to see the accused take 30 minutes or so to be strangled. Instead we had instant death, on a permanent gallows in Angel Lane. For a description of all this, see the executions of Cobbet and Wilkin on Friday 27 March 1818.

1811

(96)

1811A Sometime during January or February 1811. Harpole
Victim Sarah Benn
Accused John Chater
Trial **1811 Lent Assizes, Saturday 2 March. Mr Baron Wood**

John Chater was found not guilt and acquitted. That is all we know about this incident.

✣✣ *Sir George Wood had been a Baron of the Exchequer for four years, and before that the MP for Haselmere for ten years. Only having visited Northampton once before, for the 1808 Lent Assizes (where there were no criminal homicides on the Calendar), these 1811 Lent Assizes would be his last visit to Northampton.*

(97)

1811B Wednesday 18 December 1811. Weedon Barracks
Victim Samuel Lees, Drummer, 2nd Battalion, 48th Regiment
Accused William Jones, Sergeant, 2nd Battalion 48th Regiment

The Peninsular War had been a long one, with every regiment of the British Army taking part. On Thursday 16 May 1811, the 1st and 2nd battalions of the 48th Regiment of the line (later to become the Northamptonshire Regiment) had taken part in the dreadful carnage that history knows as the Battle of Albuhera. So severe were the casualties, that out of a total strength for the two battalions of 62 officers and 887 men, only 23 officers and 303 men survived. As a result, the remnants of the 2nd Battalion were merged with the 1st, and stopped in Spain, but the cadre, including Samuel Lees and William Jones, returned to the depot at Weedon Barracks, arriving in August 1811.

Not surprisingly, after having gone through an experience like that, nerves were still on a raw edge, even several months later. On the night of Wednesday 18 December 1811, therefore, a fight developed between Lees and Jones, but which was calmed down by their colleagues.

However, the fight flared up again in the barrack yard just before midnight, neither man gaining much advantage. Lees went back to his room, but Jones went to fetch the Sergeant of the Guard.

With Jones following, the Sergeant went to Lees' room, and knocked on the door. Immediately the door was opened by Lees, and before any word could be spoken, Jones, who had been standing behind the Sergeant, brushed him aside, and lunged at Lees with a clasp knife. The wound was three inches deep into Lees' left side. Lees collapsed immediately, bleeding profusely. He never recovered, and died at eleven o'clock the next morning.

Trial **1812 Lent Assizes, Saturday 29 February. Lord Chief Justice Ellenborough.**

Jones' guilt was obviously never in doubt, and he was found guilty before the Lord Chief Justice of England himself.

William Jones was hanged on Northampton Racecourse on Monday 9 March 1812.

1812

No criminal homicides occurred in this year

1813

(98)

1813A Sometime during January or February 1812. Brington

Victim Mary Jollings

Accused Thomas Cooch, junior

Trial **1813 Lent Assizes, Monday 1 March. *Either* Lord Chief Justice Ellenborough *or* Mr Justice Gibbs**

Thomas Cooch was found not guilty and acquitted. Again, we have no notion of the story behind this.

✣✣ *Nicknamed 'Vinegar' Gibbs because of his sour disposition, Vicary Gibbs' life story is as interesting as his judicial colleague at these 1813 Lent Assizes. Admitted to the bar by Lincoln's Inn in 1783, Vicary Gibbs made such an impression, that he was chosen to assist Thomas Erskine, acting for the Defence, in one of the sensational cases of the time. Thomas Hardy (not the novelist) and Horne Tooke were arraigned on charges of treason in 1794. The reasons are long and complicated, but Horne Tooke is the most interesting character of the two.*

Belligerent by nature (he had lost one eye in a fight with a schoolfellow), Tooke was in Holy Orders but was obviously unsuited to it, and he never wore clerical garb, and had been deprived of his livings; he also tried to be admitted to the bar, but was refused. On one occasion, before he was a Member of Parliament, he made a violent (verbal) attack upon the Speaker of the House, Sir Fletcher Norton (himself no shrinking violet, he would later be voted out of his office after a 'punch-up' with Lord North actually inside the House of Commons itself). For this, he was summoned to appear before the Commons, but managed to sweet talk himself out of any punishment.

Having contested, and lost, the Parliamentary seat of Westminster in 1790, against Charles James Fox, Tooke, published scurrilous and libellous books about Fox. This, together with a lot of other shenanigans, was too much for the 'Establishment' of the time, hence the charges of treason. For the Defence, Vicary Gibbs, assisting Thomas Erskine, was so good, that Tooke and Hardy were acquitted, bringing forth compliments from the Attorney-General, Sir John Scott, about Gibbs' ability.

After three stints in Parliament, he was knighted in 1805, becoming Attorney-General two years later. Gibbs was made a Judge of Common Pleas in 1812, so these 1813 Northamptonshire Lent Assizes were probably amongst the first he had attended. The following year he was appointed Chief Baron, and a year after that, was made Chief Justice of the Common Pleas. He would die in 1820 aged 69.

❀

(E55) FRIDAY 13 AUGUST 1813

HANGED FOR THEFT OF THE ROYAL MAIL

Huffham White
Robert Kendall

Thefts were normally tried only at Quarter Sessions or Petty Sessions. The court records are full of them, and they are generally run-of-the-mill. Occasionally however, one turns up which lifts it above the ordinary. One such is the theft from the Leeds to London Mail Coach in October 1812. And note that this is a theft, and not a robbery, as was described in the contemporary Reward Notices. Robbery is where a theft takes place accompanied by violence or the threat of it. As no person was threatened or violated, the offence was theft and not robbery.

In the early hours of Monday 26 October 1812, the mail coach from Leeds to London set off from Kettering after its mail stop there. Sixteen mail bags, together with the local mail bags (called By-Bags) were locked into the mail box at the rear of the coach.

Off the coach set, resuming its journey towards London, driving southward along the road to Burton Latimer (that is, the present day A6), with the guard sitting on top of the mail box. But between Burton Latimer and Finedon, the guard clambered over the top of the coach and went to sit and talk with the driver at the front, thus leaving the mail box unguarded at the rear. Just before Higham Ferrers, the guard resumed his proper place.

But when the coach stopped at Higham Ferrers, at the coaching stop of the *Green Dragon*, the mail box was found to have been forced open and all the mail bags stolen. Because there was no local police force to contact, (the Northamptonshire County Constabulary did not appear until 1840), the coach continued to London where the matter was reported at the General Post Office. How seriously this matter was taken, is indicated by the GPO's reaction.

Immediately, several Bow Street Runners were commissioned to investigate (no Metropolitan Police then - not until 1829). And it was a Bow Street Runner by the name of Lavendar, who was eventually to clear up the crime.

Lavendar knew his stuff, and after a few enquires, suspicion soon fell upon two local toe-rags, Huffham White and Robert Kendall. Kendall was quickly arrested at his home in Wellingborough by Lavendar, but White and his mistress Mary Howes had legged it to London. Offering the staggering amount of £200 *(£6,800 in today's prices)* as a reward for information, ensured that White and Howe were at liberty for only two weeks before eventually they too were arrested.

From the evidence given at the trial, we can piece together what happened. It appears that White, using the alias of Wallis, was staying with Mary Howes at the Keystone Tollgate House which Howes kept. Late on Sunday 25 October, Kendall collected White from Keyston in a horse and cart, and had driven through Thrapston to Finedon, where the London Road crosses the Thrapston to Wellingborough Road.

The theft was committed at the Finedon Cross Roads. The guard by then was sitting at the front of the coach, leaving the mail box unguarded, which would have been easy to break into and steal from, as the coach slowed to a crawling pace as it climbed up the long steep hill (now Irthlingborough Road, Finedon) on the way towards Higham Ferrers.

The small By-Bags of local only mail were discarded on the road near to the Finedon Obelisk, but the main mail bags were spirited away by White and Kendall to Wellingborough where Kendal lived. The next day, White returned to Howes and they ran away to London to see if they could 'fence off' any of their stolen booty of negotiable bonds and bills of exchange.

White, Kendall and Howes all appeared at the Northamptonshire 1813 Summer Assizes before the old campaigner Mr Baron 'Staymaker' Thomson. No less than 40 witnesses appeared against White, Kendall and Howes.

Howes was acquitted on a technicality, but White and Kendall were found guilty. They were both hanged on Northampton Racecourse on Friday 13 August 1813, in front of a large crowd.

1814

(99)

1814A Wednesday 6 April 1814. Aston-le-Walls

Victim Rachel Morris

Accused Thomas Morris

The body of Rachel Morris was found with truly horrific injuries, inflicted with a spade, which had been left embedded in her skull. One ear had been chopped off, one eye had been gouged out and her skull had been shattered into pieces by repeated blows with the spade.

Trial **1814 Summer Assizes, Monday 17 July. *Either* Mr Justice Chambré *or* Mr Baron Graham**

The murderer was never in doubt. Thomas Morris stood trial for the gruesome murder of his wife Rachel. No motive was ever reported for this crime, and we are left wondering at the emotions and sentiments which lay behind such a ferocious assault. The *Northampton Mercury* reported that Thomas

> 'solemnly declared that he had murdered his wife from a premeditated resolution; having deliberately gone down stairs to fetch up the spade with which he committed the horrid act.'

Thomas Morris was hanged on Northampton Racecourse on Saturday 23 July 1814, saying that 'Sabbath breaking with drunkenness had brought him to his downfall'.

✣✣ *Again, an otherwise indistinctive career; Alan Chambré was a barrister of Gray's Inn; Recorder of Lancaster in 1796; and was not made a Baron of the Exchequer until he was 60 in 1799. One year later, however, he was transferred to the Common Pleas, and as such visited Northampton for the 1800 Lent Assizes, although no criminal homicides were on the Calendar. These 1814 Summer Assizes would thus be only the second time he had visited Northampton, and he would never do so again, as he retired in 1815, and died in 1823 aged 84.*

1815

(100)

1815A An unknown date in 1815. Flore

Victim An unnamed female child

Accused Elizabeth Wadsworth

Trial **1815 Summer Assizes, Tuesday 11 July. *Either* Mr Justice Heath *or* Mr Baron Graham**

Elizabeth Wadsworth was found not guilty of the murder of her newly born baby girl, but guilty to concealing its birth. She received one year imprisonment.

❀

(E56)

FRIDAY 28 JULY 1815

HANGED FOR SHEEP THEFT

Thomas Bayson

Also at the 1815 Summer Assizes appeared Thomas Bayson. He was charged with stealing nine sheep, the property of John Mawle of Duston. No detail whatsoever is in the *Northampton Mercury*, all we have is a description of the execution.

> 'From the time of his condemnation, he appeared to be greatly affected by his situation and condition himself, as if desirous to make his peace with God - Till yesterday morning, however, he uniformly denied having committed any other but for the crime for which he was to suffer, which previously to receiving the sacrament, he confessed that some years ago he stole at different times 19 guineas from the box of a person who lived in his home, and 11 sheep from Mr C. Hillyard at Milton in 1810 when in service as a shepherd. He confessed the justness of his sentence and exhorted the spectators who were very numerous to take warning of his example.'

1816

(101)

1816A A place and date unknown
Victim John Grant
Accused William Grant
Trial **1816 Lent Assizes, Saturday 2 March. *Either* Mr Justice Gibbs *or* Mr Baron Richards.**

William Grant was acquitted of the criminal homicide of John Grant. What relationship John was to William is unknown, the *Northampton Mercury* not thinking it important enough to tell us, nor any other details, come to that.

✣✣ *Richard Richards, after the standard Oxbridge background, had been made a Baron of the Exchequer only two years previously, and in the following year, 1817, would be promoted to Chief Baron. He would only visit Northampton once more, for the 1820 Summer Assizes, when he was 68, and would die just three years later.*

1817

(102)

1817A Believed to be Friday 31 January 1817. Dallington
Victim Jane Hadley
Accused William Morris
Trial **1817 Lent Assizes, Saturday 1 March. *Either* Mr Justice Gibbs *or* Mr Baron Richards**

William Morris was found not guilty of the criminal homicide of Jane Hadley, and that is all the detail we know. Note, however, that, if the date is true, then only the 28 days of February lay between the crime and the trial. This was in 1817, 23 years before the establishment of the Northamptonshire County Constabulary (Dallington was not in Northampton Borough then), so the old police system of parish constables seems to have still been functioning efficiently.

(103)
1817B Date and place unknown
Victim An unnamed female child
Accused Edward Daniell
***Trial* 1817 Summer Assizes, Tuesday 15 July. *Either* Mr Justice Bayley *or* Mr Justice Holroyd**

No details whatsoever of this case are known, nor why a man (the father?) should be indicted rather than the mother.

✣✣ *Sir George Holroyd had been a judge for just one year. His only claim to any sort of historical importance was that he was the counsel for Sir Francis Burdett MP, who, in 1810, had spoken out loudly against the corruption in Parliament. This, not unnaturally, upset the Speaker of the House, Charles Abbot (later Lord Colchester), and the resulting court case saw Burdett being sent down to prison, despite George Holroyd's best efforts. This scandal caused quite a stir at the time, although it did not hold George Holroyd back, because he was made a judge in 1816. He would retire in 1828, and die in 1831 aged 73.*

1818

There were no criminal homicides in 1818

❀

(E57) **FRIDAY 27 MARCH 1818**

HANGED FOR FORGERY AND UTTERING

James Cobbett
George Wilkin

Because the *Northampton Mercury* did not print details of the court case, we have no idea how James Cobbett and George Wilkin were caught. They both appeared at the 1818 Lent Assizes on Saturday 28 February before either Mr Justice Gibbs or Mr Baron Garrow, charged with 'passing forged or counterfeit notes purporting to be of the Bank of England'.

As we don't know the evidence we cannot judge, but going purely on 'gut reaction' it seems there could well likely have been a miscarriage of justice in this instance. The only report we have is the report of the double hanging from the *Mercury* of Saturday 28 March :

> 'Yesterday were executed here...James Cobbett and George Wilkin for uttering forged notes, purporting to be notes of the Bank of England. At the place of execution they behaved in a manner becoming their unhappy situation. They persevered, however, in denying to the very last, having any knowledge of the notes being forged, stating that they had taken them in payment for a horse at Redbourn Fair of Mr Wenman a dealer in London. The concourse assembled to witness the awful scene was far more numerous than might have been expected, from its being generally known that interest was being used to obtain a commutation of their sentence.'

Now, admittedly we haven't all the evidence before us which the jury had, but doesn't that story ring true? If they had received the notes innocently in a former transaction, and had no idea that the notes were forged, in all probability they would have passed them over during a subsequent transaction, again in perfect innocence. And it was sheer bad luck that the recipient of the notes probably suspected they were forged, and called in the authorities.

It was probably the general feeling that a miscarriage of justice was about to happen, that caused 'the concourse assembled' to be 'far more numerous than might have been expected'. And once it was realised that no pardon was forthcoming and that the sentence was to be carried out, that may have caused the crowd to foment and seethe in anger, requiring just one spark to erupt into violent rioting. Fortunately rioting was avoided, but it was a near-run thing.

❁

It was the crowd's brinkmanship at the Cobbet and Wilkin hanging that finally caused the authorities to have a radical re-think. The drive of the cart containing the condemned, from the gaol in the town centre, up Abington Street and then up the Kettering road to The Racecourse, had been accompanied by the usual rabble of local drunks and toe-rags bawling and yawping, and kicking up the customary racket. This, coupled with the mood of the crowd at the scene, posed the threat that this rumpus could turn to full-out rioting - and the authorities knew that if rioting did *occur, then they had no means to deal with it. There was no Northampton Borough Police - this was not to be formed for another seventeen years - and so the only means of dealing with riots was to call out the militia, which took several hours to get mobilised.*

The result was the 'New Drop'. At a stroke, this solved two problems. The 'New Drop' was a permanent gallows set up at the rear of the County Gaol, in Angel Lane. And because it was a permanent structure, there was no drive from the town centre to The Racecourse, although the execution would still be visible to the crowds gathered in Cow Meadow, which is roughly on the site of the present day Victoria Promenade. Also, it was a more humanitarian arrangement.

Previously, the condemned person stood on the back of a cart under temporary gallows, with the noose around the neck. The cart would then be driven away, and the condemned would thus be set swinging. Death, therefore, came from strangulation rather than a broken neck, and the condemned would be writhing in agony for upwards of twenty or thirty minutes. But with the introduction of the 'New Drop' in 1819, where the condemned stood on a platform which suddenly opened, death came instantly from a broken neck.

It was said that the 'New Drop' was so big that it could 'hang 20 at once, quite comfortably'. Only a quarter of this capacity was needed, however, for its first outing.

❁

1819

(104)

1819A Date unknown. Wellingborough

Victim Isaac Brunt

Accused William Elson (aged 18)

Trial **1819 Lent Assizes, Saturday 27 February. Mr Justice Burrough**

William Elson received ten months imprisonment for the criminal homicide of Isaac Brunt by stabbing. No other details are known.

✣✣ *James Burrough was 69 when he attended these 1819 Assizes, having been a judge for three years. Not much more can be said, except that he retired in 1829 aged 79, and died ten years later. This was his only visit to Northampton.*

❁

(E58) **FRIDAY 19 MARCH 1819**

HANGED FOR BURGLARY

William George
William Minards
Benjamin Panther
Edward Porter
John Taffs

And it was these five who had the honour of doing the test run on the 'New Drop' in Angel Lane. They were all hung together, and the novelty of the occasion bought out one of the largest crowds ever recorded.

The *Northampton Mercury*:

> 'At the place of execution there behaviour was very suitable to persons in their unhappy situation. Soon after twelve o'clock they were launched into eternity, and after hanging the usual time, their bodies were taken down and

> those of Minards, Panther and Taffs were delivered to their friends for internment, and those of George and Porter were buried in St Giles churchyard - A very large concourse of persons (many of whom having travelled a considerable distance) assembled to witness the awful scene.'

William George (21) from Renhold in Bedfordshire and William Minards (27) a miller from Wootton were old mates, and also professional criminals. But successful they weren't.

After having been arrested for burglaries and robberies, they were confined to Northamptonshire County Gaol to await trial. And whilst there, they obviously formed an association with Panther and Taffs who were also awaiting trial, having been arrested for theft at Rothwell.

They all appeared at the Summer Assizes of July 1818, before Mr Justice Dallas. George and Minards were both found guilty and sentenced to death. But their sentences were commuted to transportation, and so they were returned to gaol to await shipment. Panther and Taffs however, were found not guilty because of lack of evidence, and were released.

So Panther and Taffs were now on the outside, and George and Minards were on the inside, which is not what they wanted, they wanted everybody to be on the outside. So, bringing along one of their mates, Edward Porter, on Friday 24 July 1818, Panther and Taffs sprung George and Minards from prison by forcing open their cell window, which ironically enough, overlooked Angel Lane.

Being an escaped band of desperados, it was only a matter of time before they resorted to crime. Just six days later, on Thursday 30 July, all five burgled the house of Mr William Marriott at Preston Deanery. But all were captured, and appeared before Mr Justice Burrough at the Lent Assizes of 1819. And the rest, they say, is history.

❀

(E59) **FRIDAY 6 AUGUST 1819**

HANGED FOR ARSON

Richard Lilleyman

By the early nineteenth century, the circulation of lurid broadsheets describing the latest scandal of the day was commonplace. But in Northamptonshire, although there were one or two before, the main series of broadsheets seems to have started with the advent of the 'New Drop' in 1819. This series of broadsheets was obviously the enterprise of one printer, because the same stock woodcut was used for all of them, as well as the same typographical layout.

Appearing at the 1819 Summer Assizes before Mr Chief Baron Richards, Lilleyman was sentenced to death. And from the broadsheet concerning his hanging we get this :

> 'Lilleyman was only 21 years of age. He was a native of the town of Northampton...and had been apprenticed to a shoemaker in Holcot...From his own confession, it appeared that he had for some time formed acquaintances with companions of idle and dissolute lives...He said that he commenced his career of thieving, by stealing a game cock, the property of R. H. Gurney Esq. at Brixworth; that he afterwards stole fowls at two separate times from Mrs Coles of Wellingborough; and also a whole cheese, and part of another, from the shop of Mr Stanton of the same place, which he induced another person to sell for him, and who gave him 2s 6d as his share of the booty.
>
> He likewise, for a supposed injury, did considerable damage to the garden of Mr Samuel Howes of Holcot; and in company with three others (a young man and two young women), robbed the orchard of Mr Cook, at the Chequers in Holcot of a quantity of apples; and also stole some ash poles. or saplings, the property of Mr Drage of the same place.
>
> Lilleyman also, with two of his companions, drew pieces of straw, as to which of them should rob the house of Mr Hilson of Holcot, and the lot falling upon

> himself, he accordingly broke open the house, and stole therefrom a quantity of lace...
>
> With respect to the crime for which he suffered, he appeared to have been solely instigated by the evil counsel of others, as he declared to the clergyman, that he was actuated by no other motive, than that of obtaining a new suit of clothes, &c which were promised him if he effected the destruction of the ricks.'

And from the *Northampton Mercury* of Saturday 7 August 1819, this is what we see :

> 'Yesterday was executed on the new drop, at the bottom of the yard of the county gaol, pursuant to his sentence at our last assizes, Richard Lilleyman for setting fire to two hayricks at Holcot, the property of Mr John Dickins;...and at the place of execution very earnestly exhorted the multitude (which was considerable) to take warning by his unhappy fate. After spending a short time in prayer, he was launched into eternity.'

1820

(105)

1820A Date unknown. Clay Coton

Victim Jane Towers

Accused John Bree (19)
Elizabeth Ward (63)
John Mount (52)

***Trial* 1820 Lent Assizes, Saturday 26 February. Mr Chief Justice Dallas**

No details whatsoever are known of this. All three defendants were acquitted.

(106)

1820B Date and place unknown
Victim An unnamed child
Accused Sarah Timson (23)
***Trial* 1820 Lent Assizes, Saturday 26 February. Mr Chief Justice Dallas**

Sarah Timson was found not guilty of the concealment of birth of her newly born infant.

✣✣ *India was the 'Jewel in the Crown' of the British Empire, but to get it, a lot of 'wheeler-dealing' went on. Warren Hastings was the Governor-General of India from 1773 until 1788 when he was charged with corruption. The causes are too complicated to go into here, but like everything in this world, revolved around financial chicanery. His trial lasted an incredible seven years before he was finally acquitted on all charges in 1795. One of his counsel during this marathon (along with Ellenborough LCJ, see 1806B) was Robert Dallas, who after education at the University of Geneva, had been called to the Bar in 1782. Robert Dallas then went on to be MP for Saint Michael's, Cornwall 1802-1805, and Kirkcaldy 1805-1806. He was made a judge and knighted in 1813 before becoming Chief Justice of the Common Pleas in 1818. His last visit to Northampton would be for the 1823 Lent Assizes, although there were no homicides on the Calendar, and he would die in 1824 aged 68.*

(107)

1820C Date and place unknown
Victim William Ingman
Accused Robert Adams (30)
***Trial* 1820 Summer Assizes, Tuesday 11 July. *Either* Mr Chief Baron Richards *or* Mr Baron Garrow**

Robert Adams received six months imprisonment for the criminal homicide of William Ingman. No other details are known.

✣✣ *One of the 'characters' of eighteenth century British politics was Charles James Fox, and William Garrow was Fox's counsel when he was scrutinised by Parliament in 1784, in one of his many 'run-ins' with his arch rival William Pitt. Garrow had only been a barrister for a year, but had already made a reputation when he had prosecuted a man called Aikles in a far-from-cut-and-dried theft case. William Garrow was MP for Gatton 1805; MP for Callington in 1806; and MP for Eye in 1812. He was made a Baron of the Exchequer in 1817. He would retire in 1832 and die in 1840 aged 80.*

Incidentally, the 'hero' of the television series Garrow's Law : Tales from the Old Bailey, *which was first broadcast on BBC 1 Television in November 2009, is based on this William Garrow. However, scriptwriters and actors can make their characters do anything they want them to do - the truth never enters into it - so the television William Garrow is far more exciting and influential than the real life William Garrow ever was.*

1821-1830

The low yearly mean average of criminal homicides is continued, as this decade contains only ten. Thus in the first 30 years of the nineteenth century, there were only 31 homicides - an easily calculated mean average of just a tad over one per year. The trend since 1720 is sustained therefore, because in the 111 years from 1720 to 1830, the total of homicides is 117, giving us a mean average of 1·05 per year

The ten homicides in this decade only resulted in two hangings - both for being concerned with the same crime. But there were eight hangings for non-homicide offences, including the last man to be hung for sheep stealing; and three young men who received their 'comeuppance' for an extremely brutal and traumatising attack.

The last four years of this decade are also exceptional, because they contain not one murder or manslaughter. This was entirely unprecedented, and had not happened before - nor since for that matter.

Also, during this decade, the proprietors and editors of the *Northampton Mercury* finally woke up. It dawned on them that a local newspaper should contain local news, and not just regurgitated news about what was happening in London. And at the same time, they realised the fascination and power of voyeurism, particularly when coupled with a smug *schadenfreude*, so that by printing the gory details of the antics of their fellow human beings, especially when displayed in that most public of all places, the court of law, they would sell a larger amount of newspapers.

Thus from the 1824 Lent Assizes onwards, the *Mercury* contains full transcripts of more and more (but sadly not all) of the cases appearing at the Assizes, not only in the criminal court, but in the civil Nisi Prius court as well. So lengthy were some of these reports, that they were sometimes spread over two editions of the paper, even appearing on the front page, which had previously been reserved for adverts and notices. As a result, greater detail of many more cases can be gained.

1821

(108)

1821A Saturday 10 February 1821. Charwelton

Victim John Clarke

Accused Mary Clarke

Philip Haynes

For a more clear cut occurrence of the old eternal triangle, it is hard to beat the murder of John Clarke. John Clarke was a farmer employing several labourers at Charwelton near to Daventry. As such, that would make him comfortably well off, if not positively wealthy. This appears not to have been enough for his wife, Mary, however, and her eye fell upon a local village lad by the name of Philip Haynes.

For almost two years, Philip Haynes and Mary Clarke were, what is euphemistically called 'carrying on', and throughout that time were consistently plotting how to get rid of John Clarke, so that Mary Clarke would inherit the property and money. Mary Clarke was foolish enough to put her thoughts into writing, and at her later trial, sixteen letters were produced which showed that she would have been more than happy to see her husband dead; and in one letter actually urged Haynes to 'do him if you can'.

For Haynes to be able to read and write in that day and age, would put him intellectually above the farm labourer class, and makes his later mistakes much harder to understand. Given so much planning time at his disposal, it is astonishing, that come the time to do the deed, Philip Haynes made such a 'pig's ear' of it.

His plan was to lie in wait in the farm yard and then shoot John Clarke when he was alone. With this in mind, he armed himself with a shot gun and settled down on top of a large pile of barley straw that was inside a farm barn. He was then level with the eaves of the barn, and so could point his gun through a gap between gutter and roof and so cover a hayrick that was opposite, which he knew John Clarke would come to sooner or later.

Not knowing how long he would have to wait, he had been provided with sustenance in the form of bread and cheese and a bottle of drink by his scheming lover. All this he put into a canvas 'bag' which was actually a large pocket that he had cut from one of his old coats.

The date chosen was 10 February, a Saturday, the thought being that few, if any, of the farm hands would be working and that Clarke was sure to be alone when eventually he came to the hayrick. True enough, Clarke did go to cut hay, but it was not until late on that winter afternoon, although it was obviously still light enough to see. However, fate now takes a hand, because John Clarke was not alone, in fact, unbeknown to Haynes, two labourers came into the very barn in which he was hiding.

Cutting hay from the rick, Clarke presented a perfect target for Haynes. He fired. But Clarke was not killed outright. Instead the shot smashed into his left elbow, and shattered it completely.

Both the labourers, Anthony Marriott and Robert Smith rushed out into the yard. Being totally surprised at this unplanned and unexpected turn of events, Haynes panicked. What could he do? If he ran, he would be detected immediately. There was no other course of action, but to stop in the barley and wait his opportunity to escape. But that opportunity never came.

Robert Canning, a neighbour of the Clarkes arrived soon after. Realising that the attacker was still in the barn, he set a number of men to watch it all night, as it was by now fully dark, and a better search could be made in broad daylight.

The next day, Sunday, the barn was searched, and in a deep hole burrowed down into the barley straw, the shot gun and ammunition, as well as the bottle and the bag of food were found. But there was no sign of Haynes.

By this stage everyone knew who they were looking for anyway. Haynes had not appeared at his lodgings, and in any case, there was more than a fair bet, that his affair with Mary Clarke had been common tittle-tattle in the village for months.

The barn was watched again on Sunday night, and it was not until the next morning that Haynes was eventually found. He was trying to burrow deeper and deeper into the barley to escape detection.

Meanwhile, on the Saturday evening, Dr Robert Wildgoose of Daventry attended John Clarke who was then still alive. Because his left elbow was so damaged, Wildgoose amputated there and then in the bedroom, and obviously without anaesthetic of any kind. It is therefore not surprising that John Clarke must have suffered enormous post-operative shock. He never recovered and died at 4am on Thursday 15 February.

Before he died however, Clarke made a Dying Declaration before a local magistrate and actually asked that Haynes be brought before him when he knew that he had been captured.
'You bloody minded fellow' said Clarke to Haynes 'how could you do to me this unkind office?' Haynes' complete indifference impressed itself on all who witnessed the scene, as had also the same attitude shown by Mary Clarke.

***Trial* 1821 Lent Assizes, Saturday 3 March. Mr Justice Richardson**

Evidence against Haynes and Mary Clarke was overwhelming. Haynes was charged with murder and Mary Clarke as an accessory to murder before the fact. The jury only took a few minutes to find them both guilty.

Philip Haynes and Mary Clark were both hung together on the 'New Drop' on Thursday 8 March 1821. 'On the morning of the execution' reported the *Northampton Mercury*:

> 'the two children, a boy and a girl, visited their mother when she appeared to be considerably affected, though she had previously evinced but very little concern at the awfulness of her situation.-Haynes met his fate with great firmness, but neither he nor his partner in guilt, said anything at the place of execution.-After the bodies had hung the usual time, they were conveyed to our General Infirmary for dissection &c.-The concourse assembled to witness the appalling spectacle, was unusually great.'

Note the speed of all this - from the actual murder to the execution, it took two days less than one month.

✣✣ *This was the one and only time that Sir John Richardson came to Northampton. He had only been a Justice of the Common Pleas for three years, and would only be so for another three. Compelled by ill-health to live in Malta, nevertheless he would survive until 1841, when he would die aged 70.*

(109)

1821B Date unknown. Islip

Victim An unnamed male child

Accused Sarah Allen (18)

Trial **1821 Summer Assizes, Tuesday 31 July.** ***Either*** **Mr Baron Richards** ***or*** **Mr Justice Park**

Sarah Allen was charged with :

> 'concealing her pregnancy, having born a living male bastard child in a privvy in Islip, with intent to conceal its birth, which child was found dead in the said privvy.'

No date was given, but Sarah Allen walked free, having been found not guilty.

✣✣ *Not to be confused with Sir James Parke (with an 'e' - see 1849), Sir James Alan Park was 53 when he had been made a Justice of the Common Pleas in 1816. In an otherwise unremarkable career, he had been a barrister of Lincoln's Inn; and the Recorder of Durham in 1802. He would continue to visit Northampton spasmodically until his death in 1838 aged 75.*

(E60) **FRIDAY 23 MARCH 1821**

HANGED FOR RAPE

James King

Just two weeks after the double hanging of Philip Haynes and Mary Clark, James King became the next offender to be introduced to the 'New Drop'. He was found guilty, before Mr Justice Richardson at the 1821 Lent Assizes, of the rape of Ann Clifton in a field at Yardley Hastings.

Fifteen year old Ann Clifton, came from Lavendon, in Buckinghamshire, which is just a few miles south east of Yardley Hastings on the road towards Bedford. Having obtained employment as a servant, she was walking from Lavendon to Yardley Hastings where her new work was to be.

But because it was late in the evening, and she had obviously lost her way, she somehow fell in with 30 year old James King who was himself walking to Yardley, where he lived with his wife and two children. King offered to show her the way to her new house.

Scarce had they gone half a mile, however, when King dragged Ann into a field, and subjected her to the most brutal of attacks. The *Mercury* declined to print any details, only saying the attack 'had left her in a state not easily to be described'.

At his trial, it emerged that King, as they say, 'had previous' :

> 'Nor is this his first offence' thundered the Broadsheet rushed out by the printers after the execution, 'having some time since been under the necessity of leaving his home and family, and enlisting for a soldier, in consequence of his having committed, or attempted, a crime of a similar nature.'

The *Northampton Mercury* of Saturday 24 March 1821 :

> 'Yesterday pursuant to his sentence, James King, for a rape, underwent the awful sentence of the law, at the New Drop at the back of the county gaol, in this town. The culprit expressed great sorrow for the crime he had committed, and repeatedly acknowledged the justness of his sentence.- From his very orderly deportment in prison since his condemnation, and his behaviour at the place of execution, there is reason to believe he died truly penitent.'

1822

(110)

1822A Date unknown. Stowe Nine Churches

Victim John Townsend

Accused William Hawkins (22)

***Trial* 1822 Lent Assizes, Saturday 2 March. *Either* Mr Chief Justice Dallas *or* Mr Justice Best**

All we know about this, is that William Hawkins was found guilty of wilful murder and was transported for seven years. No other details are known.

(111)

1822B Date unknown. Wilby
Victim An unnamed child
Accused Abigail Cotterell (30)
***Trial* 1822 Lent Assizes, Saturday 2 March. *Either* Mr Chief Justice Dallas *or* Mr Justice Best**

Absolutely no details are known of this, except that Abigail was 'delivered by proclamation' In other words, she was found not guilty.

✣✣ *The 1822 Lent Assizes, were the first time that Northamptonshire was blessed with Mr Justice Best, and he would visit periodically for the next six years. William Draper Best had the usual privileged background of the professional talker of those days. After Wadham College, Oxford and being called to the Bar by the Middle Temple, he became the MP for Petersfield in 1802 at the age of 35. He then became the MP for Bridport in 1812; Solicitor-General in 1813, and Attorney-General in 1816. He was made a Justice of the King's Bench in 1818, before being promoted to Chief Justice of the Common Pleas in 1824. Elevated to the peerage as Lord Wynford in 1829, he became the Deputy Speaker of the House of Lords. He would die in 1845 aged 78.*

(112)

1822C Date unknown. Northampton
Victim Thomas Walker
Accused John Craddock (22)
Samuel Wilson (19)
William Jones (22)
Alderman Warren (21)
***Trial* 1822 Summer Assizes, Monday 15 July. *Either* Mr Baron Graham *or* Mr Justice Holroyd**

Despite all these four being charged with the murder of Thomas Walker, the *Mercury* gave no other details whatsoever. So we do not know what evidence, or lack of it, enabled them all to be found not guilty.

❀

(E61) **FRIDAY 22 MARCH 1822**

HANGED FOR SHEEP THEFT

George Jennings, alias Jellings, alias Julyan

George Jennings was indicted at the 1822 Lent Assizes before either Mr Chief Justice Dallas or Mr Justice Best, with the theft of six lamb hog sheep, the property of Charles White of Brigstock. Apparently the evidence of Charles White 'left no doubt on the minds of the Jury as to the guilt of the prisoner'.

George Jennings himself however, appeared not to agree. The *Northampton Mercury* of Saturday 23 March 1822 :

> 'Nevertheless, he could not be induced to acknowledge himself guilty of the crime for which he was about to suffer, he said for the many irregularities in which he had indulged he could not but consider that the hand of God had kindly arrested him in a career of wickedness which most probably would have terminated in something far more serious than the crime of which he was convicted. Sabbath breaking he considered as one of the great inlets into the crime of which he had ever been guilty, and against this practise he cautioned everyone with whom he conversed.'

Why he considered himself not guilty is not revealed, as the *Mercury* chose not to print any of the evidence at the trial. Neither did it comment on the fact that also convicted for sheep stealing at the same Assizes, was William Perceval, who also received sentence of death. But Perceval was reprieved. Why Jennings hanged and Perceval did not, is not known.

❁

(E62) **FRIDAY 2 AUGUST 1822**

HANGED FOR RAPE

William Meadows
William Gent
Redmond Middleton

Sixteen year old Ann Newman was walking alone back to her home in Bozeat after having spent a happy day at Wellingborough Feast. Imagine her terror therefore, when between Wellingborough and Wollaston, she encountered a gang of six drunken yobbos, who were obviously not going to leave her alone.

And what happened to her, led all six men : William Meadows (27); William Gent (23); Redmond Middleton (20); Robert Ward (18); Thomas Bales (17) and Charles James (19), being arrested on Saturday 1 June, remanded in custody, and appearing before Mr Baron Graham at the 1822 Summer Assizes on Monday 15 July.

Meadows, Gent and Middleton were charged :

> 'On the oath of Ann Newman of Bozeat, feloniously ravishing and carnally knowing her; also for robbing her on the King's highway between Wellingborough and Wollaston of a shawl, handkerchief, a coloured silk handkerchief, two pocket ditto, a pair of stockings and some halfpence.'

Ward, Bales and James were charged with :

> 'being present at, and aiding and abetting, Meadows, Gent and Middleton, in ravishing by force Ann Newman.'

No details of the trial were printed by the *Mercury*, perhaps it is just as well. The *Northampton Mercury* of Saturday 3 August 1822:

> 'Yesterday pursuant to their sentences at our last Assizes were executed on the New Drop in this town, William Meadows, William Gent and Redmond Middleton, for having ravished and otherwise dreadfully ill-used Ann Newman of Bozeat a young girl of unimpeachable conduct.-Their behaviour since condemnation has not generally evinced a due sense of the turpitude of the crime

> they had committed, or the awfulness of their situation.-On Thursday however, their hardihood appeared to be somewhat subdued, and the idea of soon forfeiting their lives to the outraged laws of the country, induced them to seek, by penitence and prayer, pardon of their Maker through the atonement of his Son.-Their crime was of the most horrible character, and when it is considered they were all married men with families, the mind shrinks back, horror struck and confounded. Middleton addressed the multitude which was immense, with great earnestness, and particularly warned his companions and others of Wellingborough (the place of their late residence) in the habit of leading dissolute lives, to desist from pursuing a course of wickedness, which, if persevered in, sooner or later must terminate in their destruction.-Two youths one only 17 and the other 19 years of age were condemned to death as parties with the above men; and another only 18 was acquitted.-It is hoped that this youth having had so narrow an escape, will manifest his gratitude for the great lenity *(sic)* he has experienced, by sober, regular and exemplary conduct.'

Although Thomas Bales and Charles James were also found guilty and sentenced to death, in view of their age, and no doubt because they did not take part, they were both reprieved. And Robert Ward was found not guilty and acquitted.

But is there not one thing missing from this? No mention is made of poor Ann Newman. To have to undergo the ordeal she evidently had to, would have possibly traumatised her for life. What became of her? Sadly, nothing about her is printed in the Mercury, *and no mention can be found in any of the Bozeat parish registers for any clue as to what happened to her. Unfortunately, it seems that in those days not much notice was taken of the victim of crime, and it is shocking to think that in the 190 years since, nothing much has changed.*

1823

No homicides occurred in 1823

1824

(113)

1824A Date unknown. Paulerspury

Victim George Scott

Accused George May (25)

George May was accused of 'feloniously and wilfully driving over and killing George Scott'.

***Trial* 1824 Lent Assizes, Saturday 29 February. *Either* Lord Chief Justice Gifford *or* Mr Baron Hullock**

Thanks to the new enlightened policy of the *Mercury* to report on more cases at the Assizes, here is the report for this case :

> 'Thomas Wilcox examined by Mr Holbeach - Is a labouring man living at Paulerspury was in company with the deceased Scott on the night of the accident and was knocked down by the horses at the same time as the deceased. Witness was much bruised and so stunned by the blow as to be unable to distinguish anything for a length of time after the accident.-Several witnesses were then called who stated that the prisoner did not appear intoxicated and also gave him a good character.-It appeared that, after he heard of the accident, he was much affected and took a post-chaise and fetched the surgeon. - Verdict Not Guilty.'

✣✣ *Over the years several attempts have been made to kill either the monarch, the government or both. The most famous of course, is the Gunpowder Plot of 1605, followed by the Rye House Plot of 1683; and then we have the Cato Street Conspiracy of February 1820.*

A certain Arthur Thistlewood led a gang which hatched a plot to assassinate the Prime Minister, the Earl of Liverpool, and several members of his Cabinet, while they were dining at Lord Harrowby's house in Grosvenor Square. They were betrayed however, and all the conspirators were arrested at Thistlewood's house in Cato Street. Not surprisingly, they were all found guilty and hanged.

And it was Robert Gifford, as Attorney-General, who secured the convictions as he led for the prosecution. No doubt as a reward, in 1824, he was created the 1st Baron Gifford, made a Privy Councillor, and made the Lord Chief Justice of the Common Pleas.

These 1824 Lent Assizes were the only time he came to Northampton, as he would soon be made the Master of the Rolls, which is the chief judge in the Court of Appeal. He was not there long however, as he died in 1826 aged only 47.

1825

(114)

1825A Date unknown. Duston
Victim William Green
Accused William Robinson (54)
Trial **1825 Lent Assizes, Saturday 26 February. Mr Baron Hullock**
No details of this case are known, except that William Green received six months hard labour for manslaughter.

✣✣ *The 'Peterloo Massacre' of 16 August 1819 is looked upon, quite rightly, as one of the lowest points of British political life. Henry 'Orator' Hunt was due to speak at Saint Peter's Fields, Manchester on parliamentary reform. A crowd numbering about 50,000 gathered to hear him.*

Although the crowd was orderly, what Hunt was saying was considered to be subversive by the local magistrates, who started getting nervous at the size of the crowd. They ordered Hunt's arrest by the local yeomanry (which was a volunteer cavalry, and was the only group available for crowd control before the establishment of organised police forces) who stirred up the crowd by trying to do so.

The magistrates panicked, and called upon the yeomanry to disperse the crowd, which they tried to do by cavalry charging straight at them with sabres drawn. Nine men and two women were killed, and over 400 wounded.

When the dust had settled, scapegoats had to be found. Among them was Henry Hunt. He received two years imprisonment for his part in it all. On the prosecution team against Hunt was John Hullock, a barrister of Gray's Inn.

No doubt as some reward for all this, John Hullock was made a Baron of the Exchequer in 1823. He only came twice to Northampton, to the 1824 and 1825 Lent Assizes. He would die in 1829 aged 62.

(115)

1825B Date unknown. Earls Barton

Victim Joseph Stirman

Accused Joseph Tebbutt (34)

***Trial* 1825 Summer Assizes, Monday 11 July. Mr Justice Park**

Joseph Tebbutt was charged with the felonious killing of Joseph Stirman, and to which he had pleaded not guilty. However, during the trial, for some reason, he retracted and changed his plea to guilty. The *Northampton Mercury*:

> 'His Lordship addressing him said it having appeared that he had killed Joseph Stirman in self-defence and that the deceased had been the principal aggressor who had got him (the prisoner) down and was kicking his stomach, that he in defence had given the deceased a kick upon the shin which turned to mortification in two days and thus caused his death, he should fine him 1s and discharged him.'

(116)

1825C Boxing Day 1826, 12.30am. Badby

Victim Charles Bree

Accused Isaac Muddiman (18)
James Hazell (31)
William Hazell (28)
Joseph Ellard (26)

Yet another drunken punch-up after a night in a gin-palace. The Christmas cheer did not seem to affect Isaac Muddiman when he picked a fight with Charles Bree. Although Bree tried to move away, Muddiman continued fighting. Charles Bree died from internal haemorrhage into the brain as a result of the blows he had received.

***Trial* 1826 Lent Assizes, Saturday 25 February. Mr Justice Littledale**

Isaac Muddiman as the principal, was found guilty of the manslaughter of Charles Bree, and was sent to prison for one month, plus 1s fine. The rest, all charged with aiding and abetting, were acquitted.

❀

(E63) **FRIDAY 29 JULY 1825**

HANGED FOR SHEEP THEFT

William Longslow

Destined to be the last man hanged for sheep theft in Northamptonshire, William Longslow appeared at the 1825 Summer Assizes alongside his brother Thomas, before Mr Justice Park. We can do no better than quote the broadsheet circulated just after his execution.

> 'This morning we were again doomed to witness one of those solemn and awful spectacles, which we were in hopes would not for some time have agitated and harassed our feelings, but the crime of sheep stealing has become so prevalent in this and the adjacent counties, that the learned judge (Park) at our last assizes, felt it his duty to make an example of the culprit who has this day expiated his crime, by forfeiting his life to the offended laws of his country from the circumstance of his having carried on his depredations to an extent seldom met with.
>
> He was at our last assizes convicted on the clearest evidence, of stealing 40 sheep, the property of Mr Ward of Clipston. The crime itself was aggravated by the fact of the prisoner having drove the sheep only to Daventry fair, where he disposed of the whole, and actually received the money for them, which he has ever since refused to give any account of.
>
> His brother, Thomas Longslow, was indicted with him, but there was not appearing sufficient evidence against him, he was discharged.'

William Longslow was 32, and a married man living at Lubbenham. He was hanged at the New Drop at midday on Friday 29 July 1825.

1826

(117)

1826A Date unknown. Helmdon

Victim James Bull

Accused Edmund Hawkes (22)

Some places are cursed with breach-of-the-peace merchants - those individuals whose highest intellectual achievement is causing unpleasantness wherever they go, especially when saturated with fire-water. And like all villages, Helmdon held its own yearly Feast Day, a village holiday with much merrymaking. The two, if they coincide, don't mix.

Such it was that Edmund Hawkes, drunk in a village pub on Helmdon Feast Day, picked a fight with James Bull. Bull took no notice, and Hawkes was thrown out of the pub. The next day, the two clashed in a field in a vicious bare-knuckle contest.

Bull fought with his shirt on to hide ulcers on his side, which as the *Mercury* reported, was the result of being 'scrofulous in habit', presumably meaning unwashed and dirty. At one point, the two fell down heavily, with Bull underneath, causing him to lose consciousness for a short time. And a short while later, he was again knocked senseless by a blow to the side. James Bull never regained consciousness and died four hours later from massive internal bleeding into the chest.

Trial **1826 Lent Assizes, Saturday 25 February. Mr Justice Littledale**

Edmund Hawkes was sent to prison for one month for the manslaughter of James Bull.

✣✣ *Sir Joseph Littledale as well as being a judge, also had a literary streak. In 1821, and by then a barrister of Gray's Inn, he published an edited collection of poems by John Skelton, entitled* Magnyfycence, an Interlude. *John Skelton was a 15th/16th century English writer, who was considered to be the 'poet laureate' of his time.*

Three years later, in 1824, Joseph Littledale was made a Justice of the King's Bench, and remained so until he died in 1842 aged 75.

❀

(E64) **FRIDAY 21 JULY 1826**

HANGED FOR ROBBERY

George Catherall ('Captain Slash')

Because Great Britain did not have any sort of organised police force, having only to rely on the old Parish Constable system, then organised criminal gangs could maraud the countryside at will, safe in the knowledge that there was nobody to stop them. Over the centuries, Northamptonshire had suffered a long line of these, but it was the 'Captain Slash Gang' that was destined to be the last, as the Northampton Borough Police would be formed in 1836 and the Northamptonshire County Constabulary in 1840.

George Catherall came from a highly respectable family from Bolton in Lancashire. His early life is obscure, but it seems he had been dishonourably discharged from the army, as his back and shoulders were scarred with 'cat-o'-nine-tails' marks. He spurned the respectable life of his family and turned to crime, earning the disapproval of his mother who told him that 'he would die with his shoes on'.

Taking the nickname of 'Captain Slash', in imitation of an old highwayman, Catherall gathered around him a gang of violent thieves and pickpockets. Their main targets were the country fairs where large numbers of people gathered, which made thieving, pickpocketing and robbery-with-violence easy. In such activity, the gang toured around England, visiting each fair in turn, unmolested by any forces of law and order.

The 1826 Midsummer Fair at Boughton Green, Northampton, attracted the attention of 'Captain Slash' and he descended on the Fair with 100 of his gang. On the last night of the Fair, the gang moved into action, and they started attacking the booths of the stallholders, committing brutal robberies and damage. But the proprietors of the stalls, and local law abiding citizens, had been forewarned. Arming themselves with swords, muskets and cudgels, they lay in wait for 'Captain Slash'.

A tremendous fight took place, which eventually resulted in the banishment of the gang. 'Captain Slash' himself was captured, along with six of his men. In being captured, Catherall sustained a fractured skull, two broken ribs and a broken left hand.

Appearing at the 1826 Summer Assizes before Mr Justice Abbott, Catherall was found guilty of the specimen charge of 'stealing one waistcoat, one neckerchief, some half-pence, eleven half-crowns, and one crown *(£1 12s 6d, which today would be about £80)*, the property of James Henley'. Charged alongside him was Hugh Robinson, aged 18, and five other members of the gang.

All were found guilty. Catherall received the death penalty; Robinson was transported for life; and the others received substantial prison sentences.

George 'Captain Slash' Catherall, who was 29, was hanged on the New Drop at midday on Friday 21 July 1826 before a large crowd. Just before the executioner pulled the bolt, Catherall kicked off his shoes into the crowd. He died knowing that he had proved his mother wrong.

✣✣ *Charles Abbott would come to Northampton twice. Once as Mr Justice Abbott, and one year later as Lord Chief Justice Tenterden, as he had been raised to the peerage in between. Apart from that, he has the usual privileged background : public school; Oxford; Middle Temple; Recorder of Oxford, and Judge of the King's Bench in 1816. He would never visit Northampton again, and would die in 1832 aged 70.*

1827

No homicides occurred in 1827

1828

No homicides occurred in 1828

❁

In 1828, the Offences against the Person Act introduced the new offence of 'Concealment of Birth'. This was to counteract the almost impossible task of indicting a woman on the charge of murdering her offspring.

Prior to 1828 to prove 'murder' in the case of a child found dead in suspicious circumstances, and to negate the defence of being stillborn, the prosecution would have to show that the child had a completely separate existence from its mother. In other words, that the child had been capable of living a separate life (no matter how brief) physically separated from its mother, indicating therefore, the cutting of the umbilical cord.

As most (if not all) illegitimate births were in private, and un-witnessed anyway, then this 'separate existence' rule was virtually impossible to prove. Many women therefore, were literally 'getting away with murder' and were going unpunished for taking away the life of their child.

To counter this, the 1828 Act created the new offence of 'Concealment of Birth'. This was where the mother of a child found dead in suspicious circumstances, and who had attempted to conceal the body, could be convicted before a court without having to prove 'separate existence'. Appropriate legal, medical and social action could then be taken by the authorities.

The first woman to be charged with Concealment of Birth in Northamptonshire, was Elizabeth Johnson, at the 1834 Lent Assizes.

❁

1829

No homicides occurred in 1829

1830

And none in 1830 either, thus making four straight years without a single murder or manslaughter throughout the whole of the county. A four year homicide-free period had never happened before, and sadly, has never happened since. So who are we, with our supposedly enlightened society and penal system, to ridicule and deride the criminal justice system of our ancestors, where forfeiture of life was the deterrent? They managed four murder-free years in a row. Can we?

(E65) **FRIDAY 19 MARCH 1830**

HANGED FOR RAPE

Thomas White

Rape is a horrible crime, but especially so when a child is involved. Thomas White was hanged for the rape of Ann Swannell, who was not yet ten years old. On Tuesday 21 July 1829, Thomas White, a 24 year old farm labourer at Cosgrove, was at work. The rest is better told in the words of the broadsheet that was circulated at the time of the execution.

> 'He was a farmer's labourer, and it appeared that the prosecutor *(in other words, Ann Swannell)* and two other children having entered the cow-house in which the prisoner was, he shut the door, and after a little time began to take liberties with her person. From her statement, corroborated by that of her mother, and that of a surgeon who examined her, there was no doubt that the prisoner had completed the capital offence.
>
> There is reason to suppose, from the prisoner's conduct during the trial, that he expected to be convicted only on the minor charge, or that he was unconcerned as to the result. During the examination of the witnesses he smiled several times, and on the removal below with the other

> prisoners, manifested that indifference which showed that he was not aware of his awful amenableness.'

Thomas White appeared at the 1830 Lent Assizes before Mr Baron Garrow, and the minor charge he thought he would be convicted of, was obviously indecent assault rather than rape. But not to be. Thomas White was hanged at the New Drop on Friday 19 March 1830. The *Northampton Mercury*:

> 'His behaviour at the place of execution was becoming his situation, he appearing not only sensible of his awful condition, but to have benefited from the consolations of the chaplain....He appeared to suffer but little after the falling of the platform.-The concourse of people to witness the appalling scene was much less than might have been expected, considering the length of time (nearly four years) that has elapsed since an execution took place at this town. We trust the effect may be abundantly efficacious on the whole of the spectators, and especially the more youthful part, in preventing them from indulging unhallowed passions which too frequently hurry on their votaries to public shame and premature death.'

1831-1840

It is probably this decade which is the most important in the whole of Northamptonshire criminal history, because two very important things happened. Firstly, the 'Bloody Code' was abolished; and secondly, the police arrived.

With the hanging of Thomas Gee for arson in March 1835, the last knockings were heard of the infamous 'Bloody Code', the system where virtually every criminal offence was punishable by death. However, we must be wary of looking back and tut-tutting. We must realise our forbears acted with their own eighteenth century morals and logic, and not with our twenty-first century ones - they did what they thought best at the time - and at that time, the introduction of a deterrent system, the 'Bloody Code', seemed the right thing to do.

The fact that the 'Code' eventually failed because of the lack of an efficient means of detection, is now crystal clear to us with our perfect 20/20 hindsight. But this is not apparent to us by purely looking at the number of criminal homicides, as we are doing, it gives us a false impression. Although the yearly average of murders or manslaughters is just over one, the number of other crimes definitely was not, as their yearly average was rising fast.

For example, at the 1833 Lent Assizes there were 50 prisoners involved in 39 cases, and this number was not unusual. And as well as that, there were the 'lesser' offences being tried at the Magistrates' Quarter Sessions. So by the mid- to late-1820s, the thought that the 'Bloody Code' was not actually working because of the lack of an efficient means of detection, was beginning to dawn on some of the movers and shakers of the country.

It is perhaps too simplistic to state that this led directly to the formation of the 'new police' forces of the country, because there were many, many more factors involved. But it helped. The establishment of the Metropolitan Police in London in September 1829, saw the revolution in British police history - the introduction of the 'new police' concept - the full-time, professional police officer.

Eventually, for reasons which are not relevant here, the 'new police' system spread to the whole of the country. Therefore, the Northampton Borough Police was established in January 1836, and the Northamptonshire County Constabulary just four years later, in January 1840. Whether the establishment of the two bodies made any difference to the crime rates of the county, is a question which has never been investigated. Perhaps someone should do it.

Also, in November 1831, the *Northampton Mercury* received competition. The *Mercury* was a Whig influenced newspaper, and so to combat this, the Tories of the county set up their own newspaper, the *Northampton Herald*.

These two papers continued side by side until well into the 1920s, when they amalgamated, and are still with us today as the *Northampton Mercury and Herald*. Both papers reported on the Assizes, where politics was not really relevant, so from hereon-in, Assize reports will be taken from either paper.

1831

(118)

1831A Tuesday 30 August 1831, 7.15pm. Sibbertoft

Victim Mary Wright, alias Cheney

Accused William Grant (41)

Both Mary Wright and William Grant were working for Mr John Manton, who according to William Whellan's 1849 *Gazeteer and Directory of Northamptonshire* was a substantial landowner and farmer in Sibertoft. William Grant was a gardener and Mary Wright was an indoor servant. Mary Wright, because of her alternative surname, was probably a widow, and conceivably of a similar age to William.

And because of this, William thought he had formed an attachment with Mary, although it is unlikely that Mary thought so too. Having been in the Royal Marines, possibly William had never been married, but no doubt would have quite like to have been with Mary, and no doubt he kept pestering her to this end when their paths met every day. With Mary's obvious coolness, William's possessiveness turned to paranoia. Something had to give, which it did in a most tragic way.

On Tuesday 30 August 1831, Mrs Manton had sent Mary out on an errand, and at a little past 6pm was looking out for her return.

She saw Mary about 250 yards off in the lane, talking with William and walking towards the house.

When they had got to 50 yards away, Mrs Manton saw William take something from his pocket and strike Mary on the breast and then her waist. Mary screamed and Mrs Manton and a man called William Burdill who was with her, ran towards the couple.

Instead of running away, William fell to the ground at the same time as Mary, but then he got to his knees, knelt on Mary, and when Mrs Manton was but ten feet away, she saw William cut Mary's throat twice with his pruning knife. At that point she fainted.

Trial **1832 Lent Assizes, Monday 27 February. Mr Justice Bayley**

With irrefutable eye witness evidence as this, the question of William's guilt was never in doubt. When he was placed at the bar of the court, he burst into tears, and surely our sympathies are such that we can feel a pang of compassion for him. Nevertheless, he did commit murder, and he was hanged on Monday 5 March 1832.

(119)

1831B Thursday 18 August 1831. Weedon Workhouse

Victim John Wells (3)

Accused Mary Wells (35)

Mary Wells and her two children were inmates of Weedon workhouse. On the night of Thursday 18 August, her three year old son, John, was found dead, after complaining of stomach pains for the previous two days. John had been nursed by Rebecca Facer, another inmate, and one of the Matrons, Although they were highly suspicious of the pains and of the death, both women did nothing. John was buried two days later.

And that would have been that, except for one thing. On day 16 February 1832, another child died, and was buried in Northampton, and neither its parents nor grandparents attended the funeral. This so affected Mary Wells, that she broke down in tears and confessed to poisoning her son John with arsenic seven months previously. She was arrested the next day.

Trial **1832 Lent Assizes, Monday 27 February. Mr Justice Bayley**

Because the body had been buried for seven months, an exhumation was deemed pointless. And so because of lack of evidence, Mary Wells was acquitted. However Bayley J severely censured the Workhouse Matron for not reporting her suspicions in the first place.

❁

(E66) **FRIDAY 18 MARCH 1831**

HANGED FOR ARSON

James Linnell

Revenge is only sweet if you get away with it. James Linnell did not. Having been accused, and subsequently convicted, of sheep stealing by Thomas Horn, James Linnell vowed vengeance on Thomas Horn, who was a farmer in Shutlanger, and who rented his farm and his barn from the local landowner, Thomas 4th Earl of Pomfret of Easton Neston House.

On day 11 December 1830, Linnell attempted his revenge when he deliberately set fire to Thomas Horn's barn, which contained 37 quarters of barley, wheat and straw. This was obviously winter food for cattle, and the loss of it would have been the ruination of Thomas Horn.

The blaze was so huge, that it took 100 men to put it out, including James Linnell himself, who as the culprit, was re-visiting the scene of the crime. Linnell's animosity towards Horn was well known, and it was only a matter of time.

James Linnell appeared at the 1832 Lent Assizes before Mr Justice Bayley. The trial was a long one, because Linnell employed an 'excellent counsel' for his defence. But on the evidence of an accomplice, Edward Durrant, he was eventually found guilty, and sentence of death was passed. As soon as this was known, there were great exertions made by his family to get the death sentence commuted. But to no purpose.

Now this points to one thing. If a good quality barrister was employed, followed by agitation for commutation of sentence, then it points to James Linnell being from a wealthy family. No ordinary farm labourer would have the money for that. But his family obviously was out-wealthed by the Fermor family of Easton Neston Hall, the owners of the barn. The conviction stood.

On the morning of the execution, after being preached to in the gaol chapel,

> 'the sheriff's officers arrived.-The executioner came with the halter, after being bound, which he bore with great firmness, occasionally looking up to Heaven as if in prayer; thanking the Gaoler for his kindness, and shaking hands with his fellow prisoners, he walked with a slow and firm step to the place of execution, the Chaplain reading the burial service, commencing with *"I am the resurrection and the life &c"*. After a short time spent in adjusting the rope, the drop fell, and he being a heavy man, his sufferings were short. His body after hanging the usual time, was delivered to his friends for interment.'

(The Broadsheet *The Execution of James Linnell, aged 24* published by Ratnett, Printer, Northampton)

1832

(120)

1832A Date unknown. Hellidon

Victim Stephen Ralphs

Accused Sarah Cleaver (29)

Trial **1832 Lent Assizes, Monday 27 February. Mr Justice Bayley**

There are no details known about this case. All the *Northampton Mercury* printed is that Sarah Cleaver was acquitted. Who Stephen Ralphs was, how old he was, or whether he was any relation is unknown.

(121)

1832B Saturday 17 March 1832, 9pm. Northampton

Victim William Marriott

Accused Barnard McCaver (21), Private 18th Regiment of Foot
John MacSherry (21), Private 18th Regiment of Foot
John Henry (21), Private 18th Regiment of Foot

The day, the month and time of day are very significant in this case; take notice of them. And also take notice of the occupations of the three accused. The 18th Regiment of the Line, which was temporarily quartered in town, was The Royal Irish Regiment, and 17 March is Saint Patrick's Day. The rest can almost be guessed.

Sure enough, gangs of Irish soldiers had been drinking all day in various town centre hostelries, and numerous fights had occurred. McCaver and Henry had been in some of these, and had been on the receiving end several times.

At 8.30pm, McCaver and Henry had been turned out of *The Ram* public house in Sheep Street and went drunkenly up Sheep Street towards Saint Sepulchre's Church yard. There they met with another gang of soldiers. The locals had also gathered in great numbers, and were obviously trying to run the soldiers out of town. In Church Lane, the locals and soldiers clashed in a great fracas, during which William Marriott was stabbed with a bayonet to the temple, in a wound two inches deep, and from which he died instantly.

Trial **1833 Lent Assizes, Monday 4 March. Lord Chief Justice Denman**

The trial was delayed for one whole year because one of the witnesses was unavailable. And it was this time delay, coupled with the time of day of the attack, that came to be crucial. It was 9pm on a March evening remember, and it was dark, and the only street lighting being the gas lamps. Northampton had had gas street lighting since 1823, and the gas works Superintendent was called to testify that the gas lamps were on during that evening.

However, the main core of the defence was that no assailant could be identified completely because of the darkness. The defence even called Private John Maher to testify that Barnard McCaver was drinking with him in the *Light Dragoon* public house in Sheep Street at the time of the attack. Because of this confusion that no assailant could be identified exactly, all three were acquitted.

1833

(122)

1833A Date unknown. Tansor

Victim Ann Dolby

Accused Samuel Dolby (35)

Trial **1833 Lent Assizes, Monday 4 March. Lord Chief Justice Denman**

No details were printed by the *Mercury* for this case, they had used up enough space on the William Marriott murder. All that is known is that Samuel Dolby received six months imprisonment. The relationship between Ann Dolby and Samuel Dolby is unknown.

✣✣ *Thomas Denman was not the greatest of the nineteenth century legal minds, but he was certainly competent enough. During his career, he successfully defended Queen Caroline against a divorce suit bought by her husband George IV in a speech that lasted ten hours; and as Attorney-General, he drafted the Great Reform Bill of 1832. Students of British history need no reminding of what an immense landmark and breakthrough this was. If you do not know why, shame on you, go and look it up.*

Sir Thomas Denman was made Lord Chief Justice in 1832 and became Lord Denman of Dovedale in 1834, and Speaker to the House of Lords in 1835. However, what he himself considered his greatest achievement, was to reduce the backlog in the courts by getting them to sit more often, rather than only during the very short legal terms. He was so proud of this, that in his Will he directed that this fact be engraved upon his tombstone. And you can see that tombstone in Stoke Albany churchyard, half way between Corby and Market Harborough. Why he is buried here is a mystery, as he has no connection with Northamptonshire.

These 1833 Lent Assizes were the first of only two visits he made to Northampton, the other being for the 1839 Lent Assizes. He died in 1854 aged 75.

(123)

1833B Date unknown. Brafield-on-the-Green

Victim Thomas Thompson

Accused Richard White (41)

Trial **1833 Summer Assizes, Monday 8 July. Mr Justice Park**

Richard White never even appeared in court on this charge. The Grand Jury found that there was 'No True Bill', in other words insufficient evidence to go before the main court, and so Richard White was released.

1834

(124)

1834A Date unknown. Piddington
Victim Mary Smith
Accused William Tebbutt (18)
Trial **1834 Lent Assizes, Saturday 1 March. Mr Chief Justice Tindal**

Nothing is known about this case except that William Tebbutt was acquitted.

(125)

1834B Date and place unknown
Victim An unnamed child
Accused Elizabeth Johnson (36)
Trial **1834 Lent Assizes, Saturday 1 March. Mr Chief Justice Tindal**

Elizabeth Johnson makes a little bit of history when she was the first woman charged in Northamptonshire with concealment of birth instead of murder under the Offences against the Person Act of 1828. She was charged of concealing the birth by secretly burying the body. Because no post mortem could obviously be given, there was no evidence for the prosecution. So Elizabeth Johnson was 'delivered by proclamation', in other words, acquitted.

❀

(E67) **MONDAY 31 MARCH 1834**

HANGED FOR ARSON

Thomas Gee

The 'Bloody Code' had been in operation since the early 1720s, and well over 200 crimes were deemed to be capital offences. But by the turn of the eighteenth into the nineteenth centuries, people were beginning to realise that the 'Bloody Code' was not actually working.

The deterrent system only works if it is accompanied by a totally efficient and foolproof method of catching any wrongdoer, which makes anybody think twice before embarking on any crime, instilling into them the fear that being caught was inevitable and inescapable. But the only means of catching criminals at this time was the old Parish Constable system, and this had been utterly emasculated by the advance of industrialisation.

The Parish Constable system had been designed to work in small villages, where gossipy people knew everybody else's business through the parish 'grape-vine'. And because he also lived in the village, the Parish Constable was as much attuned to the grape-vine as anyone else, and so he also knew who the miscreant was if any outrage had been committed. Thus not much detection work needed to be done, and it was easy for the Parish Constable to grab the scoundrel and bounce him in before the local magistrate.

But the large cities of newly industrialising Britain gave no such luxury, and the Parish Constable system found itself entirely out of its depth and totally unable to cope. So to all intents and purposes, this country had no policing system whatsoever.

It was slowly dawning on people, therefore, what that meant. And what that meant, was a fresh evaluation of the policing of this country.

Thus it was, that by the middle of the 1820s, when the London crime statistics were so appalling, Sir Robert Peel, as Home Secretary, was able to seize the opportunity to secure a Select Committee to investigate the policing of London. And the outcome was a complete revolution in British policing.

By the establishment of the Metropolitan Police in September 1829, the concept of a full-time, paid, professional police officer, was introduced for the first time to this country - men whose sole occupation (and income) was to be a police officer, as opposed to the part-time, unpaid, amateur Parish Constables.

Thus a different means of crime control was being established, and so agitation for the relaxation and abolition of the 'Bloody Code' was started. If an efficient system of catching criminals was now being put into place, there was no need for death as the ultimate deterrent, and a more enlightened regime of punishments (especially prison) could then be used.

No longer was it acceptable to hang people for theft or burglary, or any other non-homicide offence for that matter, and although the judges still had to pass a mandatory death sentence, more often than not, this would be commuted. For instance, in 1831, 1601 people were sentenced to death throughout Britain, but only 52 were actually hanged.

Gradually therefore, offences were taken off the 'Bloody Code'. But it was not until 1835, that Sir Robert Peel, now Prime Minister, could report that the death penalty had been completely removed for all offences except murder, treason, piracy, and arson in the royal dockyards.

So it is that 23 year old Thomas Gee goes down in history as the last person to be hanged in Northamptonshire for a non-homicide crime. He was charged for the firing of a wheat stack belonging to Samuel Sharp of Guilsborough in December 1833, and appeared at the Lent Assizes of 1834 before either Mr Chief Justice Tindal.

Samuel Sharp gave his evidence :

> 'I was in bed when the fire happened, and was called up at 11o'clock; I found the stack on fire; we saved some of it;...I know the prisoner, he lives near the bottom of the village; I saw him in custody on Sunday after the fire and asked how he came to do me this spiteful trick, and whether I did him any injury? He said "No, never". I said "I cannot think how you could think of it"; he seemed confused, he then burst out crying, and said "I hope Mr Sharp you'll forgive me". I asked how long he had it in his mind to do it; he said he did not think much about it till he did it...there was between 30 and 40 quarters of wheat in the straw.'

Northamptonshire being an agricultural county, the taking away of a farmer's livelihood by stealing livestock or burning his winter stock of cattle food, was looked upon seriously. Thomas Gee was found guilty, and hanged on Monday 31 March 1834. Because of a bungled execution, his neck was not snapped cleanly, and he took twenty minutes to die of asphyxiation.

So Thomas Gee has his small place in criminal history. Eighteen years were now to pass before the death sentence was enforced in Northamptonshire again. And this time, and for all subsequent occasions, it would be for murder.

✣✣ *Nicholas Conyngham Tindal came from the usual privileged, upper class background that in those days was needed to become a professional talker. After Trinity College, Cambridge, he was called to the Bar, and then became a politician as Member of Parliament for Wigtown Burghs in 1824 and for Harwich in 1826. He was knighted and became solicitor-general in 1826, before being appointed Chief Justice of the Common Pleas in 1829. These were the first Northamptonshire Assizes he presided over, and he would visit frequently before he died in 1846 aged 70.*

1835

There were no criminal homicides in 1835

1836

There were no criminal homicides in 1836

1837

(126)

1837A Wednesday 13 September 1837. Hollowell

Victim Henry Lantsbury (7)

Accused William Lantsbury

This is one of the most heart-wrenching cases you will ever read. Thomas Good of Hollowell was approached by William Lansbury, and asked to thatch his little corn stack. This was a common practice so as to make the stack weather-proof.

So Thomas Good started work cutting straw with his scythe, whilst William Lansbury and his seven year old son Henry, picked up the stray pieces. After a little while Thomas Good had to leave temporarily, and so left his scythe at the stack. He was away for ten minutes. When he returned, he was horrified by what he saw.

William Lansbury was gone, but lying on the ground was seven year old Henry. He had a deep gash into the back of his neck, a deep gash on the back of his head, and one ear was cut off. A few feet away lay the blood covered scythe.

Trial **1838 Lent Assizes, Monday 26 February. Mr Justice Park**

The court heard that William Lansbury was formerly in the army, but then a navvy on railway construction. Whilst being a navvy, he had been buried by a fall of earth which fell heavily on his head. He subsequently suffered with paralytic fits.

Many witnesses appeared, including Doctor William Williams of Guilsborough who testified to the mental state of William. Because of this, William was found not guilty by reason of insanity, and was ordered to be kept in a secure institution.

(127)

1837B Tuesday 26 December 1837. Nether Heyford

Victim An unnamed male child

Accused Sarah Parish

Imagine giving birth to a healthy child whilst sharing a bed with a fellow servant, and not make one sound whilst doing it. This is exactly what happened to Sarah Parish.

On Boxing Day night 1837, Sarah and a fellow female servant were lying in bed. Suddenly a baby's cry was heard. The other girl was instantly awake and quizzed Sarah if she had heard the cry as well. Sarah denied doing so, but the servant was so concerned she went and fetched her employer who arrived with the cook of the house.

The employer was the Rector of Nether Heyford, the Reverend John Lloyd Crawley, who immediately searched the room. Underneath the bed he found the dead body of Sarah's newly born son. He was dead because his head had been injured as though someone had sat on it. Otherwise, he was a perfectly healthy boy.

Trial **1838 Lent Assizes, Monday 26 February. Mr Justice Park**

At the trial, according to the *Northampton Mercury*:

> 'a considerable lapse of time occurred in consequence of the suffering, exhausted and almost unconscious state of the unhappy prisoner. The Judge called for a seat for her, and sent for a prison matron.'

Sarah Parish, who was in her late 30s, was found not guilty of murder, but guilty of concealment of birth. She received twelve months hard labour.

1838

(128)

1838A Tuesday 6 March 1838. Easton-on-the-Hill

Victim Elizabeth Longfoot (40-50)

Accused Richard Woodward (28)

John Archer (23)

This case is notable because it introduces us to the Bow Street Runner, who in a couple of years time, would become the first Chief Constable of the newly formed Northamptonshire County Constabulary. Henry Goddard, for it was he, actually mentions this case in his memoirs, *Memoirs of a Bow Street Runner*, which were published in 1956.

On the morning of Tuesday 6 March 1838, the horrific murder of Elizabeth Longfoot was discovered in the cottage where she lived alone. She was lying on her back in her kitchen, with a large wound on the left side of her head, her head was extensively bruised, and there were marks around her neck as though she had been strangled with a cord. Her house appeared to have been ransacked for the money she was rumoured to have stashed away.

Easton-on-the-Hill is just a couple miles away from Stamford. So as it was only a couple of miles away, Elizabeth Longfoot's murder was reported to the Stamford Borough Police, under its Chief Constable, William Reed. Stamford, at that time, was actually split between Lincolnshire on the north bank of the River Welland, and Northamptonshire on the southern bank. But anyway, such niceties as police boundaries and magistrates' jurisdictions, never seemed to matter at the time, and the Stamford Borough Police with the Lincolnshire magistrates started investigations.

Apparently, they examined about between twelve and sixteen suspects in Easton, and in getting nowhere, it was decided to call in the Bow Street Runners. The Bow Street Runners were primarily a band of detectives who hired themselves out for private commissions; they were never a patrolling police. As such, a letter was sent, and Henry Goddard, as the only Bow Street Runner available, duly arrived in Stamford.

What happened next, is superbly told by Goddard himself in his memoirs. In visiting the scene, he saw three sets of footprints, one set of which was unusually large. He made enquiries in Easton, and was told there was a local layabout called John

Stansor, who sometimes slept rough. Stansor's sister told Goddard that she had not seen him since the night of the murder, and said that he was going to Bourne in Lincolnshire.

Amazingly, Goddard and Reed now chased all over the Fens before finally catching up with Stansor at Uppingham. And because Stansor then implicated Richard Woodward and John Archer, Goddard and Reed set off again, this time over Northamptonshire before finally cornering them, would you believe in Easton-on-the-Hill itself.

Trial **1839 Lent Assizes, Monday 4 March. Lord Chief Justice Denman**

Originally, the trial was due to be heard at the 1838 Summer Assizes before Mr Chief Justice Tindal. But on the journey to Northampton, William Reed and Mr Farrer, the Clerk to the Magistrates, were involved in an accident in their post-chaise, and were so badly injured, the trial had to be postponed.

So, the trial came on at the 1839 Lent Assizes. It had been decided not to charge Stansor, as he had turned 'approver', in other words, giving evidence against the other two.

In court, Stansor said that both men punched Elizabeth Longfoot with their fists until she fell down. Archer hit her on the head with a mason's hammer, and then 'Woodward took a cord from his pocket and strangled her with it, Archer kneeling on her stomach in the meantime'.

Another witness, a man serving a prison sentence, then appeared, and said he had heard Woodward and Archer shouting to each other from their cells about how they had strangled Elizabeth Longfoot. Denman LCJ however, made the governor of the gaol appear before him, and asked if this was possible. The answer was 'No', although after the trial, it was shown that it *was* possible. This, together with the lack of any more material witnesses, persuaded the jury to bring in a verdict of not guilty.

In the light of court procedure, however, this verdict was understandable. There was no corroboration of Stansor's allegations, and Archer and Woodward constantly denied any knowledge. The defence barrister's main argument, was that Stansor had alone done the murder, and was trying to frame Woodward and Archer. In the light of any substantial material evidence otherwise, the jury really had no other choice.

However, what the court said, and what the villagers of Easton-on-the-Hill knew to be the truth were not the same. According to the Annual Register, *when Woodward and Archer returned to their homes in Easton, the villagers formed a lynch-mob and ransacked both their houses, completely smashing everything in them. Archer and Woodward fled for their lives, and were never seen in Easton again.*

As the Bow Street Runners were disbanded by Act of Parliament in 1839, Henry Goddard was thus made redundant. Because of his expertise, not the least enhanced by this case, he was chosen as the first Chief Constable of the Northamptonshire County Constabulary, after it was established in January 1840. He was never happy in the role, and resigned in 1849, ostensibly as a result of an injury on duty, which however, never stopped him from returning to private practice as a free-lance detective, coupled with a sinecure job as doorman to the House of Lords. He died in 1883 aged 83.

(129)
1838B Wednesday 18 April 1838. Braunston
Victim Ann Chown (46)
Undetected

Ann Chown kept the village shop in Braunston. She was single and lived on her own, which is why she was obviously targeted by 'brave' desperados who had no qualms in taking the lawful earnings of a defenceless woman, and to stop at nothing to do it.

On the morning of Wednesday 18 April 1838, Mary Chown's body was found in her shop. She had been set upon with a sharp weapon, as her limbs were greatly mutilated and cut. Her throat had been slashed so deeply, that her head was almost separated from her body.

The strong box which contained her money was found intact and unlocked with the wrong key in the lock. It had been hacked about, presumably with the same weapon as killed Ann, but remained unopened.

The scenario is simple. The burglars broke into the shop, found the box and tried to open it with their weapons. Being then disturbed by Ann, they set about her with hysterical fury, and then in panic made their escape without taking the box with them.

The village constable, when the right key was found, opened the box. It contained £95/16/6 in cash *(£4,200 in 2010 prices)*, plus a savings book.

The crime was, and is, undetected.

(130)

1838C Sunday 10 June 1838. Irthlingborough

Victim John Smith

Accused John Keatch (30)

John Smith, his wife, and his fourteen year old son, were quietly sitting down to Sunday supper, when suddenly, in burst John Keatch. He started shouting and bawling, about the young boy spreading rumours around Irthlingborough about Mrs Keatch.

Not unnaturally, John Smith told John Keatch to go away, but Keatch was in a furious mood. Kicking over the supper table, he started fighting with John Smith. The fight spilled out into the backyard, and soon both men fell down heavily onto the ground, with John Smith underneath. He got up, but immediately collapsed with blood pouring from his nose. He died a few minutes later from ruptured lungs.

Trial **1839 Summer Assizes, Monday 8 July. Lord Chief Baron Abinger**

Why this case took a full year to come to court is not known. John Keatch was sent to prison for six months hard labour for the manslaughter of John Smith.

✣✣ *James Scarlett was created 1st Lord Abinger in 1835, one year after he was appointed as Chief Baron of the Exchequer. He knew Northamptonshire well, as he was the MP for Peterborough on three occasions between 1819 and 1830.*

Born in Jamaica, after Trinity College, Cambridge, he was called to the Bar by the Inner Temple in 1791. Whilst MP for Peterborough he was appointed attorney-general. He was also on the committee that looked into the 'Bloody Code' and decided that it was not working, which led directly to its abolition. Also MP for Malton, Cockermouth and Norwich, he was appointed Chief Baron of the Exchequer in 1834.

Although he had visited Northampton twice before, these 1839 Summer Assizes were the first with a criminal homicide on the calendar. He would visit periodically before dying in 1844 aged 75.

(131)

1838D Wednesday 24 October 1838. Roade

Victim Thomas Clarke

Accused Joseph King (29)

Another pub fight, or to be more precise, a beer house fight. A beer house was different from a public house. A public house was licensed to sell all types of alcohol, whilst a beer house (normally, but not always, in a room in someone's private house) sold only beer. But the purpose is the same, selling intoxicating liquor. And liquor does funny things to some people.

The front room of Mrs Tack's house in Roade was a beer house, with a keg of beer on a pair of trestles. Joseph King went to tap another pint of beer from the keg without paying, but Thomas Clarke tried to stop him. The inevitable occurred. The fight spilled out into the road, where Thomas Clarke was egged on by his brother.

Clarke was actually getting the best of King, but at one point tripped over and hit his head on some stones in the road. This made him groggy, and he would have given up, but egged on by his brother, he continued.

Not now having normal reflexes, he was a wide open target, and King hit him about the head mercilessly. After these blows, Clarke collapsed and died from brain haemorrhage.

***Trial* 1839 Lent Assizes, Monday 4 March. Lord Chief Justice Denman**

After charging the jury to return a verdict of not guilty, Denman LCJ made the acid comment :

> 'I cannot help remarking that the Coroner should have issued his warrant for the apprehension of Clarke's brother, who instead of endeavouring to stop the fight, stimulated his brother to continue it. Seconds are very frequently more culpable than the principal'

1839

There were no criminal homicides during 1839

1840

(132)

1840A Tuesday 11 March 1840, 12.40am. Long Buckby

Victim Mrs Eliza Gardner

Accused John Bree
John Holman
Thomas Vann

Was there ever such a strange case? Mrs Eliza Gardner, who was the wife of the Reverend Richard Gardner, curate of Long Buckby, died whilst she was lying in bed, without even setting eyes on the three drunken yahoos who were charged with her manslaughter. The official cause of this unfortunately lady's demise being given as 'death by fright'.

In the early hours of Tuesday 11 March 1840, the Reverend Richard and his wife were asleep in bed. Suddenly they were rudely awakened by what sounded like their front door being smashed in. Fearing burglars, Richard opened the bedroom window and pointed a gun (unloaded) into the street, and he heard footsteps running away. He went back to bed, only to find his wife totally insensible and unconscious. A doctor was called, but Eliza Gardner was already dead - literally frightened to death.

It seems that three of the local ragtag and bobtail, all in their late teens, had just been ejected from the village tavern and in their intoxicated state had decided to have some fun on the way home. This they did by kicking at peoples' front doors as they passed.

The Coroner's jury at the Inquest on Mrs Gardner (who had probably died of a heart attack) committed the three men to the Assizes on a charge of manslaughter.

Trial **1840 Summer Assizes, Monday 20 July. Mr Chief Justice Tindal**

However, at the Assizes, Tindal CJ disagreed :

> 'The deceased lady' he said 'who was in a weak state of health, died almost while the noise and uproar were

going on. But it would not be right to attribute her death to parties who neither knew of her existence nor had inflicted upon her any personal or positive injury. If there had been terror by the pointing of a pistol at her, or if a blow had been inflicted, from which death might have ensued, the case would have been a very different aspect. But to make the working upon the fears and fancy of one individual the ground for a charge of manslaughter would be too great and arbitrary a connexion between cause and effect.'

The manslaughter charge was therefore dismissed, but the Judge bound each of them over for £40 to be on their good behaviour for the next three years. Eliza Gardner was buried in Long Buckby church, and a plaque placed inside the church for all to read of the curious case of the curate's wife who was 'frightened to death'.

(133)

1840B Tuesday 6 October 1840, 6.15pm. Yardley Hastings

Victim John Dunkley (35) Gamekeeper

Accused Joseph Bedford (22) Labourer
William Downing (31) Labourer
James Underwood (21) Labourer

Bedford, Downing and Underwood after taking on copious amounts of drink at the *Rose and Crown* in Yardley Hastings, decided to go poaching. This they did on land belonging to the Marquis of Northampton, at New Hay Coppice, Yardley Hastings. After shooting a hare, they separated, but Bedford was caught by Dunkley, one of the estate gamekeepers, and heated words were exchanged. Suddenly, both men levelled their shotguns at each other - and fired.

Bedford missed with his shot, but Dunkley did not. Bedford was eventually to have 30 shotgun pellets taken out of his left shoulder as a result of Dunkley's shot, which had knocked him flat on his back. Hearing the shots, Underwood and Downing came running back, and it was Underwood who immediately shot Dunkley in the head with his shotgun from a distance of nine feet. Dunkley died immediately. But the three poachers were far from finished with him yet, and the further attacks on Dunkley's dead body can only be described as a psychopathological frenzy of uncontrolled venom and spite.

Giving his opinion at the inquest, Doctor Pell said that Dunkley had been shot once under the right ear, once in the top of the head, once in the back of the head, and once in the back of the neck when the deceased was lying face down on the ground. The back of the skull was also caved in, which could have been caused by his own gun being smashed down on his head (it had been found broken nearby) and on top of that, there were marks around the throat as though he had been strangled. Dunkley's body had then been dragged 50 feet to where it had been dumped.

***Trial* 1841 Lent Assizes, Wednesday 3 March. Lord Chief Baron Abinger**

All three men were found guilty of the wilful murder of John Dunkley, and were transported for life. Why they were transported and not hanged for such a vicious attack, is one of the shameful mysteries of Northamptonshire criminal history.

(134)

1840C Saturday 12 December 1840. Nether Heyford

Victim Martha West

Accused George West

George West was accused of the murder of his mother, Martha, by poisoning. Arsenic had been administered over a period of time, but there was no direct evidence that it was George who was the culprit. The only evidence against him was that he was a grocer who sold arsenic in his shop - he was the last person to give his elderly mother a meal - and that he stood to get some of his mother's annuity upon her death.

***Trial* 1841 Lent Assizes, Thursday 4 March. Lord Chief Baron Abinger.**

The judge said that the evidence was too slight for murder. The jury also thought it too slight for manslaughter as well, because they returned a verdict of not guilty - reluctantly it seems, because they added that they 'looked upon the case as one of very great suspicion'.

1841-1850

This decade contained 20 criminal homicides, which was the most ever recorded up until that time. Perhaps it is a bit flippant to say that by being established in 1840, this decade was the first in which the policing of the county was in the hands of the Northamptonshire County Constabulary. The 'old police' system of Parish Constables was still in operation, however, as the 'new police' did not replace them, but supplemented them, and they worked side by side until the old Parish Constables gradually faded away.

Although they do not concern criminal homicides, which still went to the Assizes, by far the biggest legal innovation of this decade, was the passing of the so called Jervis Acts in 1848. Introduced by Sir John Jervis, the Attorney-General, the three Jervis Acts were : The Summary Jurisdiction Act; The Indictable Offences Act; and The Justices' Protection Act. These Acts consolidated the workings of the Magistrates' courts, and introduced the power of Summons, as an addition to the power of arrest.

1841

(135)

1841A An unknown date. Daventry

Victim Ann Wallace

Accused Thomas Wallace (40)

Trial **1842 Lent Assizes, Tuesday 1 March. Lord Chief Baron Abinger**

Thomas Wallace was acquitted of 'feloniously killing his wife at Daventry. There are no other details known.

(136)

1841B Monday 13 December 1841. Northampton

Victim John Starmer

Accused Charles Henderson Penn (22)

Charles Penn and John Starmer were drinking in the *Wagon and Horses* public house in Northampton. John Starmer apparently, was a very aggressive character, and he started picking on Charles Penn over some disputed payment for beer.

The niggles went on for about an hour, and at one point Starmer shook his fists in Penn's face, and struck him twice on the nose. In the scuffle that followed Starmer knocked Penn to the floor. Starmer then sat down on a bench, but Penn, wanting to get his own back, came back to Starmer and they started fighting again (The *Mercury* uses the wonderfully old-fashioned term Penn 'closed with' Starmer). During the brawl, Penn hit Starmer so hard that he ruptured his small intestines. Starmer died the next day

Trial **1842 Lent Assizes, Tuesday 1 March. Lord Chief Baron Abinger**

Charles Penn received one month imprisonment for manslaughter.

1842

(137)

1842A Sunday 25 April 1842. Weekley

Victim Peggy Ward (70)

Accused Marianne Goss (22) Servant

Marianne Goss stood trial for the wilful murder of her employer, Peggy Ward. She had died of arsenic poisoning, but the only evidence against Marianne was that she had asked a fellow servant to buy her some arsenic about a week previously, which she said she would use as a mouse poison.

There seemed to be no motive whatsoever. She was a perfectly good servant and well thought of - she had not been secretive in obtaining the arsenic - and was not agitated when her mistress was taken fatally ill.

Trial **1843 Lent Assizes, Wednesday 1 March. Mr Baron Alderson**

The trial was originally scheduled to appear at the 1842 Summer Assizes, but because of the indisposition of the key witness, Mary Ward, Peggy Ward's daughter-in-law, the trial had to be postponed. So on Monday 11 July 1842, when Marianne Goss was led into court, Mr Justice Park had to tell her that she would have to spend another eight months in prison.

This naturally did not impress Marianne Goss, and she complained bitterly to Park J. However, he could do nothing, and the case was postponed.

Which is all the more ironic, because when the case finally did get to court, the case against Marianne Goss was dismissed. This was probably a tragic accident as the arsenic source was traced to some milk, and Marianne had obtained the arsenic to get rid of mice - in the dairy.

(138)

1842B Unknown date. Weldon
Victim Unnamed child
Accused Sarah Berridge
Trial **1843 Lent Assizes, Wednesday 1 March. Mr Baron Alderson**

Because the *Mercury* was intent on reporting about the Peggy Ward 'murder', it had no space to give details of this case. Therefore nothing whatsoever is known, except that Sarah Berridge was given four months imprisonment for concealment of birth.

✣✣ *Although Sir Edward Hall Alderson had been a judge for thirteen years, these were the first Assizes he had attended at Northampton, and he would never visit again. After a brilliant academic career at Caius College, Cambridge, where he won every academic prize going, he was called to the bar by the Inner Temple in 1811. He was first made a Justice of the Common Pleas before transferring to the Court of Exchequer in 1834. He died in 1857 aged 70.*

1843

(139)

1843A Sunday 26 March 1843, 12.10am. Barton Seagrave
Victim Thomas Mawby
Accused William Eayres

Following an evening's drinking bout in various Kettering gin palaces, a brawl developed on the way home. Barton Seagrave is a couple of miles south of Kettering, across the River Ise.

Eayres, in order to defend himself, stabbed Mawby and another man, called MacMain both in the stomach. Mawby managed to get home despite protruding bowels, but died the following

Wednesday of inflammation of the liver, directly as a consequence of the stabbing.

***Trial* 1843 Summer Assizes, Thursday 14 July. Lord Chief Baron Abinger**

William Eayres received twelve months hard labour for the manslaughter of Mawby and the wounding of MacMain.

1844

(140)

1844A Date unknown. Kings Sutton

Victim An unnamed child

Accused Elizabeth Russell (22)

***Trial* 1844 Summer Assizes, Monday 15 July. Lord Chief Justice Denman**

No details whatsoever were given of this case, not even the verdict. From the calendar of cases appearing, published the previous week, we do know that Elizabeth Russell had been charged with concealment of birth at Kings Sutton. But that is all we have.

(141)

1844B Tuesday 25 June 1844. Easton-on-the-Hill

Victim James Plowright (21)

Accused John Marriott

James Plowright had married John Marriott's daughter five months previously, and was living with his wife in his parents-in-laws' house. In the early hours of Tuesday 25 June 1844, Plowright and his wife were in bed, when he heard an argument between his father-in-law and his mother-in-law.

Plowright heard blows being struck, and went into the bedroom to intervene, but Marriott then started fighting him. In the scuffle, Plowright was knocked to the floor, and Marriott fell heavily upon him. Plowright lapsed immediately into a coma and died soon afterwards from ruptured lungs.

Trial 1844 Summer Assizes, Wednesday 17 July. Lord Chief Justice Denman

Marriott, who had threatened suicide several times before, received twelve months imprisonment for manslaughter

(142)

1844C Wednesday 10 July 1844. Flore

Victim James Hedge

Accused Jonathan Towersey
Stephen Oliver
Thomas Dent

Hedge and Towersey were involved in a bare knuckle fight after a brawl in *The Chequers* public house in Flore. Oliver and Dent acted as seconds.

In Round Fourteen, Towersey hit Hedge so hard on the head, that a blood vessel was ruptured. Hedge died within minutes.

Trial **1844 Summer Assizes, Tuesday 16 July. Lord Chief Justice Denman**

Towersey and Oliver both received seven days imprisonment, whilst Dent received six months. The reason for this discrepancy is unknown.

(143)

1844D Monday 22 July 1844. Billing Road, Northampton

Victim Frederick Fitzhugh

Accused Daniel Cumberpatch
John Fitzhugh
Edward Lenton
Charles Coles
Henry King

All this lot drank in the *Nag's Head* public house in Northampton. One boozy Saturday night, they were stirred up by talk on the local grape-vine about a bare knuckle fight due to take place the following Monday on The Racecourse. The beer then started talking, and Fitzhugh challenged Cumberpatch to their own bare knuckle fight, for a purse of £1 *(worth an incredible £45 today).* Cumberpatch refused.

On the following Monday, 22 July, they were all on The Racecourse watching the original fight, when Fitzhugh again challenged Cumberpatch to a fight. Fitzhugh was egged on by his drunken father, John Fitzhugh, and all the other defendants.

Finally Cumberpatch gave in, and the fight was arranged to be held in Billing Road. When they got there, the fight started.

But, in 1845, the Northampton Borough Police had been in existence for nine years, holding regular town patrols. And one of these patrols, saw the fight and broke it up. But as soon as he had gone, the fight was renewed.

After another six rounds, Cumberpatch was starting to get the upper hand. Fitzhugh was knocked down by Cumberpatch, but as he fell, his head banged against the hard ground. He never moved again.

Fitzhugh was carried to the *Milk Maid* pub frothing at the mouth. He died within minutes from a ruptured blood vessel in the brain.

Trial **1845 Lent Assizes, Wednesday 5 March. Mr Chief Justice Tindal**

Cumberpatch received three months hard labour, with all the rest receiving one month for aiding and abetting. John Fitzhugh, however, received an 'emotional life sentence' for the death of his son.

(144)

1844E Monday 30 September 1844. Northampton

Victim An unnamed male child

Accused Jane Dickins (27) Servant

Jane Dickins was a servant to Mrs Charlotte Lucas in Northampton. On Monday 30 September 1844, Mrs Lucas, who knew nothing about Jane's condition, asked after her health because she thought she looked ill. Jane replied that nothing was wrong. But so concerned was she over Jane's appearance that Mrs Lucas sent her to bed early, and called a doctor.

The doctor, however could not be fooled, he knew a newly delivered mother when he saw one. A search of the room revealed bloody bed clothes, and the body of a newly born boy. The baby was dressed in clothes, but the neck had been drawn so tight, that it had been strangled.

Trial **1845 Lent Assizes, Wednesday, 5 March. Mr Chief Justice Tindal**

Jane Dickins was found guilty of concealment of birth. She received eighteen months hard labour, which obviously reflected Tindal CJ's feelings over the case.

1845

There were no criminal homicides in 1845

1846

(145)

1846A Unknown date. Hargrave

Victim An unnamed child

Accused Sarah Clarke (24)

Trial **1846 Lent Assizes, Monday 2 March. Mr Chief Justice Tindal**

Sarah Clarke was charged with :

> 'secretly burying and unlawfully endeavouring to conceal the birth of her child'

Nothing else is known, except that she received six months hard labour.

1847

(146)

1847A Monday 29 March 1847. Welton

Victim John Capell (18 months)

Accused Thomas Kidsley

Elizabeth Capell was a widow, with an eighteen month old son, John. She was living with Thomas Kidsley, and the couple intended to get married. At 7pm on the evening of Monday 29 March 1844, the couple had an argument about Thomas Kidley's 'Certificate'.

What this certificate was, the *Mercury* did not say, but it can be deduced that it was his Banns Certificate, which had been called at Daventry. For the couple to marry, this certificate had to be produced to the Rector of Welton. But it was still at Daventry, hence the argument.

Thomas was obviously getting the worst of the argument, so he did the only thing that some men do in this situation - he struck out at Elizabeth. But Elizabeth was holding her baby John, and in turning to avoid the blow, Thomas's fist struck the baby so hard, that he was thrown against the wall. John Capell died five days later from brain damage.

Trial **1847 Summer Assizes, Wednesday 14 July. Lord Chief Justice Denman**

Witnesses were called at the trial who testified that Thomas had always treated John kindly. However, it also was revealed in court, that John's body bore marks of violence and burns, but no evidence came out as to how he had got those.

Thomas Kidsley received four months hard labour, with Lord Chief Justice Denman saying that 'intention to strike the female was no excuse.'

(147)

1847B Monday 12 April 1847. Abthorpe

Victim An unnamed male child

Accused Ruth Wills

Ruth Wills lived at Abthorpe with her brother Joseph and his wife Esther. On the morning of day 12 April 1847, the body of a newly born boy was found head first in the house privvy. Because of where he was, the baby appeared to have suffocated, and was covered in what the *Mercury*, in the euphemism of the time, calls 'night soil'.

Trial **1847 Summer Assizes, Wednesday 14 July. Lord Chief Justice Denman**

Because there was medical doubt as to whether the baby had been born alive, Denman LCJ instructed the jury to find Ruth not guilty of murder but guilty of concealment of birth. They duly did, and Ruth Wills received twelve months imprisonment.

(148)

1847C Monday 7 June 1847. Northampton

Victim William Cornfield (66)

Accused Edmund Franklin (36)
Edward Randall (19)

William Cornfield was happy, he was going out to dinner. He was going to dinner at the Temperance Hall in Northampton to celebrate an ordination. Ann, his wife waved him off, and he joined 33 other people at the dinner.

Everything was going swimmingly, until the desserts, when a blancmange appeared on the table. The blancmange was white with a green coloured topping, and a lot of men indulged, including William Cornfield.

Because he did not feel very well, William Cornfield left the dinner early and got back home at 8pm. Ann put him straight to bed, but William was very ill, being constantly sick during that night.

At 5am, William said he felt a little better and asked Ann for tea and toast. When Ann came back, William was dead.

Trial **1848 Summer Assizes, Saturday 15 July. Lord Chief Justice Denman**

It appeared that all the men who had eaten the blancmange had been ill, and although William Cornfield was the only one who had died, many took a long time to recover, hence the trial being delayed for a year. The caterers, Edmund Franklin and Edward Randall were indicted for manslaughter.

It came out in court, that Edward Randall had obtained the green colouring from a local shop, and there was a dispute as to whether the shopkeeper had said that the green was a poison - which it was.

In summing up, Denman LCJ told the jury that the case revolved on two points : did the caterers know that the green colouring was a poison, and knowing this, did they still use it? The jury found the two guilty of manslaughter and both received three months imprisonment

This was probably the first case of death by professional negligence heard at the Northamptonshire Assizes. It was however, not to be the last.

(149)

1847D Friday 24 September 1847, 5.30pm. Brackley

Victim John Bannard

Accused Frederick Fennell (27)

We think that 'drink driving' is a modern phenomenon - it isn't, it happened pre-motor car as well. Frederick Fennell was riding his horse along Brackley High Street, whilst leading another by its reins. According to eye-witnesses he was 'very drunk' and going at a 'rapid pace'.

Whether he saw John Bannard or not, is not known, but John Bannard was also in Brackley High Street, and walking in the same direction as Fennell was riding. Thus he had his back to him.

Fennel hit Bannard so hard that he knocked him down. Although Bannard got back up and walked home, in eight days he was dead from severe compression because of head injuries.

Trial **1848 Lent Assizes, March 1 March. Mr Chief Justice Wilde**

For riding recklessly, and for causing the death of John Bannard, Frederick Fennell received four months in prison.

(150)

1847E Wednesday 24 November 1847, 3pm. Lowick

Victim Emma Rands (six months)

Accused Martha Rands (32)

This is a most tragic case, and one where every sympathy must go to the mother Martha Rands, who was indicted for the death of her daughter Emma. Martha Rands was the wife of a shoemaker who lived in Southampton. They had two children, a boy aged three years, and Emma at six months.

In November 1847, Martha's sister and brother-in-law, Mary and Charles Burton, brought Martha and Emma back to Lowick where they lived. They had been so concerned at Martha's depressed behaviour, that they had actually obtained a certificate for Martha to be admitted to a mental asylum.

Whilst awaiting for her to be admitted, the family decided that Martha should never be left alone. However, at 3pm on Wednesday 24 November, by a mix up, one of the Burton children left Martha alone with Emma in the kitchen. On hearing screaming, Mary Burton rushed into the kitchen to see the baby in the copper of boiling water, feet upwards. Doctor Leete of Thrapston was called and pronounced Emma scalded to death.

Trial **1848 Lent Assizes, March 1 March. Mr Chief Justice Wilde**

After Doctor Leete had given his evidence, Wilde CJ, stopped the trial, saying 'It was one of those lamentable cases by the severe

> visitation of Providence, a person was deprived of all reason and self-control.'

Martha Rands was found insane, and was ordered to be detained in strict custody.

(151)

1847F Monday 27 December 1847, 10.30pm. Bugbrooke

Victim James Tibbs (47)

Accused John Herbert (62)

This is a bizarre case, and if it were not so tragic, you would be reminded of the modern television 'comedy' programmes when two drunken people are all over each other saying 'You're my best friend ever'. This is not being flippant or tasteless, because this is exactly what happened.

John Herbert was a baker at Bugbrooke. On Monday 27 December, he was sharing a Christmas drink with his best friend James Tibbs. At 10.20pm, George Watson, John Herbert's servant left the two men downstairs, happily 'merry' on gin and beer, and seemingly kind-hearted and well-disposed. He went to bed.

Suddenly, ten minutes later, he heard two gun shots. Rushing downstairs, he saw to his horror James Tibbs lying face down in the kitchen doorway in a pool of blood. He had been shot in the stomach and shoulder, but was still alive. Watson heard Tibbs say 'I am a dead man'. In the brew-house a few feet away, he saw John Herbert holding a shot gun.

Watson raised the alarm, and soon the house was crowded with men. Again he heard James Tibbs say 'You've shot me', to which John Herbert replied 'You're the best friend I've got in the world'.

Because the damage to his shoulder was so great, the doctor had to operate to amputate his arm. In those days before anti-biotics, James Tibbs died within hours of post-operative shock.

Trial **1848 Lent Assizes, Monday 1 March. Mr Chief Justice Wilde**

As only the two men were present at the fatal scene, John Herbert's account was uncontested. He managed to persuade the jury that it was an accident. He had only taken down the gun when he was going to show James Tibbs home, because he was fearful of who they would meet that dark night. And as he was drunk, which he freely admitted, the gun went off accidentally. Twice. The jury however, found him guilty of manslaughter, and he received three months imprisonment.

1848

(152)

1848A Wednesday 26 January 1848. Newnham

Victim John Lake

Accused John Hadland

Road accidents are the blight of modern society, but in the days of horse drawn vehicles, traffic speed was much slower, so not too many occurred. And when they did, the majority were 'damage only'. But occasionally, one came along that was more serious.

John Hadland, a horse dealer from Flore, had spent all day at Daventry Market, and was driving a horse drawn cart away from Daventry towards Newnham. His passenger was Samuel Pinfold, who was later to describe John Hadland as being 'in liquor', and the winter night as being 'very dark'.

Suddenly, another horse drawn cart appeared, being driven in the opposite direction by John Lake. Hadland did not see Lake until he was ten yards away. He tried to pull over, but the offside wheels of the two carts caught together, and both carts overturned, with everybody being thrown out onto the road.

'Damn you, I'll make you pay for all expenses - you were on the wrong side of the road' hollered Hadland at Lake. Lake denied it. He was probably feeling a bit woosy as he had a deep head wound. The following Tuesday his doctor was called in, but he died on Sunday 6 February from compression.

Trial 1848 Lent Assizes, Monday 1 March. Mr Chief Justice Wilde

This whole thing obviously revolved around the road positions of the two carts immediately prior to the collision. Two witnesses who had come upon the scene just afterwards described the positions of the overturned carts when they had seen them.

With all this information, the jury decided that Hadland had been at fault. He received three months imprisonment, plus a £10 fine.

Thankfully, deaths from road traffic accidents during the horse drawn era were remarkably few. It was not until the death of Emma Mills in 1915, that Northamptonshire was faced with its first death by motor car where a prosecution ensued. In 2008, there were 35 deaths in Northamptonshire directly attributable to raid traffic accidents.

✣✣ *If ever there was a story of how to succeed in life despite having a few setbacks, then the story of Thomas Wilde must be it. Eventually to become the Lord Chancellor in 1850, Thomas Wilde was unusual in that he had not gone to Oxbridge, nor to any other university come to that. He had been articled into his father's legal practice in 1805, and learnt the law in that way, before enrolling himself into the Inner Temple who called him to the Bar in 1817.*

However, he suffered with a speech impediment (we are not told what), which is a bit of a drawback for a professional talker. But he managed to get around it by completely avoiding the words he couldn't pronounce, and using synonyms instead. This made his speeches rather rambling, and oratory was never to be his greatest achievement.

Because of this, coupled with his lack of a degree, he was rather looked down upon by the legal hierarchy of the day. However, he managed to impress by acting as one of the defence team for Queen Caroline, when her husband, King George IV, tried (unsuccessfully) to divorce her in 1820.

He was MP for Newark-on-Trent in 1831 and 1835, and MP for Worcester in 1841. He was made Attorney-General in 1841 and 1846, and then Chief Justice of the Common Pleas in 1846.

In 1850, he was ennobled to become the 1st Lord Truro, and became the Lord Chancellor. He died in 1855 aged 73. These 1848 Lent Assizes were the first of his two visits to Northampton (the next being the 1849 Lent Assizes, when there were no criminal homicides), before becoming Lord Chancellor in 1850.

1849

(153)

1849A Tuesday 22 May 1849. Gold Street, Northampton

Victim James Turner

Accused Simon Coles

On a lovely May day in 1849, James Turner and his sister were walking in Gold Street, Northampton, when who did they see but Simon Coles. Coles was most belligerent and demanded from James the two shillings that he owed him. Two shillings today would be about £4.50.

James said he could not pay at the moment, but would pay up soon. Obviously an argument occurred, and pushing and shoving started which then escalated into punches being thrown. James Turner in falling to the ground hit his head so hard on the kerb that he lost consciousness immediately. He died later that night from severe brain haemorrhage.

Trial **1849 Summer Assizes, Wednesday 11 July. Mr Baron Parke**

The position was summed up by Parke B who asked the jury to decide whether the injuries were caused by a blow from Coles knocking down Turner and thus hitting his head; or did Turner trip during the melee without Coles hitting him, and thus fall down that way.

The jury found Coles guilty, but asked for mercy. Simon Coles received six weeks hard labour for manslaughter.

✣✣ *Again, not to be confused with Sir James Alan Park, Sir James Parke (with an 'e') had been called to the Bar by the Inner Temple in 1813. He had been knighted and made a judge of the King's Bench in 1828, before transferring to the Exchequer in 1834. He would be created 1st Lord Wensleydale in 1856, and would die in 1868 aged 86. This was his third visit to Northampton, but the first time there had been a criminal homicide on the calendar.*

1850

(154)

1850A Unknown date. Northampton

Victim Frances Waters Bates

Accused John Bates (32)

Trial **1850 Summer Assizes, Saturday 13 July. L. C. Humphrey, Esq QC**

From the *Northampton Mercury* of Saturday 20 July 1850 :

> 'The Grand Jury thought proper in the exercise of their undoubted privilege, to throw out the Bill against the unfortunate man before them. He proceeded to denounce Lobelia inflata in unmeasured language. The prisoner had acted under the advice of a well-known incompetent person.'

Lobelia inflata is sometimes called Indian tobacco and is a native plant of north America. The American tribes used to smoke it to cure respiratory conditions such as asthma, bronchitis and pneumonia. However, it is toxic and causes vomiting, hence the alternative name for it - 'puke weed'! It is still used today, but only with extreme caution.

It can be surmised that Mrs Bates had respiratory problems, and that John Bates, prompted by the 'well-known incompetent person', innocently administered it to his wife in an attempt to cure her, but with the opposite effect. There was no ill-intention, thus the finding of 'No true Bill.'

Lord Chief Justice Campbell was due to come to Northampton for the 1850 Summer Assizes, but he didn't make it for some reason. He had only been the Lord Chief Justice for a few months, and he was apparently needed elsewhere. Thus Mr Baron Platt came on his own, but he sat in the Nisi Prius court.

Therefore, sitting in the criminal court was a certain L. C. Humphrey, QC. At this time, if there was no judge available, an Assize court could be presided over by a Commissioner, who was a practising barrister given temporary judicial powers. Obviously, this action was taken only as a last resort, and it would be another 57 years before this ever happened again in Northamptonshire, when Mr Edward Atkinson who was only 29 years old, and had been a barrister for five years, presided over the 1907 Northamptonshire Winter Assizes in October of that year. By then, the number of cases going to the Assizes was so great that a third sitting had to be established. Unfortunately, no personal details of Mr L. C. Humphrey can be found.

WHAT CAN WE MAKE OF ALL THIS?

As far as we can tell, all the criminal homicides which have occurred within Northamptonshire, up to 1850, and for which documentary evidence survives, have just been described. If we study them closely, can we learn anything? We can probably attempt some interesting statistical analysis, although to have any meaning, only those cases from 1720, will be analysed. Before that date, any conclusions would be virtually meaningless, as the sparse information we have is not sufficient for any judgement to be made.

But after 1720, we do stand some sort of a chance, as we have a complete list - or as complete a list as can be obtained given the documents available.

For the 131 years between 1720 and 1850, there were 154 homicides, thus giving a yearly average of 1·18 per year. The break down for the individual periods is this :

1720-1750	38 homicides	= yearly average of	1·22
1751-1800	48		·96
1801-1810	9		·90
1811-1820	12		1·20
1821-1830	10		1·00
1831-1840	17		1·70
1841-1850	20		2·00
	154 total	= yearly average of	1·18

So we can see that we have some ups and downs, but from 1831, the yearly average rose markedly. Could we possibly find some reason for this?

It is doubtful whether the abandonment of the 'Bloody Code' by 1835 had any bearing, as the death penalty still remained possible for criminal homicide. And it is also doubtful that the establishment of the Northampton Borough Police in 1836, and the

Northamptonshire County Constabulary in 1840 had any bearing either.

With one or two exceptions, criminal homicides are especially difficult to 'hush up', and any that occurred would have come to light anyway, irrespective of what policing agency was in power. So it is difficult to ascribe the rise in homicides to the greater detection powers of the professional policemen of the Borough Police and County Constabulary over the part-time amateur Parish Constables.

So was the rise because of a larger population? When we examine this concept, we get a remarkable result.

In 1720, from published figures, the population of the county has been estimated at 55,000. If we apply our yearly average of 1·22 homicides, we get ·023 homicides per 1,000 of population.

In 1841, from published figures, the population of Northamptonshire was 220,000. Applying our yearly average of 2·0, we get ·009 homicides from 1,000 population. So despite the yearly average increasing, because of the much larger population (attributable mainly to the shoe boom), the incidence of criminal homicide per one thousand population, actually went down at the end of our period.

An analysis of the victims is also revealing. It shows that the majority of victims seem to be either members of the same family, or acquaintances, of their murderer, as it can be argued that of the 38 homicides between 1720 and 1750, 24 (or 63·1%) of the victims fall into this category.

And when we look at the victims between 1831 and 1850, again it appears that 26 out of the 37 (70·2%) were in the same category of family, or close acquaintances. An average of the two figures gives 66·6%.

Admittedly, these figures are rough and ready, unsophisticated and subjective, but they are the best we can do, and as such, appear to point to the fact that the percentage of the victims being related to, or acquainted with, their killer was near enough the same in 1720 as it was in 1850. So this rationale seems not to have changed much over 131 years.

Which means, of course, that the percentage of victims *not* falling into this category remains near enough the same as well. So, over the period 1720 to 1850, the ratio of murders (for acquisitive financial gain) to murders (for personal reasons) seems not to have changed much. And that, regarding the morals of the human race, is faintly comforting, in the fact that if we are not getting any better, at least we are not getting any worse either.

Whether this has any relevance or not, I leave up to you, but an analysis of the days of the week when homicides occurred is interesting. Of the 154 homicides described, in only 50 do we know the actual date. But of these 50, the split is remarkable :

Monday	10
Tuesday	11
Wednesday	11
Thursday	3
Friday	4
Saturday	5
Sunday	6

Going off on a tangent, an analysis of *where* the homicides occurred is interesting. The list below gives the locations where these are known. Obviously Northampton has the largest number. But what is it that makes a tiny village like Grafton Regis have the same number of homicides as the large town of Kettering, whilst Yardley Gobion, just down the road, has none at all? What is it that makes a tiny village like Welton have the same number as fairly large towns like Oundle, Wellingborough and Brackley?

It will not be wise to get into any speculation. Again, I leave it up to you.

Abthorpe	1
Addington, Great	1
Alderton	1
Aston-le-Walls	1
Badby	2
Barnack	1
Barnwell	1
Barton Seagrave	1
Boddington	1
Bozeat	1
Brackley	3
Brafield	1
Braunston	1
Brington	1
Brixworth	2
Bugbrooke	1

Byfield	1
Chalcombe	1
Charwelton	2
Chipping Warden	2
Clay Coton	1
Cogenhoe	1
Cottesbrook	1
Croughton	1
Dallington	1
Daventry	2
Denford	1
Dodford	1
Duddington	1
Duston	1
Earls Barton	1
Easton-on-the-Hill	2
Edgecote	1
Farthingstone	1
Finedon	1
Flore	2
Gayton	1
Geddington	1
Glendon	1
Grafton Regis	4
Grafton Underwood	1
Grendon	1
Guilsborough	2
Hardingstone	1
Hargrave	1
Harpole	1
Hartwell	1
Hellidon	1
Helmdon	1
Hollowell	1
Irthlingborough	1
Islip	1
Kettering	4
Kings Cliffe	1
Kings Sutton	1
Kingsthorpe	1
Kislingbury	1
Lamport	1
Little Bowden	1
Little Houghton	2
Lois Weedon	1
Long Buckby	1
Lowick	1
Marston Trussell	1
Mawsley	1
Middleton Cheney	1
Moreton Pinckney	1
Moulton	3
Nassington	1
Nether Heyford	2
Newnham	1
Northampton	20
Oundle	3
Pattishall	2
Paulerspury	3
Piddington	1
Preston Deanery	1
Pytchley	1
Ringstead	1
Roade	1
Rothwell	2
Sibbertoft	1
Spratton	1
Stamford	1
Stoke Albany	1
Stowe Nine Churches	1
Sulgrave	1
Tansor	1
Thorpe Achurch	1
Thrapston	2
Titchmarsh	1
Towcester	2
Wappenham	1
Warkton	1

Weedon	4
Weekley	1
Weldon	1
Wellingborough	3
Welton	3
Weston by Weedon	1
Wilby	1
Woodford	1
Woodford Halse	1
Yardley Hastings	1
Yelvertoft	2

JUDICIAL EXECUTIONS

The list below gives the number of known judicial executions in Northamptonshire for the 649 years from 1202 until 1850.

Murder	41
Robbery	23
Burglary	14
Witchcraft	8
Horse theft	7
Sheep theft	7
Unknown	6
Rape	5
Arson	4
Forgery	4
Theft	4
Treason	4
Sacrilege	3
Returning from Transportation	2
Attempted murder	2
Heresy	1
Riot	1
Refusing to plead	1
Wounding	1
	138

INDEX

PEOPLE AND PLACES

Northamptonshire towns/villages in **Bold**
-and ones that used to be, in ***Bold Italics***

EXECUTIONS

Godfrey of Warkton 1202 Murder
Goodman, Joseph 1745 Robbery
Gordon, Thomas 1788A Murder
Grant, William 1831A Murder
Haddon, Mary 1736C Murder
Hall, John 1785 Robbery
Hanger, Thomas 1799 Horse Theft
Harwood, Anthony 1770 Robbery
Haynes, Philip 1821A Murder
Henry of Killingworth 1316A Murder
Herbert, Sir Richard 1469 Treason
Higgerson, William 1801 Sheep Theft
Higgins, John 1794 Horse Theft
Hilliar, John 1623 unknown
Howell, William 1786A Murder
Hulbert, John 1787 Sacrilege
Jellings, George 1822 Sheep Theft
Jenkinson, Hellen 1612 Witchcraft
Jennings, George 1822 Sheep Theft
Johnson, James 1759 Returning from Transportation
Jones, William 1811B Murder
Julianne de Murdak 1316E Murder
Julyan, George 1822 Sheep Theft
Kelly, Richard 1785 Robbery
Kendall, Robert 1813 Theft
Kilsby, John 1764 Robbery
King, James 1821 Rape
Knighton, Mr 1714 Murder
Kurde, John 1557 Heresy
Lamb, William 1749 Robbery
Lavendar, John 1750 Arson
Law, Richard 1787 Culworth Gang
Lewin, Robert 1785 Horse Theft
Lilleyman, Richard 1819 Arson
Linnell, James 1831 Arson
Loale, Ann 1759C Murder
Longslow, William 1825 Sheep Theft
Love, William 1754 Burglary
Lucas, Mrs 1631 Murder
Meadows, William 1822 rape
Medlicoate, Jacob 1737 Robbery
Middleton, Redmond 1822 Rape
Minards, William 1819 Burglary
Morris, Thomas 1814A Murder
Newton Rebels 1607 Riot
Nokes, Elizabeth 1784A Murder
Paine, Samuel 1775 Burglary
Panther, Benjamin 1819 Burglary
Parker, Catherine 1780B Murder
Pearce, Benjamin 1794 Burglary
Pembroke, Earl of 1469 Treason
Pettipher, William 1787 Culworth Gang
Phillips, Mary 1705 Witchcraft
Pool, Thomas 1780A Murder
Porter, Edward 1819 Burglary
Porter, William 1742B Murder
Poydras, John 1317 Treason
Preston, Stephen 1611 unknown
Ratnett, Thomas 1722A Murder
Roberts, John 1785 Robbery
Rowledge, Russell 1764 Robbery
Seamark, Thomas 1764 Robbery
Shaw, Elinor 1705 Witchcraft
Skelcher, Thomas 1785 Horse Theft
Smart, James 1759 Returning from Transportation
Smart, William 1759 Returning from Transportation
Smith, John 1785 Robbery
Smith, John 1787 Culworth Gang
Smith, Thomas 1792 Robbery
Snarey, Richard 1723A Murder
Sparrowe, Thomas 1611 unknown
Stafford, Robert 1807 Attempted Murder
Stuart, Mary, Queen of Scotland 1587 Treason
Taffs, John 1819 Burglary
Tarry, George 1685A Murder
Tarry, James 1785 Robbery
Tresler, Elizabeth 1713A Murder
Underwood, Thomas 1789 Burglary
Unknown man 1630 Refusing to plead
Unknown 1685
Unknown woman 1645 Murder
Unknown woman 1655 Murder
Vaughan, Joan 1612 Witchcraft
Wakelin, Thomas 1750 Attempted Murder

JUDGES

ACKNOWLEDGEMENTS

It would be very remiss of me not to thank all those who, in their own way, have helped me over the years this book has been taking shape. The bulk of the research was done in the Northamptonshire Studies department of Abingdon Central Library in Northampton. So I would like to thank Mr Jon-Paul Carr and all the staff in the department whose cordiality never diminished, and whose helpfulness I continually strained with my constant demands for the next microfilm.

Also my thanks go to the staff of the Northamptonshire Record Office in Wootton Park, for similar reasons.

The photographs were taken by Mr David Bailey (no, not *the*) of the Northamptonshire Police on our visit to the Sessions House in Northampton during the recent restoration. And, of course, to Mr Roger Coleman of Northampton Borough Council for allowing us to, and for showing us round.

I must thank the Editor of the *Northampton Mercury and Herald*, for allowing me to reproduce whole swathes of his predecessors' words.

My thanks to all my colleagues and acquaintances over the years who have chipped in with their own suggestions, and experiences of the cases they have dealt with. All were gratefully received. However, I thank especially Mr Alan Richardson, Northamptonshire Police pensioner, now of Stamford, who in making a casual remark, initially set me thinking, and thus set me off on the road. So, blame him.

Lastly, of course, to my wife Valerie, whose expertise in knitting improved wonderfully during the times I was closeted in front of this word processor. To her, I give my unconditional thanks and love.

Guilty M'Lud! The Criminal History of Northamptonshire

by Richard Cowley

Northamptonshire is rich in historical criminal activity, and the documents that record it. Using these, Richard Cowley has written a fascinating and comprehensive picture of the murkier doings of our county ancestors.

Price : £16.95 plus £1.05 postage and packing - total £18.00

ISBN 0 9534095 0 3

Policing EOKA: The United Kingdom Police Unit to Cyprus 1955-1960

by Richard Cowley

The EOKA campaign in Cyprus from 1955 to 1960 is well known, but what is not appreciated so much is that the British armed forces on the island were supplemented by a contingent of British 'Bobbies' - both men and women - more used to dealing with road accidents and petty crime rather than armed insurgency!

Price £12.00 inclusive of postage and packing

ISBN 0 9534095 1 1

WHO'S BURIED WHERE
IN
NORTHAMPTONSHIRE
RICHARD COWLEY
With illustrations by
Rosslyn Nisbet-Smith

The 'Top School' The First 100 years of the Finedon Mulso School 1900-2000

by Rosemary Pearson

This book is a treasure trove of memories, especially to those Finedon families whose children have attended the school for the 100 years of its history.

Price £15.00 plus £1.00 postage and packing - total £16.00

ISBN 0 9537037 3 8

Let's go to the Pictures. A Hundred years of Cinemas in Kettering

by Maurice Thornton

In their heyday, Kettering cinemas provided over 5,000 seats. This story of the 100 years of the cinemas of Kettering is not a lament to their loss, but a celebration of their existence.

Price £16.95 plus £1.05 postage and packing - total £18.00

ISBN 0 95370372 2 X

Beyond the Five Points : Masonic Winners of The Victoria Cross and The George Cross

by Philip R. S. May, GC

Of the winners of The Victoria Cross and The George Cross, 118 have been Freemasons, including Phillip R. S. May, who died before completion of this, his life's work. Completed and edited by Richard Cowley, this will be of interest to the general reader and not just to Masonic and military historians.

Price £30.00 plus £6.00 postage and packing - total £36.00

ISBN 0 9541271 0 2